Murdering Myths

Polemics

Stephen Eric Bronner, Series Editor

The books in the Polemics series confront readers with provocative ideas by major figures in the social sciences and humanities on a host of controversial issues and developments. The authors combine a sophisticated argument with a lively and engaging style, making the books interesting to even the most accomplished scholar and appealing to the general reader and student.

Media Wars: News at a Time of Terror
By Danny Schechter

The Collapse of Liberalism: Why America Needs a New Left
By Charles Noble

Imperial Delusions: American Militarism and Endless War
By Carl Boggs

Murdering Myths: The Story Behind the Death Penalty
By Judith Kay

Forthcoming Titles

American National Identity in a Post-National Age
By James Sleeper

Animal Rights and Human Evolution
By Steven Best

Corruption
By Robert Fitch

Freud's Foes: Psychoanalysis, Science, and Resistance
By Kurt Jacobsen

No Free Lunch: How to Destroy Television as We Know It
By Philip Green

Power and Disruption
By Frances Fox-Piven

Repressive Tolerance: Second Edition
By Herbert Marcuse

Same Sex Marriage and Democracy
By R. Claire Snyder

Technopolitics and Globalization
By Douglas Kellner

*Primetime Politics: The Truth about Conservative Lies,
Corporate Control, and Television Culture*
By Philip Green

Murdering Myths

The Story behind the Death Penalty

JUDITH W. KAY

ROWMAN & LITTLEFIELD PUBLISHERS, INC.
Lanham • Boulder • New York • Toronto • Oxford

ROWMAN & LITTLEFIELD PUBLISHERS, INC.

Published in the United States of America
by Rowman & Littlefield Publishers, Inc.
A wholly owned subsidiary of The Rowman & Littlefield Publishing Group, Inc.
4501 Forbes Boulevard, Suite 200, Lanham, Maryland 20706
www.rowmanlittlefield.com

PO Box 317
Oxford
OX2 9RU, UK

British Library Cataloguing in Publication Information Available

Library of Congress Cataloging-in-Publication Data

Kay, Judith, 1951-
  Murdering myths : the story behind the death penalty / Judith Kay.
    p. cm. — (Polemics)
  Includes bibliographical references and index.
  ISBN 0-7425-2335-7 (cloth : alk. paper) — ISBN 0-7425-2336-5
(pbk. : alk. paper)
  1. Capital punishment—United States. I. Title. II. Series: Polemics
(Rowman and Littlefield, inc.)

HV8699.U5K39 2005
364.66'0973—dc22   2004030280

Printed in the United States of America

♾™ The paper used in this publication meets the minimum requirements of American
National Standard for Information Sciences—Permanence of Paper for Printed Library
Materials, ANSI/NISO Z39.48-1992.

Contents

Acknowledgments

The idea for a book on capital punishment was launched with an invitation from Professor Stephen Bronner of Rutgers to contribute to his series on controversial public issues. For his steady backing, I am most grateful.

I received so many gifts from people involved with violence who opened their hearts and lives to me. This book cannot capture what a treasure it is to have touched each person's humanity—whether they were on death row, in jail, a survivor of crime, or relatives of a homicide victim. Special thanks to Emma and Nora for their valor and to Maggie for the integrity of her fight.

Thanks also to my fellow activists in the Washington Coalition to Abolish the Death Penalty for their determination to save people's lives, and thanks particularly to Jeannette Star Howard, Neal Hulkhower, Alice Curtis, and Gayle Gower for reading chapters.

It is a privilege to learn in the classroom, and so a special thanks to my students at the University of Puget Sound, especially those who were willing to test and critique the case against punishment.

Colleagues and friends around the country read drafts at various stages. For their responsiveness and insights, I thank Howard Zehr, Linda White, Stephen Casey, Lloyd Steffen, Phyllis Hotchkiss, Stephen Nathanson, Paul Loeb, Alyce Demarais, Florence Sandler, Jane Marie Pinzino, Ronnie Friedman-Barone, Pam Roby, Vikki Verhulp, Carol Coar, and Joel Biatch. Thanks to Judith Bettelheim, who lent me her sunny home for some quiet writing time and gave me guidance about cover images.

Writing was less isolating due to the unwavering support of friends, family, and allies: David Goodenough, Stuart Gold, Marjon Riekerk, Jerry Saltzman, John Foster, Joy Kroegger-Mappes, David Jernigan, Kathy Guy, Nancy Lemon, Pauline Spiegel, Barbara Menne, Peg Brown, Alan Kay, and Hazel Henderson.

Every book has its story. Thanks to my parents, Martha and James Webb, who care about social justice and passed that on to me. The influence of my teachers—Robert Bellah, William Spohn, Martha Stortz, Thomas Schubeck, Harvey Jackins, Karen Lebacqz, and Edward Long Jr.—can be found at every turn.

Thanks to Sharon Russell for editing and improving the book's structure, Jill Greitzer for her attention to footnotes, Carol Avery, Christina Stenstrom Sulynn Walton, and Laura Bastin for production assistance, and Mary Carpenter and Laura R. Gottlieb at Rowman and Littlefield for their sure guidance.

I thank my talented and caring son, Jeremy, for his unwavering confidence and my beloved husband, Josh, who listened to me at all hours, kept our social life going, put his own projects on hold, and generally did more than his share.

Introduction

The one whose eyes
do not meet yours
is alone at heart
and looks where the dead look
for an ally in his cause.

Les Murray, "The Averted"[1]

Humans make sense of the world through stories. "For it is in telling our stories that we originally acquired our humanness; and we are not so much rational animals, as Aristotle said, or tool-making ones, as Benjamin Franklin put it, but first and foremost story-telling ones."[2] Humans need narratives to sustain their communities and sense of self. Communal narratives recount a people's origins and the hardships they endured, assert the principles that for them are worth dying for, and describe the kind of future they hope to secure. By drawing from their traditions, individuals have at the tips of their tongues language with which to interpret life events. Christians, for example, use shorthand when they speak of "wandering in the desert," "bearing their cross," or "experiencing the midnight hour." Traditions provide virtuous models. Jews emulate the courage of Deborah, the hospitality of Sarah, and the faithfulness of Ruth. Without a story to provide context and meaning, a person's life might appear as a series of inexplicable choices. Individual stories ground personal identity. They explain how a girl from Iowa became a college professor who meets with perpetrators, crime victims, and families who have lost loved ones to murder.

Careful listening to the stories of criminals results in the significant insight that perpetrators and the dominant culture operate from a shared narrative. Murderers, rather than lying outside the community, reflect society's most tenacious myths about violence. They tell the same story that the criminal justice system tells: some people are so awful that they deserve grave harm; the redress for victimization is making someone pay; harsh treatment is corrective. The community and its offenders concur that some people are inherently violent. Believing that making others suffer can be morally satisfying or is an unpleasant necessity, both murderers and state functionaries disappear into a nonhuman blankness. They exhibit a fundamental disconnection from themselves and the objects of their violence. Both embrace "doing unto others as was done unto them" as a sound moral guide. Both act as though status is regained through wielding coercive power over another. Both commit their acts of violence by targeting those over whom they have some power (or can gain some power). Both pursue justice by imposing harm.

The stories of victims and perpetrators reveal another surprise. They struggle with the same issue—to develop a personal narrative that incorporates two facts. First, they were once powerless and prostrate, helpless and humiliated. Second, they never want to feel this way again. Both victims and wrongdoers seek to regain their footing, their self-respect, and their sense of connection. The story that revenge or punishment rights the wrong is deceptive because harming others does not stop the pain. It is a narrative that lies.

The story is also dangerous. As Robert Schreiter, a Catholic priest who has worked on reconciliation in war-torn countries, observes, "What keeps people trapped in the memories of violence is precisely the dilemma of integrating the traumatic experience into their identity, on the one hand, and escaping its grasp, on the other."[3] "The narrative of the lie" stokes vindictive passions and says that making someone else suffer will cure suffering. Prison psychiatrist James Gilligan observes:

> When I speak of the motives that cause people to pursue justice by means of revenge, punishment, and violence, I am not speaking exclusively about the motives that underlie the traditional criminal justice and penal systems. I am

speaking also of the motives that give rise to criminal violence itself—that is to say, the motives that cause those whom we have to think of as "criminals" to commit their acts of violence, in the hope of attaining justice by punishing those whom they feel have punished them, unjustly. In other words, the motives and goals that underlie crime are the same as those that underlie punishment—namely, the pursuit of what the violent person considers "justice."[4]

Justice, as conceived within the story, is dangerous to society.

Even more stunning, the story is imprinted on people through mistreating them. Primary caregivers harshly punish children, acting as unwitting carriers of the community's bad habits and laboring under the misperception that brutalization teaches young people that harming others is wrong. Instead, hard treatment breaks down a subject's own sense of injustice, since violence, as Schreiter says, "destroy[s] the narratives that sustain people's identities."[5] Hence, individuals are rendered susceptible to subscribing to the narrative that revenge and retribution work. Victims, at the crucial moment of their greatest vulnerability, are handed the dominant story as a way to interpret and make sense of the injustices they have endured. Once it becomes evident that the dominant story is transmitted to each new generation in hurtful ways, it is less surprising how many people demand revenge and retribution.

Severe brutalization aims to get men, in particular, to the point of being willing to use violence, but only when instructed to do so by particular institutions, such as the military or the criminal justice system. A society does not benefit by having people become virulent killers who initiate violence on their own; it strives instead to place certain of them in a state of readiness to use violence when instructed. But it is difficult to regulate the process of getting to this state, because violence takes on a life of its own in many settings—as was demonstrated by the alleged abuse of Iraqi prisoners by an army reservist employed as a prison guard on Pennsylvania's death row.[6] Consequently, some conditioned citizens cross the line and become sadistic torturers and killers.

Since people who maim or kill at will rather than at society's command are dangerous, the state then decides that the apparent monsters it has fostered must be executed. It is manifestly diabolical and unjust to treat humans as objects to be manipulated and discarded when they no longer serve the state's purposes. Retribution lacks moral legitimacy when it blames individuals for having vices that were instilled and invoked through callous treatment. Retribution fails to hold the community responsible for its role in this drama.

The ultimate similarity is expressed in the death penalty—both murderers and the state are willing to kill in order to show who has the upper hand, who will never again be disrespected, and who has the last word. The same story sustains them both.

Timothy McVeigh believed the government was guilty of great injustices and deserved harm. Violence, he believed, was a legitimate way to secure justice. In response, the federal government concluded that McVeigh had committed a grave injustice and therefore deserved death. These two acts of justice seeking are not morally equivalent: mass murder violates the law while state-sanctioned killing seeks to uphold the rule of law. An individual took revenge, whereas the state claims sole authority to kill citizens. The 168 people who McVeigh slaughtered on 19 April 1995 in the Oklahoma City Federal Building were innocent; McVeigh was not. Strikingly, however, McVeigh and the state shared a concern to correct injustice, appealed to the same rationales to justify their decision to act upon that concern, and subscribed to a similar plot that commanded certain performances. Although many Americans wanted to expel McVeigh as a moral outsider, McVeigh used the same story line as those who rebuked him. Many family members of those killed also subscribed to the worldview that certain people deserve to die, hoping that an execution would balance the great wrong and bring closure to their pain and outrage. After the execution, some family members felt that McVeigh had not suffered enough— that retribution demanded like for like. These family members read from the same story as McVeigh, playing a familiar part in the drama of revenge and retribution.

Even before McVeigh's execution, however, fault lines began to appear in this story. Some surviving family members interpreted the situation differently. Their reading came from a new libretto, with different staging, unfamiliar lyrics, and new ways of interacting. These family members said that McVeigh's execution would make them feel not better, but worse; would increase, not lessen, the burden of their loss; and would dishonor rather than vindicate the deceased. From within their narrative, state-sanctioned killing violated rather than secured the demands of justice. Thus, surviving family member Bud Welch, whose twenty-three-year-old daughter, Julie Marie Welch, was killed while working for the Social Security Administration, forged new paths of action and connection. Appalled that the state was about to cause another family to lose a child, Welch, after much raging, grieving, and trepidation, contacted McVeigh's father, Bill. Tentative and unsure of their course, Welch and Bill McVeigh met. As Welch was preparing to leave, he met Timothy McVeigh's sister—near the age of his beloved daughter, Julie. Crying into each other's arms, Welch promised that he would do everything within his power to save her brother. He finally managed a farewell. Once inside his car, he sobbed the hardest he had been able to since the bombing. Welch and McVeigh's family remain in touch. Certainly, Welch and his fellow opponents of execution walk a different path than ideologies of revenge and retribution envision, demand, or permit.

Tragically, even some subscribers to the state's story felt they missed its moral. Jay Stratton, who lost his mother in the bombing, reportedly said, "I thought I would feel satisfied, but I don't."[7] The hole created in their lives by McVeigh's foul deed was not filled by his death. The supposedly ineluctable magic of retribution—in which state-sanctioned killing annuls McVeigh's violence—did not work for everyone.

This book exposes the plotline and character traits required in the story that so many have been willing to kill for. It invites the reader to listen to stories from victims' family members and from perpetrators who interpret reality differently. The book is intended for survivors of homicide, victims of crime, offenders, professionals, and activists as well as bystanders not yet aware of their role in the scripts of revenge and retribution.

The opportunity lies within reach to craft a narrative that fashions a better way of responding to dreadful violence, one that breaks the seemingly endless round of action and reaction, harm and retaliation. Too often, this cycle has been reified as a law of the universe, as a demand of God, or as an inevitable expression of human nature. Humans hoped that punishment would stop the cycle in ways that revenge had not. Instead, punishment became part of the cycle, and the story now says that punishment is natural. Instead of something outside history and therefore beyond human influence, the "naturalness" of punishment is a product of a story.

Once one recognizes that the cycle of crime and punishment is maintained by a particular story, the telling of a transformed story emerges as a genuine possibility. Rewriting an old script opens new emotional, behavioral, and juridical territory.

SUBSCRIBING TO THE STORY

Perhaps nothing attests more to the existence of a dominant story with a widely shared script than that harsh punishment is the status quo in the United States. Compared to other life-and-death matters, the death penalty is not an issue about which most citizens have staked out contrary, yet morally defensible, positions. For instance, while the Democrats and Republicans distinguish themselves by opposite stances on abortion, not so on capital punishment. Psychologist Craig Haney concludes that this "support is largely symbolic and generic. Americans support the *idea* of the death penalty."[8]

Ironically, even in the heyday of this most recent retributive era, the United States imposes the death penalty infrequently compared to the volume of violent crime. Of death-eligible cases that go to trial, "Juries impose the death penalty in only about 10% of capital cases, and this despite the fact that American capital juries are always 'death qualified'—meaning that death-penalty opponents are barred from hearing the case."[9] Only about 1 or 2 percent of all murderers actually receive a death sentence, since not all homicide cases make it to trial.[10] In the past twenty-five years, 11 percent of the condemned have been executed. In that same period, 36 percent of death sentences have been overturned after review at either the state or federal level, most often due to police or prosecutorial error.[11]

Although the death penalty, statistically, is rarely meted out, Americans continue to tell a story about the necessity of payback and retribution, lamenting that murderers are granted limitless appeals over trivial procedural errors while victims' families get nothing. Severe punishment remains the only way, most Americans believe, to provide closure to the victims' families.

But what happens to the families when no offender is apprehended, there is no capital trial, no death sentence is imposed, a death sentence is overturned, or the person convicted and serving time on death row is later exonerated and released, leaving the actual murderer still unidentified and at large? Are hundreds of victims' families and their communities doomed to never experience the mysterious alchemy that capital punishment is supposed to effect? If, in addition, the death penalty is *for* victims' families, it is only for a certain class of families—those who cooperate with and agree with the prosecution. Execution produces no benefit for those family members opposed to capital punishment, who are treated like "second-class victims" or even denied the status of "victim."[12] When the death penalty is the only solution offered to victims' families, then 98 percent of homicide victim families are doomed to perpetual purgatory.

Despite that fact that the death penalty benefits only a tiny percentage of survivors, polls show that the U.S. citizenry is neither morally relative nor ambivalent about the death penalty, but rather enthusiastic supporters. Law professors Stanley Gross and Phoebe Ellsworth conclude, "There is substantial evidence that those who support capital punishment will agree with almost any plausible argument for that position, and the great majority of those who favor the death penalty say that they do so 'strongly.'"[13]

When a position has been a "cultural truism" for this long, people are rarely pushed to defend their stance. Most Americans find it easier to accept the death penalty than mount an argument for it. "People have little practice in defending such beliefs and little motivation to do so."[14] Indeed, capital punishment is a topic about which educated bystanders can remain ignorant without appearing uninformed.

Such proclivities do not exist in isolation but are embedded in practices and shaped by conditioned habits that render the whole platter palatable. The story is institutionalized in the criminal justice system, undergirds the educational system, permeates religious institutions and practices, is reenacted within families, fills TV and movie screens, and is read in comic books, dime-store novels, and great works of literature. Its script comes effortlessly to mind, whether faced with instances of grievous wrong or mild insult. Third-grade girls dream of getting even with the popular girl who disrespected them on the playground. Seventh-grade boys team up against the teacher's pet. Mothers gossip, settling the score with female competitors. Habits accrued by living out the story slide in a well-worn groove down at the local police station and courthouse, as judges and juries evaluate intuitively what seems fair, what scoundrels deserve, and what will balance the scales of justice.

Humans become repeaters of platitudes, bearers of habits, and sustainers of practices that many do not know how to undo or break free of. These forms of living center on the belief that some people deserve grave, even lethal, harm. The specific kind of harm varies from century to century, culture to culture. Banishment or exile, death by flogging or beheading—no matter the choice, the response is consistent. Americans are surviving witnesses to the bitter fruits of this callous creed. Despotic regimes have killed millions because they allegedly deserved it. Of what have they been guilty? Heresy, blasphemy, physical or mental deformity, poverty, or wealth. People are targeted for harm by being the wrong gender or race, engaging in the wrong sexual practices, or threatening the moral order. Men are crushed by violence and injustice, denied the tools to recover, and then punished for wreaking mayhem and murder. The tragedy of this tangled tale causes some to cling all the more tightly to it, hoping, as George W. Bush put it, to "wage war on evil." Gilligan calls this the Moby Dick tale of punishment, the great white whale being the embodiment of evil. "Ahab pursues Moby Dick in the mad conviction that if only he can find him and kill him, he will have attained justice and destroyed evil."[15]

Punitive practices have taken new form, and people's conditioning has contemporary content. But for the most part, the story and its practices and vices are ancient, persisting not because they promote human survival or well-being, but because they are so readily imposed on the next generation.

PRACTICING THE THREE Rs

People are ingrained early with attitudes and feelings that support punitive projects known as revenge, retribution, and rectification through suffering (the three Rs). As with the three Rs expected of every schoolchild—reading, writing, and 'rithmetic—people come to master the complexities of blame and shame, merit and demerit, and winning through demeaning others. These three Rs, however, unlike education at its best, do not open doors to further insight, unleash the imagination, or stimulate creative thought. Instead, the three Rs operate like unconditioned responses so that young people well before the age of majority, play out scripted roles with one another, repeating unworkable responses. Rather than providing an increased vocabulary to write new scripts, these three Rs limit people to worn-out aphorisms, the result of a story that's been told so many times that shorthand replaces logic. Revenge, retribution, and rectification keep producing math that results in more people imprisoned and dead, failing to prevent violence while declaring that the same failed formula works.

Many Americans tend to feel like victims and mindlessly connect vindication with the ability to hurt someone of lower status. They withhold compassion from those who are thought to deserve their suffering. People are tempted to act out their painful feelings by mistreating others rather than by seeking the means to heal. These bad habits tempt them to mistake their authentic human power for the immoral power to inflict pain. Such habits also narrow full apprehension of others' humanness to a single focus on the worst thing the perpetrator has ever done.

Many Americans feel that if someone has wronged them, that person should be harmed or dropped from their universe, from their moral community of care and concern. One by one, they may exclude various scoundrels: the best friend who betrayed a confidence, the alcoholic father who was abusive, the friend who said something racist, or the worker who was irresponsible and let a coworker take the heat. A victim lets her moral community become smaller, threatening to shrink to a narrow group of intimates.

Communities also seek to protect themselves by excluding or eliminating criminals. But such exclusion offers only short-term protection. In the long term, this protection is an illusion. Prisons have a harsh and degrading effect on people. Too often, ex-convicts are returned to the community in worse shape than they were in before their incarceration. Prisoners need more than punishment to help them make good. They need a new story, new virtues, and assistance in dismantling their vices.

Banishing wrongdoers from the community does not address the harm they wrought. It merely targets those people most vulnerable to acting out the script enforced by the dominant culture. Unless individuals have recovered from their mistreatment, they are susceptible to harming others. With a few dramatic exceptions, middle-class, well-educated people who lead "safe" lives usually never face a situation that provokes lethal anger or violence. But many others, in more challenging circumstances, daily confront situations that stab at their deepest hurts, and they lash out, irresponsibly and with grave consequences.

The story about the bad guys becomes coupled with at first unwilling, and later unthinking, participation in various punitive practices, which together put the practice of punishment beyond rational debate. These experiences leave otherwise courageous and intelligent bystanders with a lack of voice and a dimness of vision. These obstacles result in certain kinds of blind polarities, as sketched below.

Nonabolitionists speak as if the death penalty were civilization's last stand against the forces of relativism and moral turpitude. The prospect of abandoning Western society's professed pieties appears to court the demise of capital punishment—the last defense against evil. In contrast, abolitionists characterize capital punishment as an anachronism that persists in the United States long after the rest of the civilized world has wisely moved forward. With either the end or the beginning of civilization hanging on its coattails, the death penalty appears able to determine the future. No wonder so much seems at stake.

Two persistent distortions in vision seem to be made, one by liberals and another by conservatives. Liberals tend to see offenders as victims of bad environments. Brutal victimization indeed is often the experience of murderers. Liberals, however, err in seeing the humanity of the offender without seeing the long-lasting effects of such brutalization. Liberals tend to underplay the murderer's resultant violent and dangerous habits, naïvely assuming that an improved environment will be sufficient for the murderer's rehabilitation. Because liberals see the community as at least partly responsible for producing violent offenders, liberals tend to buy into the idea that offenders are "victims too." Liberals fail to see the culprit's potential intelligence and integrity as well as his attachment to his vicious habits. They err by letting murderers get away with "Twinkie defenses," failing to hold dangerous people responsible for their crimes. Liberals, with their single focus, are ridiculed as "bleeding hearts" and "soft on crime." Liberals are accused of backing the early release of dangerous offenders, turning a blind eye to the pain of victims and their families.

The second error is made by conservatives, who reduce the criminals to embodiments of the worst things they ever did; misdeeds become identity. Instead of merely denouncing evil behavior, conservatives denounce certain people as essentially evil by underplaying the community's responsibility for infusing people with the same punitive, vengeful, and violent motives that drive the criminal justice system. Reluctant to name and denounce the dehumanizing social experiences that produced a human with the disposition to ravage and kill, they blame individuals as if their difficulties sprang from nowhere. Conservatives are accused of being simplistic, labeling complex humans as either purely good or evil.

Liberals and conservatives may appear to occupy opposite ends of a pole, but they actually share the same difficulty—distinguishing the human from his or her conditioning. Liberals see a limited picture of the person, not the vice; conservatives see the vice, not the person. Both share an inability to hold in view the two realities about perpetrators—that they are human beings with dangerous, debilitating, and nonintelligent habits. Thus both fail to appreciate humans' motivation to pursue the good and their vulnerability to be disrupted in that pursuit.[16] For when the human is not permitted to recover from hurt or injury, she may want to injure in return. Only when genuine human needs are *not* met do people succumb to the narrative of the lie.

Such clouded vision results from enmeshment in a story and a way of being before the age of words, which silences many before they can form independent thought and ensures complicity without ever asking for consent. It is that bad. Although the death penalty eventually may be discarded, the story, the practices, and the vices that sustain it will remain. Unless they are tackled directly.

RENOUNCING THE STORY

Because Americans are so deeply acculturated by a dominant story, it is difficult to think around it. Indeed, it is impossible to live completely outside it, because the entire culture and its institutions are so deeply entrenched in it. As social beings, we have no place entirely outside culture, even though individuals can disentangle themselves by undoing their allegiance to conditioned ways of being. Even freed just a bit from the story's habits, people have done amazing things in creating new practices of justice.

Showing great resiliency, some murder victim families and ex-convicts tell a new story that lifts them out of a life of violence.[17] Cut to the core of their being by their past and forced to deal with life's elementals, some work their way through their pain and come out the other side—aware of a new way of being and a new way of seeing, and having a new story to tell. As they seek to incorporate dreadful realities into their life stories, they also have to come to terms with the narrative that society offers them. They find it comes up short. As they seek to repair their hearts, lives, and relationships, they find that they need to tell a new story about how to respond to terrible wrongs. They challenge Americans to write a new script about justice.

Brilliant minds and courageous hearts have led Americans forward in humane directions. Whites no longer lynch African Americans at the rate of three per week and celebrate the deed by passing around souvenirs taken from the burned bodies. Vast numbers of lives are improved because this one despicable practice ended. Yet practices of punishment—including the death penalty—in the United States partake of the same mind-sets and cultural practices that supported lynching. The techniques of execution may have changed, but the habits have not.

This book illumines how the narrative of the lie shapes murderers, families of homicide victims, and bystanders. It recommends intentional liberation from enmeshment in the story that so many have been willing to kill for, identifying those practices that enable people to emerge from the wounds of the past, telling a new story about how they may act to correct injustices. As Schreiter says, "The struggle to find the way to interpret our story is frequently a gradual retelling of that story until it becomes a new story."[18] Murder victims' families who oppose the death penalty tell a new story based on a better picture of reality. Others do not. It is the difference between these two ways of seeing reality that this book addresses.

Americans face three tasks. The first is to discern those narratives that liberate from violence rather than ensure its repetition. The second task is to use liberatory narratives to heal from and transcend experiences with violence rather than getting caught in their grasp. The third is to live out of a new story and alternative practices of justice. The new story requires a commitment to refuse to pass on to others the hurts received. Needed are the expurgation of old habits and the inculcation of virtue. It requires involvement from bystanders—lending their voices to the new story, with new plots, roles, and possibilities for action.

Undoing allegiance to the three Rs will take more than educating the public about the machinery of death or abolishing the death penalty. Thus, while this book is about punishment, it is not about the techniques of death, the mechanisms of selection, the machinery of systems. It is about a society that sings the same old tune, perpetuates the play of practices, and imposes habits on each new generation—brutally, if necessary—to ensure that painful penalty remains an obvious and fitting end for some.

NOTES

1. Originally published in the *New Yorker*.

2. James Gilligan, *Violence: Our Deadly Epidemic and Its Causes* (New York: Putnam's Sons, 1996), 4.

3. Robert J. Schreiter, *The Ministry of Reconciliation: Spirituality and Strategies* (Maryknoll, NY: Orbis, 1998), 31. The phrase "narrative of the lie" is his.

4. Gilligan, *Violence*, 18.

5. Robert J. Schreiter, *Reconciliation: Mission and Ministry in a Changing Social Order* (Maryknoll, NY: Orbis, 1992), 34.

6. Ben Waxman, "Currently Employed Prison Guard Supervised Iraqi Torture," *Political State Report*, "VoterListsOnline.com," 7 May 2004, available at www .polstate.com/archives/005439.html#005439 (accessed 7 May 2004).

7. Quoted in Scott Turow, *Ultimate Punishment* (New York: Farrar, Straus and Giroux, 2003), 52.

8. Craig Haney, "Mitigation and the Study of Lives: On the Roots of Violent Criminality and the Nature of Capital Justice," in *America's Experiment with Capital Punishment*, ed. James Acker, Robert Bohm, and Charles Lanier (Durham, NC: Carolina Academic, 1998), 359.

9. "The Cruel and Ever More Unusual Punishment," *Economist*, 13 May 1999, available at psy.ucsd.edu/~eebbesen/psych16298/162DeathPenaltyArticle.html (accessed 13 August 2003).

10. "Of these 16,000 homicides [per year, as of 1999] approximately 280 get the death penalty each year. In other words, only 1–2 percent of those who commit murder get the death sentence in this country." (Mark Ostapiak, "Death Penalty Is Racist and Targets the Poor," *Socialist Action*, May 2001, available at www.socialistaction.org/ news/200105/death.html [accessed 13 August 2003]). There are many reasons for the paucity of death sentences relative to the high number of homicides. Insufficient evidence may not sustain capital charges. Prosecutors may make deals or determine that a case lacks merit. Cost matters. "Each death penalty case costs Texas an average of $2.3 million. That is about three times the cost of imprisoning someone in a single cell at the highest security level for 40 years." *Dallas Morning News*, March 8, 1992, from *Death Penalty Information Center*, available at www.deathpenaltyinfo.org/ article.php?did=108&scid=7 (accessed 13 August 2003).

Sad to say, 37 percent of murderers do get away with it. The Bureau of Justice Statistics indicates that in 2000, 63 percent of murders and nonnegligent manslaughters were cleared. See "The Percentage of Homicides Cleared by Arrest Has Been Declining," *Bureau of Justice Statistics*, available at www.ojp.usdoj.gov/bjs/homicide/cleared.htm (accessed 2 June 2003).

11. In some states, the percentage of cases overturned runs as high as 86. Tracy Snell and Laura Maruschak, "Capital Punishment 2001," *Bureau of Justice Statistics Bulletin*, NCJ 197020, December 2002, available at www.ojp.usdoj.gov/bjs/pub/pdf/ cp01.pdf (accessed 2 June 2003).

12. Robert Renny Cushing and Susannah Sheffer, *Dignity Denied: The Experience of Murder Victims' Family Members Who Oppose the Death Penalty* (Cambridge, MA: Murder Victims' Families for Reconciliation, 2002), 8.

13. Samuel R. Gross and Phoebe C. Ellsworth, "Second Thoughts: Americans' Views on the Death Penalty at the Turn of the Century," in *Beyond Repair? America's Death Penalty*, ed. Stephen P. Garvey (Durham, NC: Duke University Press, 2003), 16–17.

14. Gross and Ellsworth, "Second Thoughts," 20.

15. Gilligan, *Violence*, 15.

16. Martha Nussbaum develops the concept of the vulnerability of human goodness in *The Fragility of Goodness* (New York: Cambridge University Press, 1986), 340.

17. See such accounts in Shadd Maruna, *Making Good: How Ex-Convicts Reform and Rebuild Their Lives* (Washington, DC: American Psychological Association, 2001).

18. Schreiter, *Ministry of Reconciliation*, 43.

1

The Story We Tell

. . . with rejection comes anger, and with anger some kind of crime in
revenge for the rejection, and with the crime guilt—and there is the story of
mankind.

John Steinbeck, East of Eden

What is a communal story? It is not a fictional narrative such as one might
find in a fairy tale or an escapist romance. Rather, suggests sociologist Robert
Bellah, it is a "pattern of understandings and evaluations that a community
has worked out over time,"[1] an orienting pole that gives plausibility and
meaning to the world.

Every community has a tradition.[2] The Christian communities, for example, take the story of Jesus as foundational for their understanding of how God
wants them to live. The Jewish community is a people formed preeminently
by the story of the Exodus—the liberation from oppression and the receiving
of the law from a God who cares about human freedom and responsibility.
Similarly, the story of Muhammad informs Muslims' daily piety and pursuit
of social justice.

Some narratives become so axiomatic that their "story-ness" recedes from
view. Certain schools of philosophers, for example, write as if they occupy a
neutral perspective and as if their use of terms such as *justice* owes nothing to
the communities around them. A great deal of confusion in thinking about

1

the death penalty stems from the denial of the story dependence of any rationale for punishment. Indeed, the repudiation of story has had grave consequences for the practice of punishment.

How does story affect a community's understanding of justice?

Communal narratives need not prohibit dissent nor enforce conformity about complex questions such as justice. "Tradition is often an ongoing reasoned argument about the good of the community or institution whose identity it defines," says Bellah.[3] But such debates have parameters—wholesale rejection of forgiveness and embracing of revenge lead one outside the Christian narrative, for example.

There is no proving the truth of such founding narratives; living out their commitments tests their adequacy. Powerful traditions such as religions motivate adherents to do good as well as great evil. However, the monotheistic religions developed practices and principles of interpretation to denounce such things as unjust wars, enslavement, or persecution as antithetical to their story's true meaning. Thus even while these religions absorbed and perpetuated inequities, their prophets could call upon the tradition to speak against injustice.

Most communities develop cover stories about their own legacies of injustice and violence. Cover stories mask the ways in which a community has misused its heritage to justify exploitation or greed. Many Caucasian Americans, for instance, learned a cover story about the United States' treatment of Native Americans that says that the Pilgrims created the first outpost of civilization in the wilderness and denies the depth and richness of native cultures. Such cover stories mystify past misdeeds and promote forgetting. Atrocities are placed outside the narrative, literally becoming unspeakable events. Consequently, significant events in the lives of individuals become secrets without a name, argues psychiatrist Judith Herman. There are many ways communities try to keep the "unspeakable" unspoken and to "promote forgetting." If "secrecy fails" and victims begin to tell their dangerous memories, communities may attempt to discredit the victims. If victims continue to insist on their version of the past, many adherents of the dominant story say in effect, "It is time to forget the past and move on."[4] The traumas of injustice and violence are exacerbated by cover stories, which prevent injustices from being corrected and healing from being advanced.

In the United States, the cover story says that there is no structural injustice in the land of liberty and equality. It denies that people suffer disadvantages because of their class, sex, or race, and that such mistreatment—if left unchallenged—can ruin lives. It says: "Every American is free to rise above her circumstances. If she doesn't, well, she just doesn't have what it takes." It also denies the process by which people capitulate and go along with socially sanctioned disrespect of others. Although the losses differ for the haves and the have-nots, both groups are mistreated into accepting the disrespect of others. The story conceals the traumatic nature of this process by mislabeling it as a routine part of growing up. It says: "Boys will be boys."

Communities also tell stories about punishment. They weave worldviews that make punitive practices seem logical, true, and necessary. Within the United States, such a story is so ubiquitous and sustains so many institutions, practices, and habits that it seems intuitively right and obvious, as if there could be no other path:

- Some people are born with evil inclinations (some are bad genetically), and painful punishment steers the wayward in the right direction. When people make mistakes, they learn useful lessons from having harm inflicted upon them. But no matter how much some people are punished, they still turn out bad.
- The price paid by wrongdoers should be painful; suffering pays for wrong.
- The guilty deserve to be punished. They are bad, whereas the morally upright did not turn out bad because they have self-control and learned their lessons well.
- Revenge is a natural and inevitable response to maltreatment. The best way to defend one's honor is to fight back; vindication comes through retaliation. The world consists mainly of victims or victimizers. Given a choice, it is better to walk away the victor. In order to prevent personal vengeance, however, the state should be the agent of retribution. Punishment brings closure to the vanquished's rage and anguish.

Based on their public opinion research, Samuel Gross and Phoebe Ellsworth put the story about the death penalty in the following words:

> It doesn't matter that the death penalty is not a better deterrent than a life sentence—murderers deserve it, and besides maybe it deters some people. Poor people and minorities may be sentenced to death more than rich white people,

but that just means we should try to execute more rich white people, not abolish the death penalty. . . . A life sentence won't work because only death will guarantee that the murderer will never get free. . . .

[D]eath penalty cases were treated with exceptional care, . . . death sentences were scrutinized far more painstakingly than other legal decisions, [and] they were examined over and over again for any possible error through an interminable series of appeals, while the victims' families spent years in agony waiting for closure. Vicious killers got more help than they deserved from do-gooder lawyers intent on finding legal technicalities and creating endless delays. They lived on and on, eating free meals and watching TV at public expense, while disingenuous liberals succeeded in obstructing justice through meticulous attention to irrelevant details.[5]

Such a narrative, observes R. Sherwin, "reflect[s] a preferred sense of truth and justice" and "help[s] shape the outcome of criminal cases and predispose[s] us to play out certain scripts, schemata, and stereotypes."[6]

Nevertheless, this story paints a false picture of what is actually happening in the world. "Narratives of the lie," Catholic priest Robert Schreiter explains, "are intended to negate the truth of a people's own narratives. . . . The negation is intended not only to destroy the narrative of the victim, but to pave the way for the oppressor's narrative . . . so that people will learn to live with and acquiesce to the will of the oppressor."[7] Humans cannot survive without a narrative that sustains identity, and when their own is suppressed or shattered, in the absence of a better one, the available one must do. As German philosopher Friedrich Nietzsche says, "Any meaning is better than none. . . . [M]an would sooner have the void for his purpose than be void of purpose."[8]

Sagas from mythology recount how communities used sanctioned violence to ward off the threat of malevolent violence. The myths explain why certain people must be sacrificed in this epic struggle to save civilization. Some of these myths eventually resulted in anticipatory compliance; young virgins might be selected and offered up as scapegoats in order to protect the social order, such as in Agamemnon's sacrifice of his daughter Iphigenia, as dramatized by Euripides.

Such sacrifices were believed to function as a halt to the cycle of action and reaction. Yet Euripides shows how the sacrifice did not protect the community, but became a new wrong, needing revenge, this time by the mother, Clytemnestra, who kills her husband, Agamemnon.

What could end the cycle of harm and retaliation? The ancient Israelites sought to channel this pattern of striking back into a search for justice, sanctioned by God. As early as the receiving of the tablets from God on Mt. Sinai, Israelites were beginning to see that the cycle of revenge must have a stop. Moses demands to know more about this God who freed his people from slavery. God replies that he is slow to anger, that he shows mercy to the third and fourth generations, and that unlike in the past, revenge shall not be continued for centuries. Past injustices' hold on the present does have an end; this is God's intent. The followers of Jesus believed that the sacrifice of their beloved leader was the decisive act in history that would end forever the cycle of harm and retaliation. But within a few generations, Christians were already blaming Jews for the death of Jesus. By the fourth century, retribution for deicide was seen to justify Jews' eternal persecution and suffering. Instead of Jesus's execution ending the cycle in the Christian West, some of his followers launched a search for vengeance that lasted close to two millennia, contributing in a dark and horrible way to the Holocaust.

The Mel Gibson movie *The Passion of the Christ*, in which Jesus is subjected to the death penalty for treason, grabbed media headlines and reviews. Many moviegoers resonated with the bloody sacrifice done on their behalf. The response of some Christians has been awe and gratitude. "Look," says one, "at how much Christ was willing to suffer to save us." Another relates, "I never understood until now the depth of his sacrifice so that we might live." Jesus Christ died, they conclude, so that no other human need ever again be sacrificed to appease God and atone for humanity's sins. This brutal execution was believed necessary to save humanity, being God's decisive act in salvific history.

But within mundane history, the cycle continues. What happens when a person is wounded and that injury is left unhealed? It may originate a habitual feeling of victimization or foster a desire for revenge. Years after painful incidents, people find themselves reacting to new situations from within the framework left by old wounds so that their present actions are not fresh and creative. Instead, they react in the present to a moment that transpired long ago. Humans do not easily have access to the resources necessary to recover from such hurts. Instead, sooner or later, directly or indirectly, they may seek to avenge the injury or settle the score. Memories of past injustices—the sack of the fatherland or the slaughter of the innocent—keep painful wounds alive in the hopes that the balance is righted. For all recorded history, humans have been longing for a way out of this cycle of harm and retaliation, of action and reaction.

Many Americans believe that execution will stop the cycle and the victim's family will receive closure. But these hopes are almost as futile as those of the ancient Greeks. The execution of murderers today leaves another family wounded, creating a new set of parents to grieve the loss of a child killed. In the operatic version of the book *Dead Man Walking*, the mother of the murdered son sings her aria of grief and rage side by side with the mother of the executed killer, who sings her aria of grief and rage. Gradually, they walk closer together until their songs meld. As their voices swell, the audience realizes that the execution has not stopped violence; it has not corrected injustice, but added fresh wounds from which the current story offers no escape.

The word *myth*, historian Gil Bailie writes, has the Greek root of *muthos*, with the root *mu*, "which means 'to close' or 'keep secret.' *Muo* means to close one's eyes or mouth, to mute the voice, or to remain mute. Myth remembers discretely and selectively. Myth closes its eyes to certain events and closes its mouth." Myths, like cover stories or the narrative of the lie, can distort perception, confuse, and prompt forgetting. For example, in the case of Iphigenia, at the moment of her sacrifice, onlookers no longer saw a victim, but a heifer that bounded in joy toward heaven. The pain of her death was not recognized. In contrast, the Greek word for truth, *aletheia*, comes from the root *letho*, which is the verb "to forget" (the prefix "a" indicates a negative). "The literal meaning, then, of the Greek word for truth, *aletheia*, is 'to stop forgetting.' "[9] The opera *Dead Man Walking* invites the audience to "stop forgetting" the true harms of capital punishment.

The myth depicted "good" violence as rejuvenating the ties that bound the community against peoples or forces deemed evil. Violent punishment came to be seen as able to save the community, foster social cohesion, and protect the community against feared chaos or a more violent future. Mythic violence, Bailie says, could "ward off other violence or crush it with religious conviction when it arose."[10] However, it was not the violence that was inherently cohesive, but the myth behind it, which the violence reinforced.

Bailie claims that a similar myth informs contemporary life. The attack of 9/11 and this country's violent retaliation reveal the ability of righteous, communal violence to produce a feeling of unity, however transitory, for those enthralled by the myth. The nation's invocation of "us" versus "them" after the attack, and the president's portrayal of entire countries aligned along an "axis of evil" resulted in, for some, a gratifying sense of togetherness. Civic and economic divisions slid into the background temporarily. Concern about the violence unleashed on the Afghanis teetered in balance with the pleasure of feeling proud and unified. As Bailie notes, the myth portrays "Communal violence [as] an antidote for internal strife and the 'civil' or domestic violence to which it might otherwise lead. Campaigns against outsiders or evildoers revive the camaraderie jeopardized by internal conflict."[11] Such cohesion is perceived, however, primarily because of the power of the shared myth.

Executions serve this mythic function of unifying the community against a perceived threat. Bailie quotes a reporter's account of Ted Bundy's 1989 execution: "The scene outside Florida State Prison . . . was one of the wildest. Parents bought children; men brought wives. Hundreds of reporters camped out in a pasture. It was like a tailgate party, someone said. Or Mardi Gras." Bailie points out how the reporter concludes that it was "a brutal act," but it was done "in the name of civilization."[12] Righteous violence against evil violence secures a civilized future, says the myth.

But when the monotheistic religions emerged, they ushered in a new concern, argues Bailie. They showed a profound solicitude for victims. The ancient Israelites understood God to have special regard for the oppressed and vulnerable. As God had rescued them from bitter exploitation, so should they protect the widow, the orphan, and the stranger "for you too were once strangers in the land of Egypt." Practical compassion for victims placed important moral constraints on the sacrifice of scapegoats.

Given the great historical religions' concern for the underdog and the consequent awareness of how structural violence harms everyone, who then could be selected to be the scapegoat? Bailie suggests that "increasingly we can only lustily vent our violence against victims whom we can confidently regard as victimizers." Only "certified moral failures," who we do not perceive as victims, can be the object of our righteous wrath.[13] The story now requires that Americans deny the brutalization that leads some to victimize others. The objects of just punishment must now be seen as demons that irrationally and malevolently choose evil without any linkage to past or current injustice. They must be viewed as epitomes of evil to avoid any hint of "victim" status that would generate moral claims to compassion or protection. Consequently, rather than acknowledge a collective failure to assist all citizens to be law abiding, bystanders believe that the object of punishment bears the sole responsibility for the crime. The myth now sustains the belief that punishing "superpredators" who fully deserve their fate will save "civilization."

Nevertheless, living out the myth that punishment saves the community has proven its inadequacy, argues criminal psychiatrist James Gilligan:

> This means of attempting to prevent violence, which I will call the traditional *moral and legal* approach, far from solving the problem of violence, or even diminishing the threat it poses to our continued survival, has in fact been followed by a continued escalation of the frequency and intensity of violence, to the point that the century we have just survived has been the bloodiest in all human history, with more humans killing other humans than in all previous centuries combined.[14]

Punishment is part of the problem, not a solution.

Perhaps forswearing all stories offers an escape from archaic myths and modern story lines about how some violence is the cure-all for other violence. Beginning in the mideighteenth century, the Age of Enlightenment, reformers took this approach. They rebelled against inherited practices that were supported not by good sense, but by the traditional defense, "This is the way it's always been done." Enlightenment philosophers engaged in a great "de-storying" endeavor. They proclaimed that they would reject all traditions. Hoping to think in universal rather than socially bounded terms, ethicists such as Immanuel Kant sought to escape the limits of being, for example, German and Lutheran. They presented their justifications of punishment—the imposition of unwanted suffering on wrongdoers by a legitimate authority—as abstract truths, far removed from the annoying particularities of religion or regime, culture or class. Presented as eternal truths universal for all humankind, the rationales for punishment espoused during the Enlightenment took on a timeless quality, as if justice had always been interpreted their way.

Other reformers, such as Cesare Beccaria and Jeremy Bentham, sought to base criminal justice policies on enlightened reason alone. They argued that punishment could be justified only if it promoted the greatest happiness for the greatest number, the utilitarian formula for justice. They presented this concept as if it were story-less and value free. It should be empirically possible, they argued, for any community anywhere to formulate punishments that produced more good than harm.

But who defines "good" and "justice"? Using this Enlightenment method of reasoning, one tradition appears as arbitrary as any other, and so these crusaders ignored the different ways that such terms were interpreted in various cultures. In the Aristotelian tradition, for example, the good is not something that can be "produced." For Aristotle, the end at which a citizen of the *polis* aimed was to realize justice over the course of a lifetime. In contrast, the good in utilitarianism becomes reduced, eventually, to satisfaction of consumer preferences. Within Judaism and Christianity, justice requires that the needs of the oppressed be given special priority, which defies utilitarian calculation. Philosopher Alasdair MacIntyre argues that Enlightenment philosophers treated justice as rationally calculable apart from its governing story, ignoring the quite different meanings of good or justice in various traditions.[15]

Within the past twenty years, efforts have been made to puncture the dominance of Enlightenment discourse about criminal justice. This effort has engaged in a retrieval of pre-Enlightenment forms of justice seeking. Philosopher Conrad Brunk writes:

> Traditional cultures have developed effective ways of managing the routine offenses against the norms of the community which do not involve the imposition of "punishment" in the modern, legal sense of that term. Aboriginal peoples in North America, Australia, and Africa have used relatively informal, community-based processes for bringing the offender to accountability in the community, which do not involve the deliberate and formal impositions of pain, deprivation, alienation, and humiliation so endemic to modern law.[16]

Loosely called restorative justice, these practices make different assumptions. They focus on the harms caused by the offense. And rather than retaliate against the criminal, they ask how to repair damage and restore broken relationships.

Although justice is a universal moral good, it lacks any specific meaning without a moral narrative. Without a story, there is no guidance about how to interpret and apply justice, relate criminal justice to economic and social justice, or balance justice against other goods, such as life and liberty. A story guides what practices best embody justice, its essential rules, and its necessary virtues.

By treating ethical concepts as if they made sense apart from any story, Enlightenment philosophers' cover story became that they had no story. Today, punishment is discussed almost exclusively in Enlightenment categories. Almost every standard textbook compares retributive to utilitarian justifications for punishment. These rationales for painful penalty are discussed as if they are free from any narrative that shapes assumptions about human nature, the purpose and function of law, or the relation of the individual to society. Enlightenment discourse blocks the understanding that it, too, operates within a narrative. The denial of the story dependence of any rationale for punishment creates significant problems for death penalty discussions.

Consider, for example, the serious difficulty camouflaged by the line, "There are no stories here." This script shields the wielders of power. Who decides what is dangerous? Who decides what is a serious threat deserving of punishment? Whose actions are deemed criminal? Which victims are worthy of protection? Whose voices are excluded from these considerations? When officially there is no story (only abstract truths removed from history), the oppressive play of power in shaping criminal justice practices becomes obscured. Such forgetting deludes most Americans into believing that the death penalty singles out the worst of the worst, when such is not the case.

MURDEROUS MYTH: WHO MAY BE PUNISHED?

The rules of retribution say that only certain persons deserve to be punished harshly, namely those responsible and blameworthy for knowingly and seriously harming others. The most serious acts should receive the most serious punishments because such offenses most harm the state and its laws.

The descent is steep from these ethereal heights into the muddy rivers of history. In Europe, for example, murder was not always seen as a public offense. In pre-Christian Europe, tribal groups regarded murder, adultery, theft, slander, and assault as private affairs to be settled by the clan. Only a few actions were considered true social threats—incest, sorcery, treason, and sacrilege.[17] These travesties often invited the wrath of the entire community upon the public menace and his clan. The aim of public punishment was to eliminate the source of danger. Each member had a duty to avenge a wrong to any member of his clan. However, since "no clan recognized a wrong against another clan or the right of another clan to avenge an injury upon one of its members," "perpetual" vendettas between clans resulted.[18] Clans eventually developed ways to limit the damage from reciprocal blood feuds, one being restitution to families, such as the Germanic and Anglo Saxon system of *wergeld* (fines for murder).

Not until the establishment of kingship did harms seen as "public" and "capital" fundamentally change on the European continent. Private wrongs once adjudicated by clans became redefined as "an offence against the king's peace" and a "breach of the public tranquility."[19] The new victim became the crown (recast in modern times as the state and its laws). With this redefinition, meeting the needs of the individual, family, and community took a backseat to redress to the king. The system of restitution to victims fell away; now fines went into the king's coffers, not to families. It is easy to see that his majesty would define as serious crimes those actions that most harmed the crown's interests. Capital offenses in England steadily expanded, for example, growing from about fifty in 1700 to over two hundred in 1830. The so-called Bloody Code delivered people to the scaffold for stealing turnips and poaching.[20]

But royals did not define as criminal their wholesale exploitation of serfs and (later) laborers. Petty theft by the poor was a crime; grand larceny by the ruling elites was business as usual. The phrase "common criminal" derives from the ideology that misconduct by the lower class was especially egregious. Many synonyms for criminal are reserved for the lower classes: villain, rogue, lowlife, scamp, and knave.[21] Had commoners possessed the political power to define which forms of wrongdoing they found most onerous, the definition of crime and image of the criminal might be quite different. For example, today, if poor people dominated the U.S. Congress, a law might be passed that made it illegal to bequeath more than five million dollars to each heir.

But the underclass did not have the power then, nor do they have it now. Hence, the misconduct codified in criminal law still concerns primarily the misdeeds of the poor. Enron stole millions from its employees, but Enron's initial defense was that nothing illegal happened. Meanwhile, "Jerald Sanders, 48, will spend the rest of his life in an Alabama prison because he stole a $16 bicycle. He had a five-year history of burglaries, none of them involving violence."[22] Demands by the middling and ruling classes for severe punishment of Enron notwithstanding, philosopher Jeffrey Reiman argues, lethal actions by the ruling elites in the form of negligent worker safety or faulty consumer protection are not defined as murders, but as "regulatory violations." Newspapers do not describe lethal misdeeds by knowing corporate executives as predatory or heinous. The story portrays the gravest type of purposeful harm as unpredictably "one-on-one," encouraging people to most fear "direct personal violence." The middling classes are deeply conditioned to fear violence by the poor, as if the rabble alone were the greatest threat to their well-being. Reiman notes that although people legitimately fear death at the hands of a thug, occupational hazards as a source of death (31,218 in 1997) should cause nightmares as much as the deaths that result from knives and scalpels (13,963), firearms (10,369), other weapons (4,001), or bodily weapons such as fists (956).[23] Thus, not all forms of knowingly harmful activity are deemed criminal by the ruling elites, and the death penalty does not winnow out those people whose actions knowingly will result in "untimely deaths of innocents."[24]

Retributive systems do not punish all serious wrongdoing; they choose to ignore some. The basis of selection is nonmoral—maintenance of unjust power. Thus, as restorative justice practitioner Wesley Cragg observes,

> Retributive accounts of punishment may serve to disguise in illegitimate ways the real nature of law and punishment. . . . A system that punishes only some but not all wrongdoing is itself unjust. In fact it implies that the justification for punishment is not desert but something else. If it were desert alone, all wrongdoing would evoke the required response.[25]

Although Cragg overstates his case—not every moral wrong (lying, adultery) need be illegal—the fact remains that not all lethal activities are made criminal. The lethal activities of the "criminal class" are singled out for the severest punishment, reflecting the classism that underwrites the story of who deserves death. With unaware prejudices further biasing the operation of the system, people from a certain segment of society are most likely to receive capital charges and be executed.[26]

Capriciousness in selecting who may be targeted for punishment is shown in another way. Both revenge and retribution require that punishers communicate a message to malefactors about what they did wrong. Painful penalty, Robert Nozick argues, is meant to "*show* him [his misdeed's] wrongness" and, since the medium is the message, thus "convince [him] that it is true."[27] Offenders need to be able to receive the message—otherwise they will feel tortured, not justly punished. Opponents of capital punishment have argued that the mentally ill, the mentally retarded, and the young are not able to receive the message the state wishes to communicate. Only recently the U.S. Supreme Court ruled that the mentally retarded may not be executed; however, many states still permit the execution of children and the mentally ill.[28] One thinks of the prisoner who told his execution team to save his pecan pie because he wanted to eat it after his electrocution. The practice of executing those who cannot receive the message that punishment is intended to communicate violates the rules of revenge and retribution, revealing nonmoral factors at work.

When Enlightenment philosophers tried to de-story their concepts of punishment, they wrote as if their views were free from the constraints of culture. This pretense resulted in a lack of critical insight into the question of who decides what counts as a harm (the ruling elites) and what harms would be designated as criminal (actions that harm those interests). The result is an ideological naïveté about the harsh injustices of the criminal justice system. Most Americans repeat the delusion that the criminal law targets for prosecution all intentional lethal actions and that the death penalty is reserved for the worst of the worst.[29] These delusions are deadly.

If *Homo sapiens* really are story-dependent creatures whose narratives both create and reflect social practices, what is a second consequence of the Enlightenment project of pretending that humans operate at the level of abstract reason apart from any story? Put starkly, the result is that punishment becomes an incoherent practice.

NOTES

1. Robert Bellah, et al., *Habits of the Heart* (Berkeley: University of California Press, 1985), 335–36.

2. Bellah, *Habits*, 335–36.

3. Bellah, *Habits*, 336.

4. Judith Herman, *Trauma and Recovery* (New York: Basic, 1997), 8.

5. Samuel Gross and Phoebe Ellsworth, "Second Thoughts: Americans' Views on the Death Penalty at the Turn of the Century," in *Beyond Repair? America's Death Penalty*, ed. Stephen P. Garvey (Durham, NC: Duke University Press, 2003), 20–21, 27.

6. R. Sherwin quoted in Craig Haney, "Mitigation and the Study of Lives: On the Roots of Violent Criminality and the Nature of Capital Justice," in *America's Experiment with Capital Punishment*, ed. James Acker, Robert Bohm, and Charles Lanier (Durham, NC: Carolina Academic, 1998), 354.

7. Robert J. Schreiter, *Reconciliation: Mission and Ministry in a Changing Social Order* (Maryknoll, NY: Orbis, 1992), 34.

8. Friedrich Nietzsche, *The Birth of Tragedy and The Genealogy of Morals*, trans. Francis Golffing (Garden City, NY: Doubleday Anchor, 1956), 298–99.

9. Gil Bailie, *Violence Unveiled: Humanity at the Crossroads* (New York: Crossroads, 1997), 33.

10. Bailie, *Violence Unveiled*, 7.

11. Bailie, *Violence Unveiled*, 52.

12. Janny Scott quoted in Bailie, *Violence Unveiled*, 79.

13. Bailie, *Violence Unveiled*, 27, 83.

14. James Gilligan, *Preventing Violence* (New York: Thames & Hudson, 2001), 7. Italics in original.

15. Alasdair MacIntyre, *Whose Justice? Which Rationality?* (Notre Dame, IN: University of Notre Dame Press, 1988).

16. Conrad G. Brunk, "Restorative Justice and the Philosophical Theories of Criminal Punishment," in *The Spiritual Roots of Restorative Justice*, ed. Michael L. Hadley (Albany: State University of New York Press, 2001), 32.

17. Harry Elmer Barnes, *The Story of Punishment: A Record of Man's Inhumanity to Man*, 2nd ed. (originally published in 1930; Montclair, NJ: Patterson Smith, 1972), 41.

18. Barnes, *Story of Punishment*, 48.

19. Barnes, *Story of Punishment*, 51.

20. James B. Christoph, *Capital Punishment and British Politics: The British Movement to Abolish the Death Penalty 1945–57* (Chicago: University of Chicago Press, 1962), 14.

21. For example, *villain* comes from the Latin *villanus*, which means "farm servant." Jeffrey Reiman, *The Rich Get Richer and the Poor Get Prison*, 6th ed. (Boston: Allyn and Bacon, 2001), 170.

22. Adam Liptak, "Sentences Are Too Long or Too Short. Rarely, Just Right," *New York Times*, 24 August 2003, WK3.

23. Reiman, *Rich Get Richer*, 4, 70, 82, 88.

24. Reiman, *Rich Get Richer*, 65–78.

25. Wesley Cragg, *The Practice of Punishment: Towards a Theory of Restorative Justice* (New York: Routledge, 1992), 22, 28.

26. As James Gilligan observes, criminal courts are only interested in two distinctions about the legally guilty: separating the good guys from the bad guys and distinguishing the bad guys from the mad guys (*Violence: Our Deadly Epidemic and Its Causes* [New York: Putnam's Sons, 1996], 6). For discussion of class and race, see Reiman, *Rich Get Richer*, ch. 2. For a discussion of how gender affects perceptions of perpetrators, see Patricia Pearson, *When She Was Bad: How and Why Women Get Away with Murder* (New York: Penguin, 1998).

27. Robert Nozick, *Philosophical Explanations* (Cambridge, MA: Harvard University Press, 1981), 371, 374.

28. "Juveniles and the Death Penalty," *Death Penalty Information Center*, available at www.deathpenaltyinfo.org/article.php?did=205&scid=27 (accessed 14 July 2003).

29. Reiman, *Rich Get Richer*, ch. 2. For additional reasons why the worst of the worst are not targeted, see Scott Turow, *Ultimate Punishment* (New York: Farrar, Straus and Giroux, 2003), ch. 10.

The Incoherency (and Immorality) of Punishment

The contemporary debates within modern political systems are almost exclusively between conservative liberals, liberal liberals, and radical liberals. There is little place is such political systems for the criticism of the system itself, that is, for putting liberalism in question.

Alasdair MacIntyre, Whose Justice? Which Rationality?

The story goes that punishment is the infliction of painful penalties by a legitimate authority on those guilty of wrongdoing. Punishment affirms social values by decreeing that certain behaviors cast a person outside the society's prohibition against harming. The story says it is morally permissible to harm criminals for a variety of reasons: it removes dangerous people from society, it provides self-defense, it prods criminals to reform, it teaches valuable lessons that cannot be learned in any other way, it deters, it's what offenders deserve, it's fitting (a life for a life), it provides closure to victims and their families, it prevents crime. It doesn't matter if these agendas clash or are impossible for the criminal justice system to blend into a consistent practice. The only alternatives, says the story, are lawless failure to hold criminals responsible or a relapse into revenge.

Given widespread acceptance of this account, one might think that the morality of punishment, including capital punishment, is easy to justify. On the contrary, such rationales have been difficult to construct, and good minds disagree about how to defend the harms of punishment.

Punishment is best analyzed using the concept of practice. Philosopher Alasdair MacIntyre has painted a clear picture of practices, referring to complex social activities such as medicine, parenting, or professional sport, which consist of three components. First, practices involve cooperative projects aimed at protecting basic human goods. Medicine, for example, seeks to protect life, which is valuable in and of itself, and health as a means to preserve life. These goods provide the foundational pillars of the practice. Society entrusts medicine to protect these goods, requiring of doctors "that sort of participation-in-a-value which is never finished and done with . . . and which takes shape in a potentially inexhaustible variety of particular projects and actions."[1] The projects of medicine—preventing illness and injury, curing the sick and injured, and caring for the incurable—instantiate its foundational values. These projects in turn serve as rationales for particular tasks, such as vaccinating children or providing palliative care.

Second, a practice contains particular rules, such as "do no harm" and "protect confidentiality." There are even rules about what rules should take precedence over others, such as "Confidences may be violated to protect the public health." The rules also authorize who may legitimately practice medicine.

Third, a commitment to these basic goods in turn shapes practitioners, ideally inculcating in them virtues that support the projects and rules. By practicing medicine, professionals should acquire certain virtues and avoid particular vices (doctors ideally exhibit competence, caring, and commitment to the patients' best interests and avoid the vices of sloth, slovenliness, and sex with patients).

Today, practices reside within capitalist institutions that have quite different aims—securing a market niche and remaining competitive. But as long as these ancillary goals do not scuttle the practice by becoming its end all and be all, the practice retains its moral identity. But if all doctors, for example, were to believe that the primary good of their practices was protecting their pocketbooks rather than their patients' best interests, then the profession would lose its moral justification. If medicine's projects contradicted each other, so that curing, caring, and prevention routinely worked at cross purposes, the practice would lose its coherence. Or if the actual work of healers sickened and only rarely helped, then the practice as a whole would lose its legitimacy. Although many medical procedures are painful or invasive, patients do not consider them harmful if they have given their consent and understand that the procedures are intended to cure. When patients are harmed through deception, greed, or negligence, these bad outcomes can be denounced by appealing to the goods, rules, and virtues affirmed by the practice. But if the rules and virtues themselves justify such misdeeds, the morality of the practice is thrown further into doubt. Fortunately, medical practice realizes its goods enough of the time and has resisted full penetration by the market so that it can be called a moral, coherent, and legitimate practice.

Although the morality of practices such as medicine seems clear despite grievous errors or crass abuses of power, such is not the case with punishment. Nothing like this clear connection between empirical reality and the participation in inherent goods exists with respect to punishment. Society authorizes the criminal justice system to protect several primary goods, such as physical and communal life. Protection of life includes bodily integrity and derivative arrangements, such as property, that provide resources necessary to live. Life in community is deemed a basic good because humans are interdependent throughout their long period of maturation, throughout their productive years of work and play, and at the end of life. Humans have wellsprings of desire for human connection and, barring mistreatment, flourish in community. Mutual dependency renders humans vulnerable to abandonment and attack.

The universal need for human cooperation coupled with the universal vulnerability to violence are reflected in ethical norms. Moral standards govern life in community and come to constitute a cluster of goods, what philosopher John Finnis calls the requirements of "practical reasonableness"[2] or everyday ethics. The good of justice concerns the maintenance and repair of human relationships and the basic fairness of social arrangements, institutions, transactions, and procedures. Justice involves determinations of what is owed one another. The good of responsibility protects life in community because it denotes responsiveness to the other who makes a rightful claim. Responsibility honors the ties that bind people together and includes a commitment to the vulnerable who suffer most from structural injustices. It also refers to the individual's responsiveness to all basic human goods as one decides "what one is to be and to do."[3] In addition to being responsive to others in one's moral universe, humans are responsible for their actions. Responsible moral agents can be held accountable for their deeds. Treating people as responsive to others and as responsible for themselves respects human dignity.

In our diverse and wonderful world, different cultures interpret these goods differently and create particular practices to embody their visions. Diverse pictures of reality are not a problem. In fact, cultures are made safer when they encounter different ways of doing things and permit such encounters to help them to question received wisdom. The incoherency of the practice of punishment does not result from a multiplicity of stories, nor does the solution reside in the hegemonic imposition of one story on everyone. Rather, the Enlightenment story (that there is no story) has resulted in a practice that patches together rationales and projects from different traditions without regard for their incommensurability. People are taught to believe that there is no way to improve their picture of what promotes human flourishing. Instead, they are conditioned to conclude that the perspective one selects is arbitrarily based on preferences or taste, making it permissible to ignore the practice's incoherence.

The resulting practice of punishment is a mishmash of competing activities unable to embody core human goods. It is as if various architects were asked to design a structure and one was instructed to make the edifice look intimidating, while another said no, his instructions were to build a school, to foster learning. Yet another said it should be a fortress in order to protect those on the outside, while the fourth said no, it was to be light and airy, in order to inspire and aid those on the inside. Another disagreed with the lot of them, displaying a blueprint for a building that would have made the lives of its inhabitants as miserable as each fully deserved. These graduates of the post-Enlightenment School of Architecture did not question that they were handed incompatible aims. Each end or warrant might have been fine in and of itself (although some were of dubious merit), but the belief that one structure could be built to accommodate such competing visions never struck them as ludicrous. Never able to debate rationally the merits of each blueprint (such things, they believed, being matters of personal taste), they built a structure that followed none of their instructions well or even at all. Their employers were the only ones who stood to gain from the entire enterprise. The owners reassured the builders that they would be able to sell the project to the public by convincing citizens of its structural integrity and urgent necessity.

An analogy might clarify two different assessments made of punishment. Galloping Gertie, the suspension bridge made famous by its spectacular collapse on 7 November 1940, spanned a stretch of extremely cold and treacherous water between the mainland and the Olympic Peninsula in Washington State. The lightest, most flexible bridge of its time, it boasted a ratio between the depth of its girders and its span over twice that of the Golden Gate Bridge. However, under moderate winds (42 mph), the bridge began a wavelike motion and then fell into the depths. Photos of its demise render these facts certain. However, engineers and physicists dispute to this day the cause of the collapse as well as whether, in rebuilding the bridge, adequate steps have been taken to prevent a future catastrophe.[4]

Engineers take a pragmatic approach. Among other changes when rebuilding the bridge, they thickened the roadbed and increased the strength of the trusses. They are 99 percent certain that it will never collapse again. Physicists, however, argue that their calculations show that the bridge may fall apart again some day because they can neither predict whether or not the bridge would withstand a future wind effect nor explain why the original one collapsed.

This difference in viewpoint is key: the pragmatists think near enough is good enough; the theorists disagree, wanting to be able to explain theoretically why it fell and whether or not it would withstand a future storm. This disagreement is not a question of probable risk, comparable for instance, to flying in an airplane, which carries a risk that it will fail. With airplanes, the engineers and the physicists agree about why planes stay in the air and understand ways in which they might fail. With Galloping Gertie, the physicists cannot explain why it fell the first time, much less what is needed to keep its replacement from falling.

Killing people or storing human beings against their will in small concrete cages for extended periods is harmful. Anyone who did either of these without legitimate authority would be arrested and thrown into just such a cell. Society may legitimately restrain predators, but on what basis does it claim authority to dehumanize, deprive of additional liberties, and fail to protect prisoners from rape, mutilation, and other dangers?

Prisons and death chambers are permissible, the pragmatists argue, because competing projects of retribution and deterrence sometimes achieve punishment's noble goods. These projects are certainly better than letting predators roam freely. It is unfortunate that innocent people are sometimes incarcerated or narrowly escape the electric chair. However, akin to Gertie's engineers, pragmatists argue that even if the criminal justice system does not succeed in protecting its core values consistently—protecting life in community, correcting injustice, or fostering responsibility—it's the best the system can do.

Theorists, by contrast, want to know if the projects resting on its pillars work at cross-purposes, threatening the practice's structural integrity. They do not dispute that any human practice may be subject to error and fallibility—even the most skilled surgeon may make mistakes. But they want to know whether the practice of punishment—unlike Galloping Gertie—can stand on its own merits. This soundness seems important to determine since two million men, women, and children are behind bars, and several times a month one of them is executed.

Philosophers such as Friedrich Nietzsche argue that punishment accommodates interrelated yet conflicting desires that give rise to rationalizations and contradictory rationales. Nietzsche writes his treatise, "To give the reader some idea how uncertain, secondary, and accidental the 'meaning' of punishment really is, and how one and the same procedure may be used for totally different ends." "Purposes," he says, have been "projected into the procedure" hiding the irrationality at its core, in a vain attempt to "buttress our tottering belief in punishment."[5]

Undeterred by Nietzsche's warning, liberal philosophers have bravely sought to demonstrate coherence between punishment's projects. But are the projects of punishment—incapacitation, self-defense, rehabilitation, pedagogy, deterrence, retribution, satisfying victims, and prevention—actually compatible? And do they actually embody its foundational and justifying goods? Under consideration here is the morality, coherency, and legitimacy of the practice as a whole, not particular judgments about individual cases.

Incapacitation of dangerous people, the first of these projects, is deemed legitimate by both pragmatists and theorists. Perhaps short-term protection is achieved when the United States incarcerates a larger percentage of its population than any other nation in the world. Although restraint involves suffering and loss of liberty, it does not justify hard treatment per se or the indignities to which prisoners are exposed. It certainly does not make capital punishment morally permissible. In addition, incapacitation as a sole rationale for incarceration may result in draconian sentences of excessive duration. It also does not address how criminals should be treated while inside. Should they be forced to work? Freed from responsibility? Periods of isolation in a hostile environment often corrupt prisoners' characters, further disabling their potential to be law-abiding citizens.

When incapacitation is coupled with the project of retribution involving hard treatment and stigmatization after release, convicts' dangerousness may increase, thus defeating the project of long-term protection. James Gilligan, former head of the mental health services for the department of corrections in the state of Massachusetts and Harvard professor of psychiatry argues, "punishment beyond what is necessary for restraint . . . is an ill-conceived, misdirected societal crime for which we pay dearly in lives, suffering and social costs."[6] Once incarcerated, many are fair game for assault. (Many ex-convicts lose for their lifetimes the civil liberty of voting.) *Harsh Justice*, written by James Whitman of Yale Law School, suggests that the *telos* of the criminal justice system, having become fixated on treating criminals as a class of inferiors, is to dehumanize and demean the prisoner.[7] Gilligan observes, "When [prisoners] feel their 'honor' is at stake, and an intolerable degree of humiliation or 'loss of face' would result from a failure to fight for that honor, they may act violently."[8] Thus when incarceration is combined with degrading treatment, responsibility is not fostered, since unrepentant, unhealed, and dangerous murderers or sex offenders may be released into the community. Thus incapacitation by itself fails to provide adequate guidance for how prisoners should be treated and, when coupled with retribution, fails in the long run to protect the basic goods of protection and responsibility.

Self-defense is sometimes argued to be a second project of the practice of punishment. Self-defense and punishment, however, are distinct practices. Harming people is morally permissible, retributivists argue, because criminals deserve it. Violence used in self-defense, in contrast, is not justified because the attacker deserves it, but rather because the duty to prevent an immediate and preventable harm overrides the duty to do no harm. Also, self-defense justifies the use of force as a last resort and only as much as is necessary to stop the attack, whereas punishment often harms rapscallions even when they never pose any serious threat of harm to others, for example, prostitutes or underage beer drinkers. Self-defense is a self-contradictory project because the prison system is notorious for hardening people and inducting nonviolent people into violent lifestyles, thus failing to defend society *or* prisoners. Self-defense is a project especially inapplicable to the death penalty, because when murderers are dragged to the electric chair in leg irons and handcuffs while escorted by strongmen, they are the ones in need of defense. Self-defense provides an important argument for the use of violence, but it does not appear to be the best justification for the kinds or amounts of violence exacted by the practice of punishment.

A third project to protect life in community is the rehabilitation of offenders in order for them to become productive members of society.[9] Rehabilitation has the laudable goal of assisting offenders to become law-abiding citizens and to restore them to the community. Unfortunately, rehabilitative practices have fallen prey to a medical model, which treats prisoners as patients with no responsibility for their illnesses, and to a therapeutic model, which views prisoners as victims of larger social ills. Within a mental health system that combines both models, sick people ought not to be released until they are well. These approaches may lead to indeterminate sentences or even permanent incarceration for relatively minor crimes. By taking away all responsibility for prisoners' misconduct, these models of rehabilitation encourage the habit of victimhood, undermining the good of responsibility. These approaches are ultimately coercive, because they do not serve the interests and needs of the prisoner, but are designed to force or manipulate the prisoner to conform to predetermined ends set by those in power.

People are fond of saying, "We tried rehabilitation, but it didn't work." However, as one commentator observes:

> Human beings, whether saints or sinners, often with amazing tenacity resist being won over to any program, way of life or philosophy whose protagonists are simultaneously inflicting physical, mental or spiritual punishment on them. This is true whether such a punishment is deserved or not. . . .[10]

The very concept of rehabilitation partakes of the story's script that shame and coercion are helpful to people. As Nietzsche says, "Man is tamed by punishment, but by no means improved; rather the opposite. It is said that misfortune sharpens our wits, but to the extent that it sharpens our wits, it makes them worse; fortunately it often simply dulls them."[11] Thus the project of rehabilitation seems counterproductive.

Many people believe that those prisoners who are regarded as incorrigible are therefore dispensable. The Nazi doctors killed the incurables of their day, including alcoholics and diabetics. French philosopher Albert Camus urges "public opinion and its representatives [to] give up the law of laziness which simply eliminates what it cannot reform."[12] Protecting prisoners whose difficulties challenge society's current expertise in helping and healing is morally preferable to the project of excluding or eliminating so-called incorrigibles.

Yet another project is teaching wrongdoers the error of their ways, which is believed to make them care for social values. This project is based on a faulty premise about adults who have perpetrated heinous attacks. The argument assumes that dangerous offenders do not know what it means to be victimized and have to be shown just how wrong what they did was. However, most people capable of such violence know firsthand its ravages, throwing into the question the type of lessons violence teaches. In addition, if less painful routes of instruction are effective, then society is obligated to use them.

Utilitarians reject the above teleological approach, which recognizes inherent moral goods that may not be sacrificed for the benefit of the greater good. Instead, utilitarians argue punishment is warranted if and only if it deters or prevents crime, thus producing more benefits than costs for the greater number.[13] With deterrence, society aims to secure voluntary compliance with the law and to motivate people to obey it who otherwise would not. Fear of being caught may indeed inhibit rational people from taking actions over which they possess freedom of choice. Many reduce their highway speed upon seeing a patrol car. But evidence shows that people who commit foul acts often think that violence is a good way to handle certain situations, plan to evade capture, and would rather kill or mutilate others or risk being killed themselves than live without dignity and pride.[14] Also, given that jails serve as temporary shelters for the addicted or homeless, some commit petty crimes just to secure a bed and three square meals.

The project of deterrence is thought by many to justify capital punishment. Camus argues that the state and the public act contrary to their professed belief in the deterrent power of capital punishment. Executions occur in the dead of night, buried in the heart of isolated institutions. If the state truly believed in the power of example, it would execute on CNN, in Times Square, or at the foot of the Capitol. However, public executions, once the norm in the United States, led to public drunken debauchery and thievery, thereby generating rather than preventing crime. At the very least, rather than restricting witnesses to relatives—the people least likely to harm others—witnesses should include people already headed down the wrong path, jealous lovers, or others with a potential to kill.[15] And, finally, deterrence justifies any level of torture imaginable that succeeds in terrifying people into submission.[16] Security bought at such a steep price—as in Iraq under Saddam Hussein—is a crass form of utilitarianism, breaking human rights and other basic goods on the rack in the name of public safety.

Retribution is yet another favored project of punishment. Retributivists such as Jeffrie Murphy, Igor Primoratz, and Stephen Kershnar reject the utilitarian approach, which basically turns serious moral questions into endless empirical debates: Do prisons increase violence? Does the death penalty deter? Instead, justice requires, they argue, that the guilty suffer in proportion to the magnitude of their crime, receiving their just deserts, even if more harm than good results. By violating the rights of others, offenders lose some rights.[17] The U.S. public finds retributive violence a compelling rationale for the death penalty. "Retribution remains the major reason that people give for supporting capital punishment. In a June 1991 Gallup poll, in answer to an open-ended question asking why they favored the death penalty, 50 percent of respondents said, 'a life for a life.'"[18] People often support retribution because they want to honor the good of responsibility.

Retribution allegedly fosters responsibility by making people pay. Yet, as a backlash against blame and out of fear of imminent punishment, people resist taking responsibility. Nietzsche argues that retributive punishment fails to teach miscreants that their actions are intrinsically evil because the criminal justice system does the very acts they do: "spying, setting traps, outsmarting, bribing, . . . despoiling, insulting, torturing, murdering the victim."[19] Restorative justice advocates Dennis Sullivan and Larry Tifft write, "From experience, we all know that punishment is capable of . . . coercing a person to publicly acknowledge shame for certain acts, but because such punitive measures show little concern for the needs of the person . . . they create a vacancy or void in that person. Punishment closes people down; it incites resentment in them."[20] Thus retribution seems to undermine rather than foster responsibility.

Retribution is closely related to the last of punishment's projects, namely bringing satisfaction to victims or surviving family members. Although vengeance is taboo in civilized societies, some versions of retribution permit families to "feel satisfied" with the suffering of others. Others believe that such satisfaction smacks of vengeance and argue that, in retribution, victims feel pleasure solely because "justice has been served." A variant is the promise that murder victims' families will experience closure after the execution. The family spokesperson will give the benediction, saying, "Now we can put this whole thing behind us." However, some victims of violence are appalled that more violence will be committed in their names. Many murder victims' families attest that closure is a deception falsely promised by the criminal justice system.

In sum, unlike moral practices such as medicine, punishment lacks coherence among its projects. Even worse, its central projects fail to realize the goods of life in society, justice, and responsibility, which justify the practice in the first place.[21]

Philosopher H. L. A. Hart observes that, on the one hand, rehabilitation, by removing the "example of punishment on others," defeats deterrence and contradicts retribution. On the other hand, he points out, retributive penalties "may convert the offender to whom they are applied into a hardened enemy of society," thus defeating rehabilitation and possibly increasing violence and thereby defeating prevention of crime.[22] This fundamental irreconcilability reveals an insupportable beam between the superstructure and the pillars that allegedly support it. Yet Hart does not find problematic that punishment involves contradictory aims and activities that are not reducible to a single account. He argues that each aim, although "partly conflicting," is "relevant at different points in any morally acceptable account of punishment" and that "the pursuit of one aim may be qualified by or provide an opportunity, not to be missed, for the pursuit of others."[23]

The U.S. Supreme Court was forced to acknowledge these incompatible projects without being able to resolve the conflict, as revealed in its 1976 plurality ruling in *Gregg v. Georgia*, which stated, "The death penalty is said to serve two principal social purposes; retribution and deterrence of capital crimes by prospective offenders. . . . 'Retribution is no longer the dominant objective of the criminal law' . . . but neither is it a forbidden objective nor one inconsistent with our respect for the dignity of men."[24] The Court's effort to nail these two incompatible projects into one unwieldy frame acknowledges and fails to address the irresolvable tensions between them. On the ground floor of a prison, this higgledy-piggledy structure houses a punisher who seeks to shame while simultaneously attempting rehabilitation. On any given day, does the warden admit the drug rehabilitation specialist or subject prisoners to dehumanizing intrusions and indignities? Which is it—reform or retribution? Some will claim that suffering is a means to re-form, but anyone who spends a little time in the county jail might leave with an impression that it is either a poorly run social services agency or a ret-ributive place that has lost its moral compass.

U.S. citizens subscribe to the story and tolerate the practice's inconsisten-cies; they want punishment to uplift and degrade simultaneously, dehuman-ize without being inhumane, incarcerate and kill without inflicting suffering, and rehabilitate while satisfying the victim's family. They want punishment to do it all—incapacitate, defend, rehabilitate, teach a lesson, deter, promote re-sponsibility, and provide satisfaction to victims. This muddle-headedness is akin to the child's game Mr. Potato Head, which enables players to mix and match physical features and attire. The resulting figure would be laughable, except it is jailers and executioners being outfitted here.

With respect to the death penalty, supporters easily pinion opponents be-tween the poles of deterrence and retribution. If executions fail to deter, they argue, justice requires death. If abolitionists point out the faults of retribution, then the need for protection is invoked. Abolitionists find themselves arguing on the terms set by the status quo. They make the familiar arguments that the death penalty does not deter, it is not cost-effective, and it harms rather than helps the community. Or they attack the fairness of its application, noting, with good reason, how the victim's and the defendant's race, class, and gender often determine who is extinguished. These verbal wars are part of the liberal contest and offer no resolution to it.

The liberal project has failed. Punishment's projects conflict with each other and fail to realize its core goods.

THE STORY OBSCURES A DANGEROUS REALITY

To make matters worse, the practice of punishment not only fails to secure its goods, but also may actually promote disvalues (the maintenance of crime). It seems designed to defeat rather than protect its professed commitments. Why does society tolerate a system that fosters violence and hence fails to protect life and property? Whose interests are served by shoring up a bridge that lacks integrity?

Ironically, one interpretation of the available evidence suggests that the criminal justice system seems designed to maintain, rather than reduce, the supply of criminals. Philosopher Jeffrey Reiman argues that it is easy to design a system to produce this contrary result. First, he says, punish people for be-havior they "regard as normal" (using recreational drugs), which increases "their need to engage in *secondary* crime" (stealing for drugs). Second, give "broad discretion" to prosecutors and judges so that convicted felons know of people who did the same crime but are not doing the same time. This injus-tice will foster feelings of victimization and rage, rather than contrition and accountability. The system will seem designed to encourage their disregard of rather than respect for the law. Third, make "prison not only painful" but "de-meaning" and brutalizing, sure fire ways to increase inmates' potential for ag-gressive violence. Gilligan agrees that violence is "the predictable and even inevitable outcome of patterns of interaction between prisoners and the penal system."[25] Provide no real money is provided for drug treatment, counseling, or educational programs. Fourth and fifth, suggests Reiman, withhold educa-tion and job training and then stigmatize felons once released, preventing their integration into society. Despite the rare successes of the system—halfway houses, minimum-security prisons that treat inmates with respect, and plenty of dangerous villains who are kept off the streets—Reiman argues, "On the whole, most of the system's practices make more sense if we look at them as ingredients in an attempt to maintain rather to reduce crime!"[26]

Sociologists such as Émile Durkheim reason that, since outlaws are needed by a society to promote internal cohesion, its leaders develop mechanisms to "recruit and maintain a reliable supply of miscreants." Sociologists do not deny a criminal's individual freedom of decision or sources of criminality such as mental impairment. However, they suggest that criminals are func-tionally useful for societies, which have devised practices of punishment to control, rather than drastically reduce, crime. Since crime itself serves the good of positive community identity, then punishment "succeeds" only if "it *fails* to prevent most crime." Thus the criminal justice system actually works to maintain crime, despite some success in preventing it. Harsh punishments and prisons draw offenders more deeply into the criminal ranks instead of re-forming or deterring them. Crazy as it seems, repeat offenders, rather than signs of failure, are the system's signature successes.[27]

A crime-ridden society, of course, does not serve anyone's genuine human needs. The alleged cohesive function of crime and punishment serves mainly the ruling elites' agenda of preserving their privilege. These elites, political econ-omists such as Karl Marx allege, secured their position originally by repressing

the lower classes. Such thinkers argue that ruling groups maintain their dominance by making it permissible for those high in the class hierarchy to control—
through shame, blame, and punishment—those lower in the hierarchy. Power
elites today include the wealthiest members of society, those who own the
means of production, such as corporate executives and boards of directors as
well as the legislators and politicians who serve their interests. Class societies
have always punished people more severely for killing *up* the hierarchy rather
than down. Plato's legal code penalized a slave who killed a free man, but not
vice versa.[28] Medieval legal codes permitted Christians to testify against Jews,
but Jews could not testify against Christians. Blacks who kill whites are more
likely to receive a death sentence than blacks who kill blacks, or whites who kill
blacks.[29] In Philadelphia, a study showed that being of African heritage was a de
facto aggravating factor in sentencing. In that study, race ranked just below
"killing with torture" and "killing multiple victims" as an aggravating factor in
assigning the death penalty.[30] Death as a means of social control and instilling
fear should not be equated with the noble aims of "protecting society" or "preventing crime." According to some sociologists, the ruling elites use punishment
to serve the narrow interests of a small minority.

Reiman modifies the claims of Durkheim and Marx by arguing that it is not
the punishment of moral outsiders alone that creates social cohesion. Rather, the
story a community tells about the wonders of punishment and the nature of the
bad guys also functions like social cement. The current practice of punishment
both creates and reflects the story we tell. The criminal justice system succeeds in
"creating the *image*" that crime is almost exclusively the "work of the poor" *and*
that nothing can be done to reduce it, he argues. Selling the image that the government is waging a war on crime—without addressing the sources of violence
or supporting the few programs that actually prevent violence—serves the interests of the privileged. When the society subscribes to this distorted picture and
actually imprisons the poor, it suffers from the illusion that society has been
made a safer place, unfortunately leaving untouched dangerous activities by the
upper crust.[31]

Punishment's foundations slide further into treacherous waters in the
United States, where the ruling elites justify the world's highest incarceration
rate in the name of crime prevention, without addressing the sources of crime
or actually protecting society. As of 2003, one in thirty-seven Americans were
in prison or had served time.[32] Reiman argues this failure leads to angry pub-

lic demands for more of the same futile activities: more jails and harsher punishments. Making the fight against crime appear unwinnable helps create the dominant story that crime is primarily "the work of the poor." With the middle classes captive to the story and the poor in prison, few remain to challenge the story's deception. Leaders then benefit from the resulting preoccupation with the crimes of the poor. Reiman observes that this ideology "generates no effective demand for change."[33] He concludes:

> [T]he failure of criminal justice works to create and reinforce a very particular set of beliefs about the world, about what is dangerous and what is not, who is a threat and who is not. This does not merely shore up general feelings of social solidarity; it allows those feelings to be attached to a social order characterized by striking disparities of wealth, power, and privilege, and considerable injustice.[34]

In the absence of internal integrity, and without alignment with reality, the word *punishment* has become like the junk drawer in a kitchen. Each bit of string or discarded battery has a story behind it—but collectively, it is junk. A red light should go off in the reader's head every time he or she hears the word *punishment*. Readers should treat it like a code word and try to decipher its (usually) hidden meaning. Contained in that deceptively simple code is the story of whose actions are identified as criminal, which victims are deemed worthy of protection, and whose interests punishment serves, with a thin veneer that makes the structure appear solid enough to justify its harms.

The practice of punishment is immoral because of its role in a narrative designed to maintain injustice in the name of justice. It is immoral to pursue projects that not only fail to realize the stated commitment to core values (protection of life, justice, and responsibility) but also achieve the opposite (the maintenance of crime, injustice, and irresponsibility). U.S. citizens are accustomed to living with a practice of punishment that is mythically, but not morally, justified. The middle classes learn to spout the story, ignore the moral questions, and tolerate the contradictions.[35] The inescapable impression is that liberal philosophers are maidservants of the status quo: they attempt rationales for the infliction of painful penalties, which actually serve oppressive purposes rather than the lofty ideals they posit. By disregarding history, the story that there is no story shuts a blind eye to the powerful interests that have shaped how punishment is practiced and masks who benefits from the resulting confusion. The incoherency of punishment and its failure to prevent crime are functions of the story we tell.

The goods of physical and communal life, justice, and responsibility are too valuable to be entrusted any longer to morally incoherent projects. If the story and its projects violate core goods, how respectable are its rules of the game?

NOTES

1. John Finnis, *Natural Law and Natural Rights* (Oxford: Clarendon, 1982), 64.

2. Finnis, *Natural Law*, ch. 5.

3. Other basic human goods include life, knowledge, art, play, and friendship (Finnis, *Natural Law*, 90). For a feminist approach that results in a strikingly similar list, see Martha Nussbaum, *Sex and Social Justice* (New York: Oxford University Press, 1999), 41.

4. Yusuf Billah and Robert Scanlan, "Resonance, Tacoma Narrows Bridge Failure, and Undergraduate Physics Textbooks," *American Journal of Physics* 59, no. 2 (February 1991): 118–24.

5. Friedrich Nietzsche, *The Genealogy of Morals* 2.11–14, in *The Birth of Tragedy and The Genealogy of Morals*, trans. Francis Golffing (Garden City, NY: Doubleday, 1956), 212, 214.

6. James Gilligan, *Violence: Our Deadly Epidemic and Its Causes* (New York: Putnam's Sons, 1996), 140.

7. James Q. Whitman, *Harsh Justice: Criminal Punishment and the Widening Divide between America and Europe* (New York: Oxford University Press, 2003), 23.

8. Gilligan, *Violence*, 97.

9. Karl Menninger wrote about the need for treatment, not punishment. See his *The Crime of Punishment* (New York: Viking, 1969).

10. Alan F. Kay, "A New Framework for Our Prisons," *America* 141, no. 3 (August 1979): 46–48.

11. Nietzsche makes this point in *Genealogy of Morals*, 215, 216.

12. Albert Camus, "Reflections on the Guillotine," in *Resistance, Rebellion, and Death*, trans. Justin O'Brien (originally published in 1957; New York: Vintage International, 1995), 232.

13. Jeremy Bentham and John Stuart Mill make the classic arguments. For a critical review, see Lloyd Steffen, *Executing Justice: The Moral Meaning of the Death Penalty* (Cleveland, OH: Pilgrim, 1998), 49–87.

14. Gilligan, *Violence*, 110.

15. Camus, "Reflections," 187.

16. Stephen Nathanson, "Why We Should Put the Death Penalty to Rest," personal copy, 4.

17. Jeffrie Murphy, *Retribution, Justice, and Therapy: Essays in the Philosophy of Law* (Dordrecht, Netherlands: Reidel, 1979); Igor Primoratz, *Justifying Legal Punishment* (Atlantic Highlands, NJ: Humanities Press International, 1989); and Stephen Kershnar, *Desert, Retribution, and Torture* (Lanham, MD: University Press of America, 2001).

18. Samuel R. Gross and Phoebe C. Ellsworth, "Second Thoughts: Americans' Views on the Death Penalty at the Turn of the Century," in *Beyond Repair? America's Death Penalty*, ed. Stephen P. Garvey (Durham, NC: Duke University Press, 2003), 33.

19. Nietzsche, *Genealogy of Morals*, 215.

20. Dennis Sullivan and Larry Tifft, *Restorative Justice: Healing the Foundations of Our Everyday Lives* (Monsey, NY: Willow Tree, 2001), 5.

21. For an effort to reconcile these projects, see Lenn E. Goodman, *On Justice: An Essay in Jewish Philosophy* (New Haven, CT: Yale University Press, 1991), 60–61.

22. Herbert L. A. Hart, *Punishment and Responsibility* (New York: Oxford University Press, 1968), 26–27.

23. Hart, *Punishment and Responsibility*, 3. John Rawls sought to reconcile conflicting approaches by suggesting that the practice as a whole, by embracing retributive rules, produces the greatest good ("Two Concepts of Rules," in *John Rawls: Collected Papers*, ed. Samuel Freeman [Cambridge, MA: Harvard University Press, 1999], 20–46). However, many critical theorists dispute that punishment serves the greater good; instead, they say, it serves the narrow interests of the ruling elites. For a good summary of the literature, see Jeffrey Reiman, *The Rich Get Richer and the Poor Get Prison*, 6th ed. (Boston: Allyn and Bacon, 2001), chs. 1, 4; appendix.

24. Excerpts from the opinion of Justices Stewart, Powell, and Stevens can be found in "Gregg v. Georgia, 1976: The Death Penalty Is Not Per Se Unconstitutional," in *The Death Penalty in America: Current Controversies*, ed. Hugo A. Bedau (New York: Oxford University Press, 1997), 200.

25. Gilligan, *Violence*, 164.

26. Reiman, *Rich Get Richer*, 3, 4. Original in italics.

27. Reiman, *Rich Get Richer*, 47–48.

28. Plato, *The Laws II*, 872b–c.

29. Amnesty International USA, "Killing with Prejudice: Race and the Death Penalty" *Amnesty International's Campaign on the United States May 1999*, available at web.amnesty.org/library/index/engamr510521999 (accessed 11 June 2003).

30. Richard Dieter, "The Death Penalty in Black and White," *Death Penalty Information Center*, June 1998, available at www.deathpenaltyinfo.org/article .php?scid=45&did=539 (accessed 11 June 2003).

31. Reiman, *Rich Get Richer*, 4, 5, 58–68, 159.

32. Paige Harrison and Allen Beck, "Prisoners in 2003 (NCJ-205335)," *Bureau of Justice Statistics*, available at www.ojp.usdoj.gov/bjs/abstract/p03.htm (accessed 5 January 2005).

33. Reiman, *Rich Get Richer*, 6. Also see all of ch. 4.

34. Reiman, *Rich Get Richer*, 48.

35. Reiman, *Rich Get Richer*, 12–57.

3

The Rules of the Game

Punishment is resentment universalized.

Henry Sidgwick

The victim's voice must not be heard lest the ritual sacrifice go awry and lead to cultural disaster. Furthermore, the victim's glance must not be allowed to awaken sympathies in those whose role in the ritual is essential. . . . So intense is the actual moment of the killing, however, that [the onlooker] reports it in a stammering and halting way. . . . "The rest I did not see, Nor do I speak of it."

Gil Bailie, Violence Unveiled

What rules does the practice of punishment use to guide its daily operations? Within the story, justice is stated as a formal rule—give to each what is due. The communal story guides ruling elites in filling out each part of the formula—who is authorized to harm, on what basis the wrongdoer's deserts are determined, how much harm may be imposed, and why the response must be painful.

The story says that whereas premodern societies used the rules of revenge, modern civilizations now employ the rules of retribution to effect justice. Revenge, the story says, is passé and anachronistic. A leitmotif of great drama and literature, revenge is often portrayed as the downfall of deluded leaders, the corrupter of communal bonds, or a potion that poisons all protagonists, such as in the tragedy of *Hamlet*. The story says that communities that permit their members to wrest personal revenge have regressed morally. In most ethnic conflicts, both sides resist the characterization of their mutual retaliatory strikes as revenge, convinced that retribution is far removed from such bloody scenes. Conversely, writers such as Friedrich Nietzsche, Susan Jacoby, Robert Solomon, and more recently, Peter French suggest that, without revenge, condemnation of wrongdoing, essential to morality, would not exist.[1] Revenge, they say, channels moral outrage at evil toward the highest achievement of civilization—justice. Thus, while the dominant story says the legal system uses only bright, efficient rules of retribution, which are allegedly far removed from the dark passion of revenge, American practices of punishment are actually steeped in these two Rs and are not as far apart as moderns would like to believe.

Movies and TV shows such as *Falling Down, The Godfather,* and *The Practice* reaffirm the story's full mythic power. In genre Westerns, Americans romantically embrace revenge in the form of vigilante justice. In shows featuring courtroom drama, Americans affirm their allegiance to due process. An action outside the script—such as community mediation by a neutral third party— would fail to conjure the necessary symbols: the Marlboro man standing alone in the sunset, the vigilantes smoking cigarettes while the outlaw swings on a tree behind them, or the lawyer securing the defendant's confession on the stand in a burst of tears. Vigilantes and vigilant lawyers are admired for having secured justice (allegedly) despite a corrupt or inept legal system.

What are the rules that govern vigilantes such as those portrayed in *Dirty Harry,* and how are they similar to and different from retribution, portrayed in *Law and Order*? The adequacies of the two Rs in securing justice can be assessed by examining their responses to the questions posed by the story's notion of justice (give to each what is due): (a) Who is authorized to give harmful treatment? (b) On what basis are penalties due? (c) How much harm is due? and, (d) What may be imposed?

WHO IS AUTHORIZED TO HARM?

Most forms of revenge grant rights of retaliation to victims or their representatives (usually family members). Individuals settle scores without recourse to bureaucracies. Victims must meet the moral criterion of having been insulted or injured, thus justifying the retaliation done in their name. This criterion distinguishes avengers from malefactors, who allegedly harm others for no good reason.

The metaphors of vigilante justice so deeply permeate American culture that George W. Bush, a Texan president, resorted to them when responding to the quite new threat of Osama bin Laden. "Round up the posse, and let's go get 'em," he said after the horror of 9/11.[2]

In the old West, the lone avenger, confronting the outlaw in a shootout, was given tacit support by the community. Retaliation followed swiftly on the heels of humiliation or injury. At other times, vigilante squads were entrusted with exacting penalties. Rangers operated outside the legal system, yet on behalf of the community. Legal scholar Franklin Zimring observes that these community-authorized avengers knew the victim and his or her family and could identify interlopers into their community; they also knew the local values. They were trusted to identify the guilty party without a great deal of fuss and deliver the appropriate penalty, affirming their concern for the victims over the criminal justice system's preoccupation with the rights of wrongdoers.[3] Vigilantes acted with the bystanders' passive support, because "they get in return a *representation* of their collective sense of injustice." Through such avengers, "the bulk of the community 'sees justice done,'"[4] even if a particular act of revenge was unjust because the wrong person was killed, for example, or the harm was out of proportion to the originating offense.

Despite the lure of a romanticized past and Americans' reluctance to turn in their holsters, most have sworn allegiance to the state. Retribution, they swear, is better than—and different from—revenge. Yet according to Zimring, Americans have never abandoned their attraction to vigilante justice pursued by the local community out of distrust of the federal government. The guns are still in the closet. Psychologically, he argues, Americans are ready to demand a return to local justice when the government's delivery of justice seems too unwieldy or too lenient. Vigilante justice also addresses Americans' concern with the exclusion of crime victims from the legal process.[5]

Retribution restricts retaliation to the state; when the state's laws are violated, it becomes the new victim, displacing crime victims from the criminal justice system. The victim's desire for satisfaction is supposed to be met vicariously through judicial proceedings and sentencing.[6] Aggrieved parties now must take complaints to the courts rather than to the town square for a shootout or behind the courthouse for a lynching. With the consolidation of punitive power by ruling elites, eventually nations established that only state officials might punish.[7]

Retributivists believed that if the government exacted punishment, the practice would be freed from reliance on avengers of dubious character and effectiveness. The desirable traits of objectivity and neutrality, they imagined, were more likely to be exhibited by bureaucrats than by those close to the traumatized. Through controlled and centralized procedures, retribution offered better protection against vastly differing subjective judgments of what is due the person responsible for the crime. Government-sanctioned execution also stood, it was believed, a better chance of reducing irreversible error by killing only the legally guilty. In addition, retribution would ensure that punishment would not be left to the whim of the victim. If the victim or the family of the deceased did not want to proceed, the state could prosecute anyway. In addition, the amount of punishment given would not vary with the feelings of the victim or her agents—forgiving victims might not exact any payment, whereas demented ones might kill off entire families. It was believed that the state would be better able to secure justice, since not every person would be properly habituated to become an avenger. Many Americans believe that the United States is more just without vigilantes, although this confidence in the fairness of the state sits uneasily alongside a resonance with vigilante-style justice.

Zimring argues that this dual allegiance—to vigilantes' swift and certain justice and the state's retributive concerns for due process—explains Americans' lack of concern about authorizing the state to kill its own citizens.[8] He notes that, in contrast, Europeans question the consolidation of punitive power into the hands of the nation-state. European countries experienced states' power to kill those it thought deserving during the Holocaust of 1939–45. In the decades after the war, European countries one by one forbade their governments to execute their own countrymen. In 1957, French philosopher Albert Camus wrote:

> State crimes have been far more numerous than individual crimes. I am not even speaking of wars, general or localized, although bloodshed too is an alcohol that eventually intoxicates like the headiest of wines. But the number of individuals killed directly by the State has assumed astronomical proportions and

infinitely outnumbers private murders. . . . Hence our society must now defend herself not so much against the individual as against the State.[9]

A few conservatives, such as George Will, on this point link arms with abolitionists. However, Will has not been able to rally his fellow conservatives around their traditional objections to an overweening federal power treading on private interests. Zimring suggests that neither abolitionists nor conservatives have been able to use the European argument, because most Americans do not see capital punishment as an abusive exercise of state power. Although the theory of retribution argues that the state becomes the victim because its laws are violated (thus denying the real victims any real voice in the criminal justice system), since the 1970s and the emergence of a victims' rights movement, Zimring argues, the state has stopped declaring itself the victim and has begun portraying itself as serving the interests of the victims. Ten, fifteen, or twenty years after the sentence, executions are portrayed as offering "closure" to victims' families, despite the fact that many survivors abhor the term, because for them, the abyss that murder creates is never sealed over. Nevertheless, Americans now cite closure as a major rationale for punishment. The story says that the death penalty is good for homicide survivors and done in their name, masking the state's exercise of brutal power, too often unjustly targeted at the guilty poor.[10]

Even those abolitionists who oppose the state's license to kill focus less on the question of state power and more on the issue of government ineptitude. Plenty of evidence supports their concerns about fairness.[11]

Ten years ago, government officials uniformly denied that innocent people have ever been executed. In 2000, Governor George W. Bush of Texas, while running for president, went on record with the claim, "I'm absolutely confident that everybody that has been put to death . . . [is] guilty of the crime charged, and, secondly, they had full access to our courts."[12] Yet Texas has neither public defenders nor an office dedicated to postconviction review. And as recently as March 2003, the U.S. Supreme Court stayed the seventeenth scheduled execution of Delma Banks Jr. ten minutes before he was to be executed, arguing that the Texas Court of Criminal Appeals had failed to consider the merit of the final appeal, which it refused because the attorneys had missed a deadline. Also, the Texas Board of Pardons and Paroles rejected a clemency petition without reading it because it was too late. "I think this case goes to show, unfortunately, in Texas, substance and merit and concern about due process and possible innocence don't hold any water compared with technical procedures and rules," NAACP attorney Miriam Gohara told the *Houston Chronicle*.[13]

Opponents of capital punishment would like to radically shrink the pool of eligible punishers. The human inability to fully understand another person's motivations, character, history, and mental state makes retributive punishers morally illegitimate, they argue. Christian abolitionists appeal to Jesus's caution, "Let those without sin throw the first stone." Recognizing human frailty, self-interest, and susceptibility to error, abolitionists suggest that neither the state nor local community nor private avengers should be authorized to take human life. As Camus puts it, "But precisely because he is not absolutely good, no one among us can pose as an absolute judge and pronounce the definitive elimination of the worst among the guilty, because no one us of us can lay claim to absolute innocence."[14] However, unlike the Europeans who join Camus in arguing that imperfect entities ought not to impose absolute sentences, Americans continue to embrace harsh penalties, especially the death penalty.

Frustration with governmental ineptitude ironically renders the rules of vigilante justice compelling to Americans, convinced that the state's authority derives from the local community, which acts on behalf of the victim. Zimring argues, "There is no other developed country where citizens believe that official punishments are an extension of the community rather than a function of the government."[15]

The publication of *The Virtues of Vengeance* in 2001 by philosopher Peter French illustrates the desire to embrace retribution's procedural rules while affirming vigilantes. He argues that victimization alone does not entitle a person to seek revenge. Rather, avengers who embrace retribution's concerns for not punishing the innocent and for proportionate penalties are morally authorized to hunt down and kill offenders if the state fails in its job. They are forbidden from being sadistic, but instead must be willing to maim or kill motivated by the high moral purpose of repelling wrong.[16] As long as they meet these criteria, private citizens should wait for the state to act, and if they discover justice was not delivered, then they can harm offenders, giving them their "true deserts."

Advocates of a conscious blending of revenge and retribution, such as French, seek to enlarge the number of authorized punishers (to those with the stomach and level head) beyond the government, while adopting retribution's other rules about punishing only the deserving and making the punishment fit the crime. His book reveals the profound conditioning that has led Americans to accept these two Rs and blend them in distinctly American ways.

Thus, despite criminal justice's theoretical distinction between revenge and retribution on the question of who may legitimately punish, the story links the two Rs. The state punishes, but as an avenger who is motivated by concern for the victims and their families (allegedly). The state as avenger exploits victims in order to mask its capricious use of power against those too poor or too unlucky to escape its ultimate punishment.

ON WHAT BASIS SHOULD PAINFUL PENALTIES BE METED OUT?

Another rule of both revenge and retribution is that only the guilty, not the innocent, may be harmed. The two Rs utilize the criterion of moral desert or merit. It would be wrong, according to their rules, if people were punished based on other criteria, such as their ability to pay, their contributions to society, or their needs. (Recall that the cover story obscures from view that the state abandons this rule when it fails to criminalize lethal actions of the upper classes, immortalized in Woody Guthrie's song "Pretty Boy Floyd": " Some rob you with a six gun, and some with a fountain pen.")

How should moral merit be determined? Philosopher Stephen Nathanson distinguishes two kinds of moral merit: a robust concept of moral blameworthiness versus its gaunter cousin, "payback" or "getting even."[17]

Revenge often interprets moral desert as payback, "an eye for an eye," the *lex talionis* (or *jus talionis*). Peter French, for example, accents heavily the action, not the motive. "What a person does to others matters more than why he or she does it."[18] When punishers consider the act narrowly and exclude considerations of history, intentions, and motives, they use a payback schema, not a full-bodied concept of moral blame.

The distinction between blameworthiness and payback does not neatly align with the distinction between retribution and revenge, although payback is most often associated with the crude assessments of merit within revenge.

Nathanson observes that Kant, a retributivist, expresses a notion of payback when he says that persons should be executed because they have killed:

> Any undeserved evil that you inflict on someone else among the people is one that you do to yourself. If you vilify, you vilify yourself; if you steal from him, you steal from yourself; if you kill him, you kill yourself. Only the law of retribution, *jus talionis*, can determine exactly the kind and degree of punishment.[19]

Despite the significance of Kant's influence, most retributivists agree that actions alone are insufficient for determining moral blame. Imagine a man slapping his wife. Without a narrative, the observer has difficulty interpreting the meaning of the action. In scenario A, an angry husband lashes out at the wife, whom he blames for his feelings of shame. In scenario B, the loving husband saves his wife's life by slapping a bee off her face, thus preventing a sting to which she is fatally allergic. In each case the action is the same, but moral merit varies with the motives and intentions (humiliated rage versus loving protection). Thus, when using the criterion of moral blame, the phrase "murderers deserve death" is empty, because punishers need to know minimally the murderer's circumstances, motives, and powers of self-control and deliberation. Every action has a history, and before punishment can occur, the context must be understood. This reasoning underlies the presentation of mitigating evidence during the penalty phase of a capital trial.[20]

But the determination of blameworthiness is complex and imprecise. Since "no man is an island" and habits have social roots, people are a complex mixture of individual freedom, cultural socialization, and unwanted painful conditioning. Although it is unfair to characterize courts' assessments of merit as purely subjective, it would also be inaccurate to characterize them as self-evidently clear. Grasping the complexity—if not the impossibility—of evaluating blameworthiness, abolitionists such as Nathanson conclude that determinations of moral merit are beyond what a legal system should be entrusted with when a human life hangs in the balance.

Absent a reliable way to assess moral blameworthiness—and a fondness for vengeful payback—assessments of criminal merit deteriorate into evaluations of social merit. Class societies rank people in a hierarchy of who should receive more of society's resources. Punishment, like capitalism, does not strictly distribute benefits and burdens according to people's personal merit (how hard they have worked, the value of their contribution, their abilities), because people are rewarded or penalized unfairly for arbitrary and irrelevant reasons—status, color of skin, lineage—their social desert. People's social worth is partially dependent on wealth, and the misdeeds of the wealthy often evade criminalization or harsh punishment.

Social desert, like moral merit, is polar, involving both rewards and punishments—the upper crust deserve riches, the poor deserve prison. Not all dangerous moral agents are treated severely by a society due to considerations of social merit. In the hierarchical medieval world, the life of a bishop was more valuable than that of a serf. When restitution was the response to murder, the higher the rank of the injured party, the more money had to be paid.[21] Punishment was selective based on the status of the victim *and* murderer. Philosopher Jean Hampton writes, "punishment for those who injure the less valuable people is lighter than for those who injure the more valuable people."[22] Ironically, the state's imposition of the death penalty became a symbol of the victim's worth, usually determined by class standing, gender, or race. The reservation of capital punishment for less-valuable killers of more-valuable victims is unfortunately evident in the U.S. criminal justice system. In a society where race determines worth still, black-on-black murders are not prosecuted as capital crimes as often as black-on-white homicides.[23] When appealing to intuitions about merit, bystanders, juries, and judges often conclude that the severest punishments are deserved by those whose social deserts are most negative—poor, uneducated African American men whose victims are white.

The criminal justice system absorbs and creates the surrounding culture's confusion of social with moral merit. Ironically, status-bound punishment puts victims into the position of demanding harsh penalties to show their worth. Many Native Americans support the death penalty, perhaps because they want the homicides of Natives to be taken seriously, after a legacy of devastating mass murder according to the unofficial U.S. policy, "The only good Indian is a dead one."[24]

The idea that certain people deserve grave harm appears intuitively true because American relationships and institutions are shaped by this very notion. The story depends upon a populace conditioned to feel that to be at the bottom is to be worthless, the ruling elites deserve their rank and wealth, and that "when someone fails at an endeavor . . . he or she deserves whatever pain, loss, burden or punishment derives from his or her misguided actions and efforts."[25] Neither revenge nor retribution is able to ensure that judgments about social desert do not distort assessments of blameworthiness. For this reason alone, juries should be barred from imposing capital sentences using the murky, imprecise, and easily prejudicial criterion of moral blameworthiness.

Restorative justice practitioner Wesley Cragg says that retribution "leaves no room for other values to which we are equally committed, values whose focus is human needs rather than human deserts. It is this element of exclusivity or 'moral imperialism' that renders it seriously suspect."[26] The narrative of the lie remains silent about the possibility that other criteria of what humans owe one another—need or equal human worth—could override moral demerit.

HOW MUCH SUFFERING DO WRONGDOERS DESERVE?

Retributivists such as Kant think strict equality is due. The punishment inflicted should be equal to the harm committed. Kant adopted the biblical restriction on the excesses of revenge, the *lex talionis*, which limits the payment for murder to only one life, not a bus full. The measure "a life for a life" seems to imply that equality is achievable, at least with respect to murder.

However, such a criterion violates the rule of blameworthiness. If "life for a life" were the measure, then all killings—regardless of circumstance— should receive the same sentence. However, the criterion of equality cannot be applied easily to many crimes, including treason, fraud, and serial murder. Kant, like the ancient Hebrews, recognized that equality actually provides little real guidance. Rather than raping the rapist, Kant advocated castration, while the ancient Hebrews advocated death for those who ravished the betrothed. On what basis can either justify their recommended punishment as equal to the offense?

Retributivists who endorse the approach of German philosopher Georg Hegel argue that the amount of harm due is based on a notion of balance. They assume that at the time of the crime, perpetrators and victims start on an even playing field, in a just situation. The injury lowers the victim while benefiting the criminal. By inflicting painful suffering on the wrongdoer, society removes the benefit and lowers the offender to the victim's level. Victim and offender are now equal, if at a lower level than before. It is permissible to harm the offender to restore fairness.[27]

This approach can be challenged on a number of grounds. It errs in assuming that harming others is a truly human benefit to the criminal. Although economic advantage may result, unjust accumulation of property does not necessarily enrich the soul, promote virtue, or lead to the good life in a fully human sense. This approach also proceeds from two false views about humans. First, it assumes that people are looking for opportunities to be "free loaders"—violating the law while expecting others to be obedient. Second, it assumes that people are "itching" to commit serious moral wrong—plundering, raping, or murdering. Humans who have had a chance to develop in good enough environments neither find such laws constrictive nor want to exploit others.

Also objectionable is the fallacy that the original playing field is level. Much crime is a reaction to existing inequalities, an attempt to get ahead or secure dignity when legitimate avenues are closed. Dennis Sullivan and Larry Tifft write:

> His or her actions threatened existing deserts arrangements. Since deserts-based justice has to do with equalizing unequal situations, it is believed that this equalization can be best achieved through the equalization of loss, through the creation of equal ill-being. Only through the imposition of a counter-debt can the original debt be paid. . . . The counter-debt lets the [person] know that property rights and distributions are to be upheld even if they disallow the [person's] needs from being met.[28]

Thus punishment within an unjust society reinforces existing inequalities, rather than correcting injustice.

Punishment shows that the community has the power to demean offenders. This lose-lose model communicates the legitimacy of those with the privilege to exercise power over others. Justice grounded in merit lets each person know "who is in power and that power relationships are acceptable."[29] When the rules of merit are violated, the system moves to punish so that these hierarchies can be reestablished.

Retributivists offer another argument for punishments equal to the crime. Hard treatment allegedly defeats the wrongdoer's false claim of superior human worth, Hampton argues. By inflicting suffering on the rapist, the state's retribution shows him, the victim, and the community that his dehumanization and devaluation of the victim was wrong. It demonstrates that the victim is a person of equal value and did not deserve to be subjugated or used as a thing. "The retributivist . . . aims to defeat the wrongdoer in order to annul the evidence provided by the crime of his relative superiority."[30]

Prison psychiatrist James Gilligan challenges the retributivist view that affirming equal human worth constitutes the good motive behind retribution, whereas criminals have the bad motive of asserting their false superiority. Instead, he argues that the motives behind the crime and the punishment are identical:

> That the greatest fear in each instance is that of being shamed or laughed at; that the subsequent wish or need to dominate and humiliate others is in the service of gaining a swelled sense of pride and power by having dominion over others, including the power to inflict pain on them, punish them, and "give them what they deserve."[31]

In Gilligan's view, it is the lack of recognition of equal human worth that fuels both crime *and* retribution: "The emotion of shame is the primary or ultimate cause of all violence, whether toward others or toward the self."[32]

The two Rs are based on the dubious proposition that the crime's false message of unequal human worth is defeated by wielding coercive power. Such power is a tool of class oppression—"I have power over you and am able to exploit you." With it, punishers and avengers hope to communicate a non-classist message—"We all have equal human worth."

But ultimately, neither revenge nor retribution can be forced into a non–class-based framework. "The master's tools will never dismantle the master's house," as Audre Lorde writes in an influential essay.[33] Both Rs use the tools of class hierarchy—coercive power to demonstrate relative rank and status—ostensibly in the service of equality. What is the lesson of painful penalty? That the ability to make another suffer establishes worth. But a society cannot affirm that humans never deserve grave harm if it is willing to harm them gravely to demonstrate the point.[34]

The retributivists' rationales for punishing people equal to their crimes are both practically and conceptually unsound. Defeated in a demand for equality, advocates of revenge and retribution have proposed the measure of proportionality. The avenger may exact his pound of flesh according to the deed, but no more. The notion of proportionality or fitness, as French is the first to admit, is an aesthetic judgment, much akin to determining how dirty a pair of jeans has to get to warrant laundering.[35] Making the punishment fit the crime remains an elusive goal, since assessments of what is "too much" or "not enough" vary with shifting cultural mores. Vengeance in particular seems destined to spill out of bounds due to the powerful pain that motivates retaliation and the differing evaluations of what desperadoes deserve.

Camus argues against capital punishment, stating that it is excessive rather than equal or proportionate. Although the public may be deluded that "a life for a life" is a straightforward exchange, Camus points out that confinement on death row subjects prisoners to torments beyond what the typical homicide victim faces:

> Let us admit that it is just and necessary to compensate for the murder of the victim by the death of the murderer. But beheading is not simply death. It is just as different, in essence, from the privation of life as a concentration camp is from prison. It is a murder, to be sure, and one that arithmetically pays for the murder committed. But it adds to death a rule, a public premeditation known to the future victim, an organization, in short, which is in itself a source of moral sufferings more terrible than death. Hence there is no equivalence. Many laws consider a premeditated crime more serious than a crime of pure violence. But what then is capital punishment but the most premeditated of murders, to which no criminal's deed, however calculated it may be, can be compared? For there to be equivalence, the death penalty would have to punish a criminal who had warned his victim of the date at which he would inflict a horrible death on him and who, from that moment onward, had confined him at his mercy for months. Such a monster is not encountered in private life.[36]

Cragg notes, "The inability of retributive accounts to generate a determinate scale of sanctions or to help us evaluate the appropriateness of proposed or existing sanctions like capital punishment points to a gap which the account itself cannot fulfill."[37]

Fundamentally, each of these rules to determine how much is due—equality, proportionality, or excess—uses wrongdoers' bad behavior as the measure for harm. That is, they use the dictum "do unto others as was done unto you" as the guideline. This dictum is a distortion of the golden rule because it instructs the avenger or the state to treat the malefactor by the same bad maxim upon which he acted. When individuals, communities, and sovereign nations act on such a terrible rule, they replicate humanity's worst behavior.

In contrast, the true form of the golden rule (do unto others as you would have them do unto you) sets ideal behavior as the norm (even when stated in its negative form—do not do unto others as you would not have them do to you). The golden rule inspires people to treat others as one wishes all humans to be treated—responsively and in ways that promote their flourishing. It is a worthy moral guide in all spheres of human activity. It is true that humans want wrongdoers stopped, to take responsibility for their conduct, and to help repair the harm done. But the golden rule does not justify giving offenders hard treatment comparable to the damage they have done. Both revenge and retribution are morally bankrupt because they replicate heinous behavior rather than model effective, nonviolent, and helpful ways to respond to perpetrators' and victims' needs. But since the distorted golden rule permits harm that imitates the sadism of the sadist, a new moral criterion is morally imperative, a bold standard that no human deserves death.

Although revenge and retribution differ somewhat, the above analysis supports those who conclude that retribution drinks deeply from the well of revenge and, like revenge, is morally bankrupt. The state acts as avenger of victims, targets people for punishment based on ruling elites' definition of what is a threat to society, cannot prevent unconscious biases about social merit from distorting its assessment of moral merit, and justifies harming people with the despicable rule "do unto others as was done unto you." The determination of how much punishment to inflict is ultimately an aesthetic judgment resting not on moral principle, but on cultural relativism.

The case of Jim Elledge, executed in Washington State in 2001, illustrates how murderers and the state tell the same story and attempt to follow the same rules of the game. Both used a distorted golden rule requiring them "to do unto others as was done unto them." Both used excessive rather than proportional responses. Both used the criterion of payback rather than moral blameworthiness. Just as the state, Elledge believed that some people deserve grave, even lethal harm. Ironically, his fervent belief in the two Rs forced the state to reveal its own reliance on the rules of revenge.

Jim was born into a family of slim resources in Louisiana in 1943. Things for the whole family took a turn for the worse when young Jim and his little sister Annie went into the hospital to have their tonsils removed. Jim awoke the next morning; his beloved sister did not. He never got over her loss; his family lacked the communal, financial, and emotional resources to grieve her death adequately. Jim began drinking when he was seven or eight and said later, "That's what ruined me." The father soon disappeared from the scene into a mental hospital. Jim was first jailed at age ten for breaking and entering. His father died when Jim was thirteen, and two half-siblings killed themselves shortly thereafter. His mother declined into alcoholism and neglect of Jim and his remaining siblings.

Jim, given no help in dealing with his losses, blamed himself in some inchoate way for the disintegration of his family. By the age of twelve, Jim was in a group foster home. While there, he was accidentally scalded when a kettle of boiling hog's fat fell on him, severely burning his feet. Jim lay in the hospital, convinced that God was punishing him for a bad thought he had had the day before. Some forty years later, Jim could not give up his conviction of God the punisher. His young life had been so out of control, so cruelly subjected to others, that he clung to a belief that there was an order to the universe, an order that he ultimately controlled through his own bad behavior. With great poignancy and understatement, he would later tell the court, "I like to be in control of my own destiny."[38] After his stint in reform school, he begged the staff to keep him rather than send him home. Returned home, he starved. For one period, he was paid for sexual services, money he needed for food. "I didn't mind so much," he said. "It was better than being hungry."

At the age of fifteen, he was without education, family, or money. At age twenty-one, Jim committed an armed robbery in New Mexico in which "he took a woman clerk hostage, hit her over the head with a gun, rendering her unconscious, and poured gasoline over her."[39] Jailed for that crime, he later escaped and was captured. While on parole nine years later, he hammered to death a sixty-three-year-old female hotel manager, Bertha M. Lush, in an argument over a bill.

Jim was "institutionalized," not really able to function on the "outside."[40] Jim kept to himself in prison, once saving the life of a guard during the 1987 prison riots in Atlanta.

On parole for his first murder, Jim, now in his fifties, landed a job as a custodian at a Methodist church in Lynnwood, Washington. He had flirted with a woman, Eloise Fitzner, forty-seven, who lived upstairs from him, but their relationship soured. Jim had his own interpretation of what happened, prompting him to conclude that Ms. Fitzner had turned on him. By then, he was dating a woman named Sue, whom he had met while working briefly at Boeing as a custodian.[41] Ms. Fitzner wrote a letter to Sue, urging her to not "stay with that awful man any more" and asserting that Elledge "does not even love you" and that "He is just using you for sex, and because he needs the income from your job." The letter further accused Elledge of making sexual advances toward Ms. Fitzner. Jim later married Sue, but he felt that the vindictive abuse did not cease. A defining moment for Jim came when the church usher, with obvious disgust on his face, handed Jim a note just prior to Sunday services, allegedly from Ms. Fitzner. Jim felt it insulted him. He was convinced that the usher had read it; the perceived public humiliation was too much. He concluded that the only way to ward off future humiliation was to "take care of her once and for all." "I had been carrying around . . . anger inside of me for over a year [and it] just got to the top and it just spewed out."[42] On 18 April 1998, he lured Ms. Fitzner and one of her friends to the church on the pretext of a tour of the building followed by dinner. He tied up both and strangled Ms. Fitzner. Before strangling her, he delivered the "vengeance message," which communicates to the victim, "You are about to die for the harm you did to me." Jim simply said, "You talk too damn much." To make sure she was dead—and perhaps to ensure that she would never humiliate him again—he then stabbed her in the throat. He took the other woman to his home. The next day, he drove her to her car and released her. He then drove to a nearby motel room and tried to electrocute himself by putting his feet into a pail of water and sending electric current through the water (perhaps burning feet still seemed to him like the punishment he deserved). The next day, he called the police to surrender quietly.

By the time of his execution, he had been incarcerated over thirty-eight of his fifty-eight years.

Jim Elledge's second murder was motivated by revenge—consciously, for wrongs done to him in the present and, unconsciously, for wrongs done to him long ago. Even though Jim knew that he shouldn't kill his friend, he deeply believed she deserved what she got for having shamed him. According to the rules of revenge, Jim had authority (as the alleged victim of slander), he had identified the right transgressor, he communicated the vengeance message that the recipient received, the criterion was moral merit, and his victim deserved harm. According to revenge's rules, Jim's error was lack of proportionality. Doing unto her what she had done to him is revenge's correct measure for determining how much pain she deserved. She did not deserve death for maligning him, although within his internal world, on his subjective scale of his humiliation and memories of former powerlessness, he felt that she did.

No human deserves to be deceived, tied up, strangled, and stabbed. There was nothing Ms. Fitzner did to deserve death. She could have written Jim a thousand disparaging letters and still deserved no harm. But because both bystanders and the murderer subscribe to the same story and the two Rs, victims are often stigmatized as if they had done something to deserve death. Because social desert and moral blameworthiness are so confusingly intertwined for Americans, bystanders tend to assume that those who "get themselves murdered" must have deserved it. "They were in the wrong place at the wrong time." "They should have known better than to befriend ex-convicts." Surviving family members suffer cruelly from the community's failure to affirm that their beloved never deserved death.

Although Jim employed the rules of revenge in arriving at his murderous plot, once he was arrested, he was in the state's retributive grip. But he knew the story and the practice, and he could manipulate its rules. He wanted to be executed, and he wanted a lawyer who would usher him into the executioner's hands as soon as possible. He found such an attorney, the trial proceeded with quiet speed, and the jury tidily delivered the desired sentence. Jim had deeply internalized the belief that certain people deserve grave harm and believed that the only way to set things right was through his death. Jim had considered suicide many times, but lacked the nerve. He had now created the circumstances in which he would get the state to kill him.

The Washington State Supreme Court, in conducting its mandated review of every capital case, found itself in the questionable position of having to hire a lawyer to argue against its own lawyer (because Jim's lawyer was not going to argue with the state). The court proceeded to hear arguments from both its appointed lawyers. Elledge's lawyer sat with the prosecution.

The lawyer hired to mount an attack on Jim's death sentence—against Jim's wishes—concentrated on two key arguments. First, he observed that Mr. Elledge had not received a fair trial because the state violated the first of retribution's key rules (my language). The state's authority to punish partly derives from its commitment to due process in the form of an adversarial process. With both the defense and prosecuting attorneys seeking the same outcome—death—there was no adversarial process to determine responsibility and moral merit. The state's lawyer did not extend his argument, because it would have led to the observation that the state was acting more like an avenger than a state committed to procedural justice. Second, he argued the sentencing phase of the trial was not fair because no mitigation packet was prepared. A mitigation package contains carefully researched information about the defendant's social history, which is considered essential to determining moral merit or "legal blameworthiness."[43] This hired lawyer also refrained from pointing out that the penalty trial's failure to evaluate Jim's moral merit forced the jury to use the criterion of payback that is most associated with revenge—he killed, he dies. Both of these errors moved the court into the role of avenger rather than retributive agent. The state further undermined its legitimacy as a punishing authority by letting the criminal determine his own sentence.

The self-contradictions of this judicial review were not lost on the state supreme court justices. How could they determine if death was proportional to the crime without a review of mitigating circumstances and a full consideration of Elledge's moral blameworthiness? Could death really be construed as the worst punishment if it was Jim's preference?

Jim's case called upon the State Supreme Court to clarify exactly what its aim was and what rules it would use. Perhaps worried that overturning his sentence would reveal that Jim had cleverly manipulated the whole system, the court upheld the death sentence, with the chief justice issuing the lone dissent. Interestingly, this dissent was based on the issue of proportionality. This murder was not comparable to the other murders that had been deemed capital by the same court. When the state was forced to reveal its hand, it chose payback over consideration of blameworthiness. By dispensing with due process, letting the offender's wishes control the procedures, and unfairly evaluating proportionality, the court played more by the rules of revenge than by retribution. Jim liked this outcome; these were the same rules he lived and died by.

The ease with which the state uses the rules of revenge does not imply that legal retribution ought to be replaced with a return to private vigilantes, as French suggests. The choice is not between these two projects and their governing rules. Both revenge and retribution are morally suspect, and their solidity collapses when they have to mount a defense for why wrongdoers must be harmed.

WHAT SHOULD BE GIVEN?

Here revenge and retribution face their stiffest challenge. Proponents want the person to suffer, even if no other good comes from it (although most believe that good will come of it). They want evildoers to "pay" with their pound of flesh. Since harming people is always a grave moral wrong, the burden of proof falls on those who advocate the two Rs. Why can't the two Rs rest content with the messages that society condemns the misdeed, that the victim has value, and that the offender needs to accept responsibility for the harm she did? If punishment creates a moral debt, malefactors are due something. Why must the payment be in pain? The answer lies further in the story.

NOTES

1. Friedrich Nietzsche, *The Genealogy of Morals* 2.11–14, in *The Birth of Tragedy and the Genealogy of Morals*, trans. Francis Golffing (New York: Doubleday Anchor, 1956); Susan Jacoby, *Wild Justice: The Evolution of Revenge* (New York: Harper and Row, 1983); Robert Solomon, *A Passion for Justice: Emotions and the Origins of the Social Contract* (Lanham, MD: Rowman and Littlefield, 1995); and Peter A. French, *Virtues of Vengeance* (Lawrence: University Press of Kansas, 2001).

2. A study of the practice of revenge in Texas by Pietro Marongiu and Graeme Newman helps explain that state's entrenched support for killing public enemies. Marongiu and Newman focus on Texas's revenge cycles after the Civil War, in a two-year period of general social breakdown immediately after the Confederate defeat (1868–1870) when "more than 900 (and possibly as many as 1500) feud-related murders took place." These figures translate into one to two revenge deaths per day. Marongiu and Newman characterize these feud executions not as lawlessness but as occurring out of a need for order in which a substitute is sought for legal redress when "written law . . . has not yet arrived" or where "legal remedies are not embraced" because of a distrust of federal and state authority. *Vengeance: The Fight against Injustice* (Totowa, NJ: Rowman & Littlefield, 1987), 104.

3. Franklin E. Zimring, *The Contradictions of American Capital Punishment* (New York: Oxford University Press, 2003), 119–23.

4. Marongiu and Newman, *Vengeance*, 119. Italics in original.

5. Zimring, *Contradictions*, 137.

6. However, about 40 percent of homicides never result in a conviction. Those many surviving families will never receive this alleged punishment benefit. U.S. Department of Justice: Office of Justice Programs, "Bureau of Justice Statistics: Homicide Trends in the U.S.," available at www.ojp.usdoj.gov/bjs/homicide/cleared.htm (accessed 2 June 2003).

7. Restorative justice advocates argue that community representatives, the victim, and the offender ought to be authorized to determine, jointly, the appropriate sentence. They argue that this victim-centered approach predates state punishment, citing practices among aboriginal peoples.

8. Zimring, *Contradictions*, 45.

9. Albert Camus, "Reflections on the Guillotine," in *Resistance, Rebellion, and Death*, trans. Justin O'Brien (originally published in 1957; New York: Vintage International, 1995), 227.

10. Zimring, *Contradictions*, 61. He cites an April 2001 poll statement by ABC News/Washington Post: "The death penalty is fair because it gives satisfaction and closure to the families of murder victims." A total of 60 percent of the respondents agreed either strongly or somewhat with that sentiment. The rhetorical force of the story obscures several realities. First, some families do not want the death penalty for the murder of their beloved, and hence the exercise of state power is not being done in their name. Second, often the victim and perpetrator come from the same family, so that destroying a family is done in the name of that family. Third, often defendants come from a family that has experienced murder, yet their homicidal urges and actions are not interpreted as being motivated by revenge. Rather, murderers are portrayed as having "acted for no reason," without provocation.

11. See, for example, the death penalty projects and arguments of Amnesty International, American Civil Liberties Union, American Friends Service Committee, Catholics against the Death Penalty, Citizens United for Alternatives to the Death Penalty, Death Penalty Focus, Equal Justice USA, Fellowship of Reconciliation, Institute for Economic and Restorative Justice, the Moratorium Campaign, National Coalition to Abolish the Death Penalty, Religious Organizing against the Death Penalty, and Washington Coalition to Abolish the Death Penalty.

12. Derrick Z. Jackson, "Bush's Death Factory," *Boston Globe*, 25 October 2000, A17.

13. Hugh Aynesworth, "Banks' Execution Expected to Proceed," *Washington Times*, 12 March 2003, A05.

14. Camus, "Reflections," 222.

15. Zimring, *Contradictions*, 120.

16. Even those most frustrated with the criminal justice system are not likely to be persuaded by French's arguments for a self-appointed class of avengers. French, *Vengeance*, 169–172.

17. Stephen Nathanson, *An Eye for an Eye? The Morality of Punishing by Death* (Totowa, NJ: Rowman & Littlefield, 1987), 77–82.

18. French, *Vengeance*, 187.

19. Immanuel Kant, *Metaphysical Elements of Justice*, trans. John Ladd (Indianapolis: Bobbs-Merrill, 1965), 101.

20. Moreover, "the criminal law is notorious for its extremely narrow focus on decontextualized criminal acts. . . . Much that a social scientist would want to know about the historical, social contextual, and even immediate situational influences on criminal behavior . . . is deemed irrelevant by criminal law" (Craig Haney, "Mitigation and the Study of Lives: On the Roots of Violent Criminality and the Nature of Capital Justice," in *America's Experiment with Capital Punishment*, ed. James Acker, Robert Bohm, and Charles S. Lanier [Durham, NC: Carolina Academic, 1998], 351).

21. Harry Elmer Barnes, *The Story of Punishment: A Record of Man's Inhumanity to Man*, 2nd ed. (originally published in 1930; Montclair, NJ: Patterson Smith, 1972), 49.

22. Jean Hampton, "The Retributive Idea," in *Forgiveness and Mercy*, ed. Jeffrie Murphy and Jean Hampton (Cambridge: Cambridge University Press, 1988), 141.

23. Stephen B. Bright, "Discrimination, Death and Denial: The Tolerance of Racial Discrimination in Infliction of the Death Penalty," *Santa Clara Law Review* 35 (1995): 437.

24. Based on conversations with Native Americans who oppose the death penalty, who tell me that they feel like a distinct minority within their community.

25. Dennis Sullivan and Larry Tifft, *Restorative Justice: Healing the Foundations of Our Everyday Lives* (Monsey, NY: Willow Tree, 2001), 103–104.

26. Wesley Cragg, *The Practice of Punishment: Towards a Theory of Restorative Justice* (New York: Routledge, 1992), 20.

27. Herbert Morris makes a similar argument. This justification for punishment works only within a story that believes coercive power over another is a truly human benefit. "Persons and Punishment," *Monist* 52 (October 1968): 475–501.

28. Sullivan and Tifft, *Restorative Justice*, 106–108.

29. Sullivan and Tifft, *Restorative Justice*, 107.

30. Hampton, "Retributive Idea," 137.

31. James Gilligan, *Violence: Our Deadly Epidemic and Its Causes* (New York: Putnam's Sons, 1996), 182.

32. Gilligan, *Violence*, 110.

33. Audre Lorde, "The Master's Tools Will Never Dismantle the Master's House," in *Sister Outsider: Essays and Speeches* (Trumansburg, NY: Crossing, 1984).

34. Hampton, "Retributive Idea," 138.

35. French, *Vengeance*, 227.

36. Camus, "Reflections," 199.

37. Cragg, *Practice of Punishment*, 18.

38. Clemency Petition on Behalf of James Elledge, 6 August 2001, 16.

39. Supreme Court document, State of Washington v. James Homer Elledge Concurring Opinion, docket #67342-0, 5 July 2001: 8.

40. Rebekah Denn, "Dispute Embroils Killer's Request to Die," *Seattle Post-Intelligencer*, 7 July 2001, 3, available at seattlepi.nwsource.com'local/30451_elledgex07.shtml (accessed 18 July 2001).

41. "Sue" is a pseudonym.

42. Supreme Court document, State of Washington v. James Homer Elledge Dissenting Opinion, docket #: 67342-0, 5 July 2001: 2.

43. There were significant mitigating factors that should have resulted in a reduced sentence. But because of Jim's ability to muzzle his lawyer, these factors were never presented to the jury. His lawyer said, "We certainly don't want to ask the Court to do anything else, but in my opinion, I think that Mr. Elledge could well have received a life sentence" (Clemency Petition presented to the Clemency and Pardons Board, 6 August 2001, 12). One juror, Jon Sherrell, after learning about Elledge's personal history from the newspaper said, "I could have seen changing my mind." Denn, "Dispute."

4

Rectification through Suffering

A thing is branded on the memory to make it stick there; only what goes on hurting will stick. . . . [F]or every damage there could somehow be found an equivalent, by which that damage might be compensated—if necessary in the pain of the doer.

Friedrich Nietzsche, The Genealogy of Morals

The story insists that pain "sets a person right." If painful punishment does not adequately condition a person to refrain from wrongdoing, reads the script, then pain, at the least, has the ability to make her recognize the error of her ways. Since an offender does not comprehend viscerally the magnitude of her sins, suffering shows her "this is how wrong what [she] did was."[1] Rectification through suffering aims to correct the human and set her on course. Failing that, the penalty will rectify the wrong and balance the scales.

Rectification, the third R, is not a project of punishment, but it is what makes the two Rs allegedly effective—it offers the hope of correcting the miscreant. But why are pain and suffering thought to effect this change?[2] Since unwanted pain is not good for humans, how did the notion arise that inflicting harm on unwilling persons would work for or lead to good?

Slap a small child's hand for reaching for a flaring match. She is unlikely to reach out again. Pain seems to have a pedagogical usefulness; pain aids memory, overriding the childish temptation to play with fire. On a personal level involving minor infractions, such common experiences confirm the story. People who harm others allegedly do not know what it means to suffer and therefore need to endure distress "to get the idea." If murderers grasped fully the pain they created for others, the story beguilingly suggests, they would not do it.

The apparent success of pain to instill a memory of "thou shall not," however, deceives. The child has not learned anything useful about matches or fire; she's only been conditioned to react with fear. Such conditioning is of marginal, short-term usefulness. Under dire circumstances or imminent demise, a child can use such conditioning and rigidly avoid fire—perhaps it will save her while the parents are busy defending the village. But in more secure circumstances, children should be given the tools to think about matches and understand their dangers and proper functioning. Hence the goal should be a child who can think, not one who has an inelastic knot of feelings and rigid prescriptions. So, if painful conditioning seems temporarily useful for instant obedience, in the long run, it is antithetical to human intelligence, survival, and flourishing.

Advocates of the three Rs, particularly in Western cultures, believe in the magical power of suffering to improve character and turn a person toward God. Of course, the death penalty does not aim at correction but at extermination. Nevertheless, at that pivotal moment when the condemned is strapped to the gurney, the family members of the murder victim await the "last words" to demonstrate that imminent death can soften even the most hardened heart.

A primitive notion of economic exchange within class societies underlies the modern projects of revenge and retribution. Wrongdoing, the story goes, creates an unequal exchange, a moral debt. A despoiler has seized unfair advantage by not following the rules of the economic game; the victim may have lost ground in a competitive economic sense. Or the overreacher may appear falsely superior in worth or power; the dominated may appear falsely worthless or demeaned. An inequality of shame and fear often results from crime. Payment of a debt is an ancient metaphor for justice, and this debt must be paid through the currency of pain.

But why pain? Why must suffering be the symbolic dollar that trades hands? German philosopher Friedrich Nietzsche tackles this question directly in his treatise *The Genealogy of Morals*. Brushing aside all later rationalizations for punishment, Nietzsche seeks to understand its origins.

Nietzsche breaks the argument down to basic economics. He analyzes economic exchange and the emergence in the marketplace of commutative justice, which serves as a model for other forms of justice. Barter and trade brought the need to make good on deals gone awry. Necessary for continuance of this system, Nietzsche argues, was the prior human ability to make a promise. The town market rested on the willingness of two people to engage in the practice of promise keeping, which specified what a promise is and established rules governing how its terms would be fulfilled. And in order for such a practice to develop, he says, humans needed memory to remember promises made to them as well as their obligations to others. More important, people needed to remember what would happen if they reneged on their promises. Pain, the most powerful memory aid, he claims, sears experiences into the body, etches events into the mind, and causes a distant memory to seem as fresh as yesterday's.[3]

A class system built upon exchanges of property relies on "making good" through suffering. The way to enforce a deal was painful penalty, even death. Nietzsche observes:

> In order to inspire the creditor with confidence in his promise to repay, to give a guarantee for the stringency of his promise, but also to enjoin on his own conscience the duty of repayment, the debtor pledged by contract that in case of non-payment he would offer another of his possessions, such as his body, or his wife, or his freedom, or even his life.[4]

In turn, the creditor "had a right to inflict pain," to take even body parts. For instance, Shakespeare has the creditor in *The Merchant of Venice* secure the debtor's promise with flesh to be cut from his chest. The creditor, instead of getting paid in money, would be paid in *pleasure.* "That pleasure is induced by his being able to exercise his power freely upon one who is powerless . . . the pleasure of rape. That pleasure will be increased in proportion to the lowliness of the creditor's own station . . . a foretaste of higher rank."[5]

Hurting another human may *feel* pleasurable as a reduction of prior pain, but no undamaged human would find such an action genuinely pleasurable. Pleasure in debasing a person of higher rank occurs primarily by painful injustices spawned by inequality. This pleasure would not exist without the kinds of systematic mistreatment fueled by maintaining class hierarchies—humiliation, isolation, denigration, raw economic exploitation, material deprivation, and violence.

The story behind the death penalty helps explain the fondness for rectification through suffering. Nietzsche's further comments make the story's desert basis clear: "For once [the creditor] is given a chance to bask in the glorious feeling of treating another human being as lower than himself—or, in case the actual punitive power has passed on to a legal 'authority,' of seeing him despised and mistreated. Thus compensation consists in a legal warrant entitling one man to exercise his cruelty on another."[6] The habit of seeking release from the pain of one's own mistreatment through the mistreatment of others finds its way into this third "R."

Cosmological stories reinforce the belief that moral debt can be paid off through suffering. Jesus's life and death are perhaps the most well-known Western account of rectifying wrongs through suffering and execution. Jesus's death upon the cross is familiarly interpreted as God's effort to save sinful humankind. Although not the most adequate moral and theological interpretation of Jesus,[7] this view "supposes that a wrathful God demanded that a victim pay in blood for human sin . . . and that God chose to take a human form and pay for the sin 'Himself.' "[8] Consistent with the economic model, the execution of this particular Jew by the Romans was seen as God's willingness to pay the ultimate price—the death of his son—in order to redeem the entire world. Jesus's death becomes understood as the will of his father. This father, rather than condemning the state-sanctioned torture and execution of his beloved child, uses imperial violence for the purpose of salvation. In this way, the power of the oppressive empire is left uncondemned.

This doctrine of the atonement—Jesus's death pays the debt for all humanity's sin—implicitly exonerates the violent power of the state and establishes that executions can achieve good. Albert Camus dryly observes: "The unbeliever cannot keep from thinking that men who have set at the center of their faith the staggering victim of a judicial error ought at least hesitate before committing legal murder."[9]

Protestant theologians Rebecca Parker and Rita Nakashima Brock challenge this interpretation of Jesus's death, which condones violence as God's way of setting things right. They particularly challenge the claim that God intended Jesus to be executed. They build their objection on Abelard, who in the thirteenth century questioned the "debt payment" interpretation offered by his predecessor, Anselm. Abelard asked:

Who will forgive God for the sin of killing his own child? . . . How cruel and
wicked it seems that anyone should demand the blood of an innocent person as
the price for anything, or that it should in any way please him that an innocent
man should be slain—still less that God should consider the death of his son so
agreeable that by it he should be reconciled to the whole world![10]

Instead, Parker argues, God did not want Jesus to die: "This was not the will
of God to do this to any human being. His execution was an act of great evil.
It would have been better had Jesus lived."[11] In a Lenten sermon, Parker says,
"Jesus' crucifixion was a consequence of domination, not its cure. An oppressive system killed him to silence him and to threaten others who might follow
him." She continues:

The spiritualizing of suffering makes God the author of all pain, who uses pain
to edify or purify human beings. . . . The mysticism of the cross teaches that violence is God's way of transforming people and communities into greater spiritual well-being. It clouds the realities of human violence in a haze of spiritual
glory. . . . God . . . does not sanction cruelty and torture. To inflict pain on ourselves is not virtuous and to inflict it on others is not edifying or transforming.
Sparing the rod does not spoil the child. It is not godly to beat our children or
ourselves.[12]

As we saw at the end of chapter three, Jim Elledge learned the story well. In-
ternalizing the idea that he "deserved" the abuse he received, he believed that
others deserved the abuse he in turn doled out. Elledge had lived his whole life
by this story. And he died by it. He thoroughly believed that his death would
work its magic—bringing relief to the victim's family, securing God's forgiveness, and bringing peace to his tortured soul.

Nietzsche concludes, "With the aid of . . . [painful] memory, people eventually 'came to their senses.'"[13] He puts "coming to our senses" in quotation
marks because by this process he means the abandonment of their supposed
nature of instinct and aggression. This willful nature is replaced by civilized
conformity to custom. Whereas some might see this process of "civilizing"
brute nature as a net gain, Nietzsche does not. It is a net loss, a process of losing our nerve and verve in exchange for conformity and mediocrity. Nietzsche
challenges his Enlightenment predecessors who regarded the process of civilizing humans as a step in the right direction. Yet, while reversing the usual

evaluation of this process, Nietzsche supports the dominant story that humans are "by nature" brutish, selfish, and aggressive.

Outside the confines of community, the story goes, humans once were free to do as they pleased. The process of entering covenantal agreements chalks up a net loss of liberty, the storytellers say. Perhaps Nietzsche mistakenly inverted the "true" story. A clearer account envisions humans as groomed for life in community, beings who flourish in the care and nurture of others and find mutual bonds fulfilling and freeing. Well tended and loved, safe in the bosom of an extended network of beloveds, people have the freedom to pursue the highest flights of thought and creativity. Group living—that is, group living without mistreatment and oppression—is not alien to humans, but it is as necessary to them as air and water.

Nietzsche meant to rail against this legacy of oppression, but he ended up attacking all civilization, which isn't the enemy. Life in community itself does not limit the fulfillment of human potential. In contrast, injustice, all manner of mistreatment, and exploitation are delimiting. Humans flourish and function brilliantly without these enemies. Unfortunately, most societies are saddled with a heavy inheritance of practices that lead to mistreatment of self and others, such as rectification through suffering. Such deforming practices—not "civilization"—are the enemy.

Pain, rather than "bringing us to our senses," accomplishes precisely the opposite. Pain renders intelligent people brutish, dulls the mind, mutes the senses, and causes the brain to seize up just when most needed. But the practice of rectification through suffering does not understand these effects of pain on humans; instead, it assumes that humans respond to pain as do wild animals—by taming the beast within. People are not animals requiring taming, however. Humans require care and nurturance to achieve the goodness that is their birthright.

Pain is a primitive tool of conditioning. Ask horse lovers who have observed a mare grazing contentedly while her foal, on its four spindly, widespread legs, nurses energetically, sucking in big gulps. But sometimes the foal approaches nursing as a preparation for conquest. He'll race at the mare and pound on her side with his front hooves. Several warning nips from the mare may not register. Finally, a mare might raise both hind legs and deal a breath-defying kick to the foal, which crumples to the ground, winded and shocked. The foal forms a rigid recording that is encoded with pain and in a conditioned manner now associates too aggressive attempts to access mother and milk with painful blows.

Nietzsche has such animalistic forms of conditioned responses in mind. Pain, he says, is a way to "triumph" over our "base instinct," "brutal coarseness," and "plebian instincts." With an unreflective use of the word *nature* (meaning here, like the brutes), Nietzsche writes that painful punishment conquers nature and the "individual was finally taught to remember five or six 'I won'ts.'"[14]

Pain does sear human memory but not in a way that ends violence. Rather, it encodes and reproduces violence. Nevertheless, many people continue to assume that an inflictor of pain can be rectified through pain, despite many centuries of evidence to the contrary.

French philosopher Michel Foucault documents what he calls the "return effects of punishment." Rather than rectification, painful punishment produces "hardness of heart," shame that fuels vengeance, and "ferocity." Foucault traces how most civilized countries have abandoned punishment through bodily torments, such as drawing and quartering, dismemberment, disembowelment, burning at the stake, or boiling in hot oil. Physical torture, he suggests, has been replaced with a "universal pedagogy of work, which would revive for the lazy individual a liking for work, force him back into a system of interests in which labour would be more advantageous than laziness. . . ." New forms of penal colonies sought the "pedagogical and spiritual transformation of individuals brought about by continuous exercise." With this new model of suffering, "the length of imprisonment became tied to correction and the economic use of a corrected criminal." The English, he notes, added isolation as a punishment in the 1500s. "Isolation is a terrible shock" aimed at spiritual conversion, which sought to "rearrange not only the complex of interests proper to *homo aeconomicus*, but also the imperatives of the moral subject." The new symbol of this form of rectification was the monastic cell, which "became the instrument of 'reconstituting' workers and the 'religious conscience.'" The goal was to create an instrument that would transform mind and soul and produce an "obedient subject."[15]

Despite efforts to make killing look humane, death rows remain brutalizing.[16] The public hopes that murderers will come to understand the pain they inflict. Unfortunately, murderers often disengage from the suffering of their victims, unable to hear their cries with sympathy or feel compassion for their trembling bodies. Given the emotional numbness and dissociation evident in many violent offenders, the script says that horror will jolt them back into seeing, hearing, and feeling. Jolt. This is what it feels like to suffer. Jolt. This is what it is like to be terrified. Jolt. This is what it is like to feel at the mercy of someone more powerful. Once jolted out of numbness, the story goes, the offender will apologize to the victim's family and to God.

There are two confusions here. First is the mistaken belief that the victimizer has not suffered, so he needs to suffer in order to understand what pain is. The reality is often just the opposite—most victimizers have been heavily brutalized; they are the embodiment of what unhealed trauma can do to humans. The second is that the executioner does not have to engage in a distancing ritual at the very moment that imminent violence allegedly jolts the offender back into his humanity. The ability of the myth to sustain this mirage of magical suffering has grown weaker over time. The arbitrariness of the distinction between the violence of the executioner (used to awaken another at the cost of deadening himself) and the violence of the offender (a product of having been deadened by violence) has become increasingly obvious. Violence renders the humanity of all victims invisible. Violence harms all humans, both illegal and legal killers.[17]

The moral pathology of believing that humans can be made right through painful penalty abides deeply within us. The comic strip *Calvin and Hobbes* frequently laments how this trapping is imposed on children. Calvin grumbles often about his parents' belief that "suffering builds character." Not so. Virtues may be acquired through facing challenges and learning to do difficult things against feelings that otherwise might keep some in bed with the cover over their heads. But doing the right thing despite feeling lazy or scared is not suffering per se: it's just feeling bad. The kind of suffering inflicted during retribution and revenge is meant to either degrade the prisoner or diminish his false sense of superiority. As Jean Hampton says, "Both responses involve the desire to inflict pain as a way of mastering another, and both see such mastery as making a point about the relative value of offender and victim."[18] In practice, however, Hampton recognizes that these different aims—degrade the offender versus annul the false information about the superiority of the offender—may be too subtle for most punishers or avengers to discern or implement.

Rectification is, in part, an empirical claim: "suffering tends to provoke repentance." Hampton suggests that "suffering tends to bring people low, to reduce them, to humble them."[19] Suffering may reduce the offender to begging for mercy. However, such coerced repentance is hardly a sign of inner change.

Instead, domination, as restorative justice practitioner Wesley Cragg observes, interferes with accountability:

> Violence . . . ignore[s] and undermine[s] the moral status of those on whom their violence impinges. . . . Violence . . . reduces the ability of those affected by it to plan, to assess the consequences of their actions, or to predict how their actions will be understood by those affected by them. . . . [It] undermines [the moral agency of persons] by threatening their security and thereby forcing a shift to a self-interested perspective. . . . Violence gives an urgency to self-interest that, if it comes to dominate, severely inhibits the capacity of agents to assume a moral point of view.[20]

Violence, rather than rectifying wrongdoers, drives people inward, turning them away from the relationships that could help and repair. It isolates. Feelings get cut off, shrinking the sphere of caring. Violence voids human presence; it restricts or shuts down thinking. Violence possesses, Cragg concludes, "an *anti-moral* character."[21] Thus to dominate victimizers is to use means that are immoral.

The story that punitive violence achieves justice is false. Hard treatment neither rectifies the criminal nor protects life over the long haul, nor restores relationships, nor heals the survivors, nor enhances responsiveness and responsibility. The so-called magic of execution is not powerful enough to heal the wounds caused by murder. People are not restored by humiliation, defeat, threats of violence, isolation, or execution. Instead, these things harm everyone.

Society needs to denounce serious wrongs. But inflicting pain is a messy, imprecise, and morally depraved mode of communication. On what grounds can the imposition of painful penalties be justified, if at all?

NO ONE DESERVES HARM

A familiar expression of the concept that moral merit justifies harm is the belief that God will bless the virtuous and punish the vicious. Various voices in the Bible express the belief that the upright deserve to experience a level of well-being that the degenerate do not, if not in this world, then in the next. Because wicked actions do not automatically produce negative consequences for the sinful (so-called poetic justice)—and God's punishment in the hereafter is not known with certainty (divine justice)—many humans have felt the need to ensure that the depraved receive harm here and now.

Central to the perspective that it is permissible to harm offenders is how the three Rs relate moral merit to human worth.

The monotheistic religions proclaim that humans possess equal worth. The vision of equal human dignity is captured in the Jewish, Christian, and Muslim affirmation that humans are created in the image of God.[22] Secular natural law thinkers affirm that humans deserve to be treated well simply by virtue of their being human—a common humanity establishes human worth. The American Constitution appeals to inalienable rights. Such assertions about the worth of all humans, always made within a narrative tradition, seek to provide the best picture of the human person available. As such they are subject to error and improvement. But functionally, if a society deems a group deserving of discrimination or death, opponents can appeal to the requirements of human flourishing, a common humanity, God's law, or human rights to denounce the injustice.

The practice of capitalism, in contrast, denies equal human worth.[23] Instead, it confers or withholds human value based on what is understood to advance the interests of capitalists. With the advent of the industrial revolution, people were primarily prized for their ability to labor long and hard. People who could not keep up—the physically impaired, the very young, and the very old—became less valuable. These people became known as the "undeserving poor," since they were poor through no fault of their own. People who refused to enter into factory service or stole rather than worked were labeled the "deserving poor." Since presumably their own choices had landed them outside the realm of wages, they did not merit assistance. Criminals, since they are unproductive, remain second-class citizens in capitalist economies. In all cases, a person's value is determined by her merit—her instrumental value to the capitalist economy—not her human worth.

Does one's moral demerit diminish one's human worth? Is there a floor below which one's human worth cannot fall, or can one's moral blameworthiness reduce one's human value to less than zero? Despite some differences on these important questions, the three Rs assume that wrongdoers merit *harm.*

Advocates of revenge such as French argue that human worth rests entirely on moral merit; humans have no worth independent of what they do. By reducing people to their behaviors, French extends classism to its ultimate, logical conclusion: humans have value only if they do well. Since there is no minimum floor of respect due humans as humans, the avenger is free to do to the villain exactly what the wretch himself did to the victim.[24]

The rules of revenge deny that dangerous, violent criminals are human at all and permit treating them as if they were evil monsters. The rules of retribution make a slightly different assumption; although perpetrators may have once been humans of worth, their vices have replaced any human potentiality—the more of one, the less of the other. In everyday parlance, some people are "rotten to the core"; there is no humanness left in them.[25] As Emmett Barcalow summarizes, "Their evil deeds show that they are evil people, and evil people who have done evil deserve to be punished."[26]

The three Rs often assume that some humans merit harm because their habits and actions constitute who they are as persons. *Punitive desert ascribes to human's essential nature or entire personhood external, acquired features.* "If you look like X, act like X, then you are X." This is tunnel vision and a tremendous error.

Significantly, when murderers kill, they fail to see the humanity of their victims. In words echoing French philosopher Emmanuel Levinas, "Murder . . . renounces absolutely all 'comprehension' of the other, for one no longer wishes to include the other in the 'same,' that is in one's own project of existing."[27] The three Rs urge offenders to lose sight of their own humanness—"I am thoroughly bad and unredeemable." And when victims demand revenge or retribution, they also fail to see the humanity of the offender. Partial vision, the inability to see the other's human face, harms everyone. A lack of discerning vision enables murderers and executioners to kill (and bystanders to endorse execution) without recognition of whom they are harming.[28]

Discerning vision is the ability to see the humanity in every person while recognizing the habits that may make it difficult for the person to look or act humanly. How does discerning vision alter the perception about what perpetrators deserve?

Advocates of painful rectification misconstrue the human person who shares a form of primitive learning with animals—we, too, can be conditioned like Pavlov's dogs to fall silent at the sight of an angry authority figure. Any human typically has several complex forms of conditioned responses, acquired as a result of unhealed maltreatment. Habits are recognizable by their inappropriate emotions, rigid insensibilities, and distorted perceptions. Such habits lack human intelligence in that they contain unworkable solutions without regard for present circumstances. But unlike most other mammals, *Homo sapiens* have a qualitatively different form of intelligence capable of genuine human learning that is quite distinct from brute conditioning. The unconditioned human is able to think outside such habits, craft effective responses, and act. The person's heart and mind can work, able to size up situations accurately, feel appropriately, and interact with others respectfully.

Distinguishing the flexible and virtuously developed person from her painfully conditioned and antihuman vice is neither dualistic nor a reversion to an abstract, qualityless concept of the universal human. A person's human potentialities can only be realized in particular ways—she thinks, loves, and initiates in her own unique way. The human aspects of her self are socially developed and culturally situated. "There is no 'ahistorical essence' lurking deep within untouched by culture. . . . Instead there is a thoroughly historical, socialized person burdened by a thoroughly historical, conditioned set of imposed patterns."[29] Realizing that a criminal is neither "summed up" nor determined by her habits (patterns or vices) recognizes her freedom and responsibility as a moral agent. She can choose to act based on her habits or her own innovative thinking.

Distinguishing the person from her vices signals an important difference between saying "she is violent" versus saying "she has a habit of violence." The former denies that she has any capacity to act outside her habits. The latter affirms her moral agency and intelligence and their availability to be acted upon. Human beings are not potential killers. Rather, they are vulnerable to acquiring violent habits if they are mistreated and not enabled to recover. Only humans conditioned in particular ways are potentially violent. The virtuously developed aspects of their being may always be distinguished from nonhuman accretions acquired through maltreatment.

Hampton wonders if a commitment to differentiate the human from her vice in every person stems from religious faith or requires Godlike qualities.

However, nothing superordinary is required, only discerning vision that keeps two utterly different objects in view.

In the *Return of the Jedi*, Luke Skywalker refuses to believe that his father, Darth Vader, has turned completely to the dark side, despite his father's conviction that he has. At the movie's climax, Luke removes Darth Vader's mask and finds the human face of his father, barely alive. Hardened criminals cannot be decloaked so easily, because habits are not like masks or capes, but Luke's conviction that even Darth Vader is not rotten to the core is an example of discerning vision.

It is possible and certainly desirable to differentiate a person's humanness from the agglomerations that obscure it. Discerning vision enables people to see the dignity due the person himself, not just respond to a crime. Hampton perceives that such a distinction is plausible:

> One who opposes and wants to correct her wrongdoer will experience and convey disapproval of the wrongdoer's action, and disapproval of any of the characteristics from which his action flowed, but still insist that there is a core of decency within him. She will believe, not that he is rotten, but that he has only "cloaked" himself in evil, where his character or dispositions or habits may be taken to be part of the cloak. This belief will allow her to sustain a belief in his inherent decency.[30]

At the extreme are figures such as Hitler who appear to have completely identified with the "dark side." It's not certain whether or not they can access any of their potentialities for human functioning. No one can say definitively, however, that they are rotten to the core. Given this uncertainty, it is plausible and morally preferable to assume that their potential humanity lies deeply buried, not destroyed. As philosopher Lenn Goodman puts it, "Complete loss of [human] desert would be tantamount to non-existence."[31] Humanness is an ontological reality out of which one cannot fall or be expelled. (Even fallen angels such as the devil, Thomas Aquinas reminds us, retain the ontological goodness of their creation.)[32] Even Hampton says, "moral hatred of people . . . is always wrong because people never become so rotted as individuals that they lose" all potential for decency.[33] Thus there is no paired term such as "reward and punishment" or "praise or blame" for human desert. One's humanness always deserves respect and protection from harm and is present, if only in potential, even in people who have not developed it.

Even if some retributivists are willing to distinguish the humanity of the agent from the vice, they argue that the agent still merits harm.[34] Moral merit overrides human worth, making it permissible to harm wrongdoers.

Most retributivists affirm equal human worth. All humans, simply by being human, deserve to be treated with dignity. Retributivists vary, however, on whether this inherent worth protects the individual from extreme punishments. Kant, for example, thinks society shows respect for human dignity by imposing the death penalty upon the deserving; Jeffrey Reiman, in contrast, thinks that human dignity limits the abuse society can heap on an individual. According to him, a murderer may merit dreadful treatment, but his human worth forbids torture or execution.[35] Nevertheless, both Kant and Reiman believe that murderers *merit* death, despite their different conclusions about the maximum sentence that may be imposed.

Retributivists and avengers insist on painful penalties because they recognize that failure to respond to evildoers would be a grievous wrong.[36] Both revenge and retribution rest on the correct conviction that holding people responsible for their actions is a needed form of human respect. Viewing people as responsible presumes a deep inner connection between the deeds and the person's moral agency. A moral agent is a person whose intentions and motives correlate with his actions; a person is able to respond to his environment in ways he intends. Retributivists, particularly of the Kantian sort, are particularly keen on treating humans with the full respect they deserve, which includes treating them as responsible moral agents, not as powerless victims. This responsiveness to others is a basic human good. The three Rs err in treating painful penalty as a form of respect. It is illogical and unnecessary to argue that executing someone is the best way of responding to the other or respecting her humanity. These projects neglect to see that particular responses—such as suffering or death—are merely conventional agreements about ways to express communal outrage and holding someone accountable.[37] There is no innate connection between a person's moral merit and the imposition of suffering or death.

Evil behaviors count, not as criteria of why and how much perpetrators should be harmed in return, but as prime indicators of what is needed to protect the community, help the victims, and restore offenders to themselves and to useful lives. Their misconduct provides vital information about their difficulties, how their vices might have been acquired, and what they might need to be able to live within the law. "When a crime occurs, the victims are owed and the offenders owe," writes restorative justice advocate Howard Zehr. "What we're differing on is what currency will fulfill that obligation. Retributive theory says punishment will do it. Restorative justice says it takes an active effort by the offender to make things right."[38]

Malefactors' human dignity requires that they be helped to see that their harmful actions matter because they as humans matter. Bad moral merit does not mean forfeiting one's claims to having one's needs met or being expected to act like a human. Humans deserve to be helped to become accountable and responsive and to address their real problems, rather than be isolated, shamed, dehumanized, or killed. Morally, humans deserve to be treated as if they have the potential to act thoughtfully, despite any destructive habits. A human being never deserves harm, even though a person acting in the grip of a violent vice needs firm and decisive restraint. Human desert obligates bystanders and criminal justice practitioners to respond to the human presence of criminals, while working feverishly to help them undo their enmeshment with vicious habits. This is what humans deserve—guilty or innocent.

Consider what is required of the young murderer who is brought before the victim's community to be sentenced using discerning vision, within the Sioux narrative, as recounted by anthropologist Ella Deloria:

> The angry relatives debated the kind of punishment fitting the crime while the wise elder listened. After a good while he began to speak. Skillfully, he began by going along with them. "My Brothers and Cousins, my Sons and Nephews, we have been caused to weep without shame. . . . No wonder we are enraged, for our pride and honor have been grossly violated. Why shouldn't we go out, then, and give the murderer what he deserves?"
>
> Then, after an ominous pause, he suddenly shifted. . . . "And yet, my Kinsmen, there is a better way!"
>
> Slowly and clearly he explained the better way. It was also the hard way, the only certain way to put out the fire in their hearts and in the murderer's.
>
> "Each of you bring to me the thing you prize the most. These things shall be a token of our intention. We shall give them to the murderer who has hurt us, and he shall thereby become a relative in place of him who is gone. . . . And from now on, he shall be one of us, and our endless concern shall be to regard him as though he were truly our loved one come back to us."
>
> . . . [T]he council's speaker offered [the killer] the sacred pipe saying,

"Smoke now with these your new relatives, for they have chosen to take you to themselves in place of one who is not here. It is their heart's wish that you shall become one of them; you shall go out and come in without fear. Be confident that their love and compassion which were his are now yours forever." And during that speech, tears trickled down the murderer's face. He had been trapped by loving kinship . . . and you can be sure that he made an even better relative than many who are related by blood, because he had been bought at such a price.[39]

This response to the killer and his crime did two important things. First, it required something constructive of the murderer in contrast to harming him and rendering him passive and irresponsible. He needed to come to terms with the wounds in himself that led him to wound others. Second, it responded to his humanness, not only his actions based on his vice. It responded to what he is capable of in the best sense as well as his loss of integrity in acting out of his conditioning. This fundamental difference in the object of response—the human person *and* the vice—suggests that there are alternatives to revenge, retribution, and rectification through suffering.

In the end, claiming that criminals deserve grave harm ignores the person's (obscured) humanness. The blindfolded goddess of justice balancing her scales is unable to see or affirm the humanity of the individual who awaits her judgment.

Something is *due* humans who harm humans, but the three Rs have not demonstrated why that response must be hurtful. Determining what is due is a moral choice: to respond to evil deeds with calculations of punishment or with evaluations of what will redress harms, meet human needs, and help humans emerge from their vices. What kind of people do Americans want to be?

From a historical perspective, the choice is clear. Humans have tried painful penalty for four millennia, and it has not prevented violence or corrected injustices. As the husband explained about his battered wife, "I just kept hitting her and hitting her and she never seemed to get much better." Instead, the United States could embrace new projects that affirm the humanity of everyone, resolve conflicts with minimal violence, seek to correct injustices, and meet needs.

Punishment has yet to be shown a moral practice. First, it fails to secure the goods it promises to protect. Second, its rules fail to justify the harm it perpetrates. These rules foster singleness of vision, a dangerous blindness to human worth. By treating people as if they were only their habits, the three Rs are built on the false conclusion that some humans *merit* harm, even death. Humans by virtue of being human never *deserve* harm (self-defense is not a question of what the attacker deserves). Stunningly, the distorted perspective that some people deserve grave harm fuels crime *and* punishment.

In order for such blinkered perspectives to become this pervasive and feel "intuitively right," everyone must undergo painful conditioning, reinforced by a dominant story. No one escapes "schooling" in the three Rs. Sadly, the practice of punishment, rather than fostering virtues, spawns the very vices that it tries to squelch.

NOTES

1. Robert Nozick, *Philosophical Explanations* (Cambridge, MA: Harvard University Press, 1981), 370.

2. Pain and suffering are not identical. A person might willingly undergo a long fast and not suffer. Suffering is unwanted pain or pain that is accompanied by emotional distress.

3. Friedrich Nietzsche, *The Genealogy of Morals*, in *The Birth of Tragedy and The Genealogy of Morals*, trans. Francis Golffing (Garden City, NY: Doubleday Anchor, 1956), 193.

4. Nietzsche, *Genealogy of Morals*, 196.

5. Nietzsche, *Genealogy of Morals*, 196. Most humanists would assert that this is not a genuine human pleasure but one rooted in painful conditioning.

6. Nietzsche, *Genealogy of Morals*, 196–97.

7. For alternative understandings of atonement, see Timothy Gorringe, *God's Just Vengeance* (Cambridge: Cambridge University Press, 1996), ch. 8, and J. Denny Weaver, *The Nonviolent Atonement* (Grand Rapids, MI: Eerdmans, 2001).

8. Gil Bailie, *Violence Unveiled: Humanity at the Crossroads* (New York: Crossroads, 1997), 37.

9. Camus, "Reflections," 224.

10. Rebecca Ann Parker, "Away from the Fire," in *Proverbs of Ashes*, ed. Rita Nakashima Brock and Rebecca Ann Parker (Boston: Beacon, 2001), 30.

11. Rebecca Parker, "The Cross, the Death of Jesus, and a Violent Culture" (lecture delivered at the University of Puget Sound, Tacoma, Washington, March 2000).

12. Parker, "Away from the Fire," 37, 44.

13. Nietzsche, *Genealogy of Morals*, 194.

14. Nietzsche, *Genealogy of Morals*, 193–94.

15. Michel Foucault, *Discipline and Punish: The Birth of the Prison*, trans. Alan Sheridan (New York: Vintage, 1977), 91, 122–123, 128.

16. For a creative examination of how what strikes moderns as "violent" depends on the perspective of the victim, victimizer, or observer, see William Ian Miller, *Humiliation and Other Essays on Honor, Social Discomfort, and Violence* (Ithaca, NY: Cornell University Press, 1993), 52f.

17. For one executioner's account of his trauma, see Donald Cabana, *Death at Midnight: The Confession of an Executioner* (Boston: Northeastern University Press, 1996).

18. Jean Hampton, "Forgiveness, Resentment and Hatred," in *Forgiveness and Mercy*, ed. Jeffrie G. Murphy and Jean Hampton (Cambridge: Cambridge University Press, 1988), 138.

19. Jeffrie G. Murphy "Forgiveness and Resentment," in *Forgiveness and Mercy*, ed. Jeffrie G. Murphy and Jean Hampton (Cambridge: Cambridge University Press, 1988), 27.

20. Wesley Cragg, *The Practice of Punishment: Towards a Theory of Restorative Justice* (New York: Routledge, 1992), 88–89.

21. Cragg, *The Practice of Punishment*, 88. Italics in original.

22. Genesis 1:26. See also, "There is neither Jew nor Greek, there is neither slave nor free, there is neither male nor female for you are all one in Christ Jesus" (Galatians 3:28) and the Muslim tenet, "We have conferred dignity on the children of Adam, borne them over land and sea, and provided them sustenance out of the good things of life, and favored them far above most of our Creations" (Quran 17.70).

23. Stephen Nathanson, *Economic Justice* (Upper Saddle River, NJ: Prentice-Hall, 1998), 65.

24. Peter A. French, *The Virtues of Vengeance* (New York: Addison-Wesley, 1990), 189, 192. He considers the idea of equal human worth "fundamentally flawed" (188). He imposes some limits on what harms avengers can inflict, which stem from the effect of vengeance on the avenger's character, however, not from the desert of the wrongdoer.

25. Jean Hampton, "The Retributive Idea," in *Forgiveness and Mercy*, ed. Jeffrie G. Murphy and Jean Hampton (Cambridge: Cambridge University Press, 1988), 153.

26. Emmett Barcalow, *Moral Philosophy: Theory and Issues* (Belmont, CA: Wadsworth, 1994), 245.

27. Roger Burggraeve, "Violence and the Vulnerable Face of the Other: The Vision of Emmanuel Levinas on Moral Evil and Our Responsibility, *Journal of Social Philosophy* 30, no. 1 (Spring 1999): 38.

28. Jerry Saltzman suggested the phrase, "discerning vision."

29. Judith W. Kay, "Politics without Human Nature? Reconstructing a Common Humanity," *Hypatia: A Journal of Feminist Philosophy* 9, no. 1 (Winter 1994): 41–42.

30. Hampton, "Retributive Idea," 152.

31. Lenn E. Goodman, *On Justice: An Essay in Jewish Philosophy* (New Haven, CT: Yale University Press, 1991), 67.

32. Thomas Aquinas, *Summa Theologiae*, Ia–IIae, 85.1 and 85.2.

33. Hampton, "Retributive Idea," 152–53.

34. Murphy, "Forgiveness," 33.

35. Igor Primoratz also holds that murderers deserve death but it ought not be imposed because torture is prohibited (*Justifying Legal Punishment* [Atlantic Highlands, NJ: Humanities Press International, 1989], 168). See Jeffrey Reiman, "Why the Death Penalty Should Be Abolished in America," in *The Death Penalty: For and Against*, by Louis P. Pojman and Jeffrey Reiman (Lanham, MD: Rowman & Littlefield, 1998), ch. 2.

36. Goodman is a good example of such a retributivist. See his *Justice*, ch. 2.

37. "Thus punishment, for example, might be deserved by the criminal only because it is the customary way of expressing the resentment or reprobation he 'has coming.'" Joel Feinberg, *Doing and Deserving: Essays in the Theory of Responsibility* (Princeton, NJ: Princeton University Press, 1970), 82.

38. Howard Zehr, quoted by Scott Nowell in "Face to Face," *Houston Press*, 27 September 2001, available at www.houstonpress.com/issues/2001-09-27/feature.html (accessed 8 May 2004). Kathleen Daly ("Revisiting the Relationship between Retributive and Restorative Justice," in *Restorative Justice: Philosophy to Practice*, ed. Heather Strang and John Braithwaite [Burlington, VT.: Ashgate, 2000], 33–54) disagrees with Zehr and argues that restorative justice is an alternative form of punishment, not an alternative to punishment. Because of the wide diversion within restorative justice theory about the role of moral merit and punishment, I have not used *restorative justice* as a rubric in this book.

39. Quoted in Larry Brendtro, Martin Brokenleg, and Steve Van Bockern, *Reclaiming Youth at Risk: Our Hope for the Future* (Bloomington, IN: National Educational Service, 1998), 66–68.

5

The Story's Vices

People stand before suffering like those who are color-blind, incapable of perception and without any sensibility. The consequence of this suffering free state of well-being is that people's lives become frozen solid. . . . But more important than this consequence of apathy is the desensitization that freedom from suffering involves, the inability to perceive reality. . . . Then walls are erected between the experiencing subject and reality.

Dorothee Soelle, Suffering

A moral practice is supposed to protect basic human goods, safeguard important principles and rules, and foster particular virtues. The conventional story says the practice of punishment is good for us. It builds character, making all involved better people. Survivors, without being cruel or brutal, may be filled legitimately with resentment because they were made to suffer undeservedly. They may brim with hatred for perpetrators. With moral anger, the story says, survivors demonstrate their self-respect. Armed with these powerful emotions, survivors make justice work by being willing to meet wrongdoers with hostility. The story accuses survivors who seek forgiveness of failing to love themselves or the deceased adequately. Forgiveness is suspect because it shows a lack of resentment. Yet, wary of the power of emotion to undermine objectivity, the story prefers its legal punishers to be above such feelings; instead, they must be passionless. The punisher's motivation? Duty, because "somebody has to do it." In TV law-and order shows, protagonists save their emotion for behind the scenes. The story permits prosecutors to have powerful emotional motivations to "put the bad guys away forever," but must be able to transform outrage into biting legal argumentation moderated by dispassionate distancing.

Survivors glowering with hostility accompanied by lawyers distanced from the harm they seek to have the state inflict—are these traits truly virtuous? Most discussions of the role of emotion in virtue fall into two rival camps. The first treats emotion as a source of ethical judgment, while the second regards emotion as its obstacle.

Proponents of vengeful passions such as Robert Solomon, Susan Jacoby, and Peter French argue that it is permissible for punishers to be motivated by hostility, hatred, or resentment. These emotions, they argue, cause the wronged to rise up and defend themselves. Underlying such convictions is the perspective that emotion—not reason—is the basis of the moral life.[1]

In contrast, retributivists perceive the dangers of unbounded vindictiveness; they are fearful, rightfully, of the power of feelings to derail good sense. They distinguish vengeance from retribution because the latter should be grounded not in passion, but in reason. Justice emerges from a sense of duty; it gives no pleasure.[2] Ethics, in this view, must emanate from reason, aloof from the wild roller coaster of feelings.

Do emotions make men moral? Or does reason? Is hatred a sound basis for action? Or a barrier to morality? Enlightenment philosophers regarded emotion (David Hume) or reason (Immanuel Kant) as distinct sources of moral authority—and hence the Enlightenment story offers no way forward. Again, the story that there is no story results in most moderns being content with an inconsistent amalgam of the two views, willing to ignore the incompatibility of these competing visions.

Both viewpoints are confused: they wrongly assume that ethics must be a matter of either reason or emotion, but not both. Consequently, they assume that an emotion's presence or absence is a sign of virtue; if a person does not feel vindictive, then he is not a vengeful person. Both perspectives misconstrue the nature of virtue and the role of emotions in the moral life. To understand the inadequacy of their rival accounts, it is useful to invoke a different story.

Drawing from the Aristotelian classical tradition incorporated into the Christian West, a discussion of virtue must begin with practical reason. Practical intelligence is that distinctively human ability to see reality clearly, discern appropriate and fitting responses, generate action, and learn from engagements with others. Virtuously developed practical reason involves seeing what is good for humans, in the sense of what promotes their flourishing and well-being. Virtues are acquired ways of being that embody the goods appropriate to humans and are those excellences of character that correspond best with what we have the potential to be—creative, caring, and daring.[3]

Virtues require that emotions be appropriate to the situation, based in accurate perception, and expressed in the right manner to the right person to the right extent at the right time. Emotions involve beliefs; hence the better the alignment of thought with reality, the more likely that emotions will follow suit.[4] Since virtue employs both practical reason and appropriate passion, one without the other cannot be a virtue. What matters, morally, are the accuracy of the perceptions that move humans, and what moral agents do with their feelings. Morally, the painfulness (or pleasurableness) of emotions or their presence (or absence) are never alone adequate guides to right action. Most painful feelings need to be physically released and healed (e.g., through crying) in order to free practical intelligence to craft a fitting action.[5]

Vices are habits, completely nonhuman in character, consisting of pseudo-thinking and inappropriate feelings. They show a lack of the gifts of practical reason and therefore a lack of clarity of vision. Instead of creative thinking, they yield conditioned responses. Instead of freedom of perspective, they are confined to a narrow view. Instead of appropriate emotional response to the present, they replay feelings attached to the past. Instead of expanding freedom of choice, they limit the individual to one of two choices, often opposite extremes. The individual may feel as though she is making a fresh decision, but within the vice, choices appear as well-worn dualities: "Fight back or submit," "Avenge or be humiliated," "Insult or be insulted."[6]

Based on the view that both emotion and reason are essential to the moral life, emotions can be morally evaluated to determine whether or not they are a sound basis for action.[7] Is the emotion based on an accurate view of the situation? Is it rooted in distressing experiences from the past? As a rule of thumb, practical reason can assess the fittingness of an emotion by evaluating its congruence with what promotes human flourishing and with what is presumed true of humans. Such premises include that humans have the potential to be critically intelligent and initiators of respectful responses. Humans want things to go right for themselves and others and seek the goods that enable them to flourish. They are grieved and outraged when their needs and others' needs go unmet, their humanness is violated, or they are treated disrespectfully. They can recognize when feelings are out of alignment with such attitudes. Any inappropriate feelings, whether pleasurable or painful, need to be released appropriately. This catharsis frees people to decide how best to act. Feelings that often stem from past painful situations rather than from current realities include a preoccupation with getting even, a failure to care that others suffer, powerlessness (a feeling that nothing can be done), and hopelessness (a feeling that nothing will change).

Feeling good is not the point of the virtuous life. Sorrow and anger are appropriate feelings in response to murder and mayhem. Painful emotions, guided by the virtues of courage, temperance, and fairness, should be expressed to an appropriate person (a caring friend or counselor), at the appropriate time (with the attentive person's permission), in the right manner (verbally *and* through emotional release), and to the right extent (until the painful emotion is drained away, which may take hours or years). Actions should be based on one's best thinking that is cognizant of when the presence or absence of an emotion may prompt one to act against one's own best judgment.

Vices, in contrast, build defensive rationales for doing what painful emotions direct one to do. Rather than take responsibility for their recovery process, most people, in a desperate attempt to avoid feeling bad, act out their feelings in abuse of self or others.

People acquire habits that are held in place by painful emotions or the inability to feel. In contrast to the belief that retribution is reasonable whereas revenge is passionate, in fact retribution involves the same habits as revenge, only camouflages them better.

VICE #1: VICTIMHOOD

Rape and virulent assault are horribly traumatizing. In addition to suffering physical wounds, victims are damaged by distressing scripts of powerlessness, fearing for one's life, and humiliation. Broken bodies and painful emotions of rage, grief, and terror take decades to work through. Murder leaves a yawning hole in the world of surviving families, whose lives are altered forever. Their sense of safety is shattered; having someone precious taken from them results in overwhelming anger and grief. Trauma damages, yet it is possible to mitigate its effects through a sustained recovery process. Losses are permanent; feelings can be repaired. Many victims avoid the term *healing* because it implies a preestablished endpoint to a journey, but emotional recovery *is* possible.

Being traumatized, however, is different from having a *habit* of victimhood that involves chronic feelings of powerlessness, even for those who occupy a powerful and privileged place in society. Victimhood involves perceiving every new event and circumstance through a distorting lens that denies real power, often leading to a denial of how one might be complicit in the mistreatment of others.

The story reinforces a mind-set of victimhood in almost everyone. Within the habit, people are allegedly right to take others' behavior as personally demeaning. When people hurl insults, their targets conclude that the behavior truly has something to do with them, rather than considering that such behavior reveals much more about the aggressor. Within the yoke of the habit, victims see the world as acting upon them, rather than seeing themselves as actors. They become objects rather than subjects. Seeing themselves as always in danger of losing status, being humiliated, or vulnerable to attack, they do not feel secure about their inherent moral worth, ability to handle others, or personal safety.

Victimhood also involves the fear that others may believe they truly deserved the maltreatment. This can engender a desire to blame back. Given the surfeit of unearned demerit in society, people often seek to defend themselves by blaming others for making them feel bad. A fixation on blame thus is the counterpart of victimhood. People rarely blame another unless they have lost a sense of their own power and ability to act with consequence. This lost sense is a lingering effect of unprocessed helplessness.

A story that nurtures victims by training them to blame others rather than assume responsibility must be thoroughly challenged. There is no need to interpret the experience of trauma through the eyes of victimhood; indeed, most people who emerge from their wounds realize the essential truth that their mistreatment had nothing to do with them (or their beloved) as a person, even though it happened to them. In contrast, a habit of victimhood locks them into believing that there is something shameful or disgusting about them. This shift in perspective is possible for victims of individual harm as well as of structured violence such as racism or sexism.

People who believe that the victimizer communicates a true message about their inferiority feel obligated to retaliate.[8] Jim Elledge could have shrugged off his female friend's slander. But he interpreted her behavior from within the trappings of victimhood—her conduct had to do with him.

The practice of punishment reinforces this propensity, even in relatives of homicide victims. Although the state declares itself the victim, it, in fact, relies on sustaining such families in a state of victimhood. Families, made to wait many years for a promise of closure through an execution that may never happen, are encouraged to remain fixated on their anger and to define themselves in terms of their loss. The deceased is often maligned during the trial, the implication being that she deserved death because she had the wrong friends, was in the wrong place at the wrong time, or was an addict or prostitute. Faced with the possibility that no one will assert the worth of their beloved, families employ the three Rs to buttress their belief that violent punishment is necessary for vindication. In this way, "the motives behind crime and punishment are the same"—an attempt to ward off blame and shame.[9] Residing in victimhood is essential to the rules of the game.

Most discussions of whether the survivors' vengeful feelings are virtuous implicitly assume that the wronged must see themselves as demeaned. But those surviving do not need to interpret horrific offenses through the lens of victimhood. If provided with tools to recover, victims can begin to see themselves as powerful in the present, even if they were rendered powerless in the past. Some even come to the perspective that the perpetrator was more scared than they during the assault, and grieve that another human could be so damaged that he would feel compelled to attack. Both the civil rights and women's movements, for example, affirm the agency and initiative of their constituents without denying the genuine difficulties created by a legacy of being treated as less than fully human. Survivors can adopt such perspectives without condoning the crime (or ongoing discrimination) and without minimizing one iota of the damage wrought. The story remains silent about these possibilities.

A person's inherent human dignity should never be in doubt. Giving up a habit of victimhood challenges the story of social desert and moral blame and is essential to envisioning alternatives to revenge and retribution.

VICE #2: SATISFACTION IN SEEING ANOTHER SUFFER

The story about revenge is clear. It's a sweet and satisfying fruit. "The taking of revenge usually produces an emotional or psychological state in the avenger, a feeling of pleasure, a sense of accomplishment. . . . [T]he avenger typically wants, in fact needs, to savor the sweetness of revenge in order to bring closure to his or her act of vengeance."[10] Revenge promises a release from powerlessness and shame. This emotional kick is perceived by advocates as a real high.

But grown-ups, the story continues, have abandoned such naughty little pleasures, and as serious adults, duty alone motivates them. Most Americans deny ever gloating over a prisoner's suffering or death. Philosopher Trudy Govier cannot emphasize this point enough: "*Legal punishment carries no implication that the point of the offender's suffering is to satisfy the victim.*"[11] By allowing the state to kill fellow citizens, bystanders allow "the state to do vengeful battering for us" and assert that not one of us takes pleasure in it.[12] If there is any pleasure to be had, it's confined to "seeing that justice is done," to a discharge of duty.

Even modern advocates of revenge wish to distance themselves from vindictive motives. For instance, revenge advocate Peter French forbids avengers from being motivated by a desire to inflict suffering or by the seeking of pleasure in it. For he wants avengers to treat wrongdoers with hostility and to inflict pain from the motive that "It's the right thing to do."[13] Here, the avenger merges with the state bureaucrat: "It's a nasty job, but someone has to do it."

The sad reality belies this cover story.

However much advocates of retribution deny that the state's task is to give satisfaction to victims, the actual practice of punishment is still measured by its ability to satisfy. Prosecutors tell family members that an execution will bring closure, ending their ordeal. The murderer had the supposed pleasure of dominating the victim; the state promises that the family's humiliation and shame can be fixed by demanding this satisfaction for them, too. Any prominent execution has a gleeful group, giddy about the pending ritualized death. And then there are bystanders who silently applaud and support the action of the state. Contemplating the suffering of criminals makes bystanders feel good because "we're not bad like them" and "they deserve what they are getting."

Prison psychiatrist Gilligan asks this penetrating question: "What emotional gratification are people seeking when they advocate punishing other people harshly, as opposed to quarantining them in order to restrain them?" He continues: "punishment has always been consciously intended to mirror crime. . . . Namely, a defense against the fear of being shamed or laughed at, and the positive attainment of feeling pride, even honor." However, murderers ultimately realize that "even killing someone cannot truly eradiate the feelings of shame. . . . [T]he [additional] rituals surrounding violence [such as mutilating a dead body] . . . enable the murderer to stave off the tidal wave of shame that threatens to engulf him and bring about the death of his own self."[14] Many homicide families come to realize that even the ritualized magic of an execution is not powerful enough to stave off the stigma that murder carries in a blame-based society.

Some philosophers have seen such satisfaction as the rightful assertion of victims' self-respect. Without the desire for vindication, the story goes, the victim would simply be left there, naked and numb. Anyone with self-respect must demand the comeuppance of the despoiler. However, the three Rs proceed past condemnation to making the perpetrator suffer. Only through becoming a victimizer, says the story, can the victim (or his representative) reestablish the perceived loss of status.

Making another suffer is believed to be integral to ensuring this emotional payoff, of asserting the value of the victim. Americans usually scoff at Socrates' insight that it is better to be humiliated than to humiliate, to be oppressed than to oppress. In the story they know, there is nothing good about being at the bottom. Anyone who remembers pangs of helplessness or powerless rage longs to escape. How could being "top dog" have a higher cost than being worthless trash? Isn't power where one gets real status? It is hard for some to see the costs to society's soul of inflicting harm. Instead, punishment promises sweet relief from the terrible feeling of having been "had."

Yet, despite this promise of satisfaction, as Pietro Marongui and Graeme Newman conclude, one cannot restore "the sense of equilibrium that is the driving force behind the elementary sense of injustice—that is, the equal exchange of one violent act for another, the switch from being the oppressed to the oppressor."[15] Violence as therapy does not work, because it creates new victims rather than healing anyone. Gilligan says that for the man who commits murder, execution is not a threat.

> Many [offenders], . . . so as to settle at last their accounts with the world [have] the fantasy of dying in a shoot-out with the police in which they would take at least as many people as possible into death with them before they die. . . . If anything, death is a promise of peace, which makes it understandable that executions and capital punishment encourage more murders than they deter.[16]

The projects of revenge and retribution offer only three roles—victim, victimizer, and bystander. It is time to be none of these.

VICE #3: NONHUMAN BLANKNESS

What virtues should punishers possess? The story says that the police, defense attorneys, prosecutors, juries, judges, and attorney generals should strive to exemplify justice, honesty, and integrity, all of which require practical reason. Ideally, state executors of justice do not butcher justice; they secure it.

This ideal is far from reality, mainly because the three Rs emerged from within oppressive societies and are unavoidably tainted by them. Retribution is practiced within institutional structures—the state bureaucracies—that continually infect, distort, and derail the best efforts of the most virtuous individuals. As Christian ethicist Reinhold Niebuhr observed in his 1932 classic, *Moral Man and Immoral Society*, institutions always have their own self preservation as a priority, which requires accommodation to the status quo.[17] The criminal justice system inevitably helps protect existing inequalities.

In addition, individuals grow up within an oppressive society and are thus unavoidably tainted with habits imposed through lies and mistreatment, despite their valiant resistance. Despite committed efforts to exercise the best virtues of the profession, experts' judgments too often are racist or classist. Unfortunately, the practice of execution is an instructive case study in how professionals adapt to institutional irrationalities and oppressive relationships.

Onlookers should not be deceived by the lack of passion in tenacious prosecutors or execution teams. Dissociation while seeking the destruction of another human is a key element of violent habits. The understanding of emotions must be widened in order to understand what feelings might lie beneath the calm demeanor of people who wield death machinery with deceptive ease.

As Hannah Arendt's book *Eichmann in Jerusalem* demonstrates, Adolf Eichmann, in organizing the transports that sent millions of Jews to the killing chambers, invoked the attitude that they deserved it, comforting himself with the reminder, "I myself had no hatred for the Jews."[18] As Gil Bailie argues in *Violence Unveiled*, during performances of ritual sacrifice, the tendency to disconnect means that the human being seeking death neither notices nor feels nor recollects it. This habit and its supporting story, in Bailie's words, "make it possible to participate in, observe, or recollect certain violent events without having to actually *witness* them in any morally significant sense."[19] Participants are unable to "see" what they are doing because they are addicted to replaying a ritual, unresponsive to the genuine needs of victims, their families, or the accused.

George Kateb, Ervin Staub, and Victoria Barnett, in their analyses of the roots of evil in the modern world, struggle to name the troubling character flaw exhibited by perpetrators of bureaucratic killing and by their indifferent bystanders. Kateb labels this habit "nonhuman blankness." He suggests that this habit is neither "depravity [n]or inhuman blackness of heart. It may not be radical evil in the Kantian understanding: a Satanic disposition 'to adopt evil *as evil.*' It may not be Milton's Satan saying, 'Evil be thou my Good.'"[20] Rather, nonhuman blankness is a form of not being there, of being disconnected from the reality of what one is doing, and failing to grasp the import of one's actions. It is a failure to attend to the suffering human in one's presence. It is a form of looking but not seeing, hearing but not listening. This habit involves profound internal disconnection, a lack of justice in the soul, a lack of integration of reason and emotion. Kateb links this proclivity directly to the kinds of dispositions Protestants in particular are encouraged to acquire, especially the willingness to put principle before human connection. Observing this pattern in German perpetrators and bystanders during the Third Reich, he faults the harshness of the Lutheran Kant, a supporter of capital punishment. Kateb writes, "I believe that thoughtlessness of the Nazi sort and scale is possible only in a culture that can produce and respect a sentence like the following," by Kant:

> Even if a civil society were to dissolve itself by common agreement of all its members (for example, if the people inhabiting an island decided to separate and disperse themselves around the world), the last murderer remaining in prison must first be executed, so that everyone will duly receive what his actions are worth and so that the bloodguilt therefore will not be fixed on the people because they failed to insist on carrying out the punishment; for if they fail to do so they may be regarded as accomplices in this public violation of legal justice.[21]

Kateb thinks this view values a hard-hearted rigor more than human life.

This kind of nonnoticing, nonthinking, nonaware embrace of violence permits participants to feel nothing while perpetuating the killing machinery of the state. The personal price for participating in legal retribution is nonpresence, a way of being disconnected from one's humanness.[22]

Encased in such a story and modes of being, victims, punishers, and bystanders become immune to the pain of others. We prefer "our own status to [others], even when these others are suffering considerably."[23] Retribution may be worse than revenge, because it requires from participants and bystanders a type of complicity with evil that revenge did not require. Not only does retribution fail to prevent the habits involved in revenge, but it also reinforces this additional one that in the modern world has deeply disturbing ramifications.

VICE #4: STATUS RESTS ON WIELDING COERCIVE POWER

A vice is obscured by the superficially easy question "Who should be the punisher?" Both revenge and retribution falsely believe the wielding of coercive power to be essential to affirming power and dignity. In the story that makes both plausible, dignity is interpreted only as the possibility of having "power over." Self-respect involves being able to demean or defeat others.

Imposing punishment on others is a way of saying, "I, too, possess the power to harm, which is the essential trading card in this community." Within the story that encourages people to see themselves as victims, the only apparent way to regain a powerful position is to harm in return. Jim Elledge's only perceived way to deal with humiliation was through victimizing another. Murder is never a fitting response to humiliation and gossip, but Jim sought to ward off overwhelming shame through gaining the upper hand.

Retribution differs from revenge in this matter only in that privileged victims or their families can sometimes get the state to do their dirty work for them.

Thus, when defenders of the three Rs evade discussing the story in which they are imbedded, they manage to ignore the most salient questions. Are there roles beyond victim or victimizer? On what does human worth depend? On what does dignity rest? What is power? If one's dignity has been despised, how can one assert it? These are the essential questions for every survivor of hurtful mistreatment. And since *no one* escapes some kind of hurtful mistreatment, these are questions everyone carries close to her heart.

The story traps people in a power-as-domination worldview in which everyone allegedly must harm others in order to feel human and valuable.

Unfortunately, ultraviolent offenders share this story, although they make errors using the practice (as does the state). As with Jim, they may fail to find the "right" fit and use excessive force. Or maybe they don't find the right person and harm an innocent bystander. Or maybe their motives are wrong—pure interest in harming, not a proper sense of duty. As with many moral agents, they often are not virtuous. But they have the belief—they have had it beaten into them—that if they don't strike back, they may be worthless worms at the bottom of the dung heap. Since that's where most murderers on death row come from, the tight fury with which they cling to the only story they know, which advocates violence as a means of overcoming humiliation, ought not be too surprising.

VICE #5: EQUATING PERSONS WITH THEIR VICES

Proponents of revenge and retribution begin with the intuition that "*wrong-doing* must be met with hostility." They then subtly shift to a quite different claim, namely "*wrongdoers* must be met with hostility," without addressing the vast difference. For example, French writes, "People who do evil—simply, evil people . . . should be targeted for penalties that are painful to them."[24] Here he makes evil an ontological aspect of their being. Even though some proponents of retribution affirm equal human worth, they still believe that *humans* deserve punishment.

Being hostile to murder is different from being hostile to a human who has murdered. It is always possible and certainly desirable to use discerning vision and see both the person's humanness and her second nature. Humans are oriented to the good, have the capacity for practical intelligence, and seek caring, cooperative connections with other humans; they have the capacity for fresh, creative problem solving. Discerning vision requires remembrance that a person's vices are *always* antithetical to that person's potential humanity. Vices lack human intelligence; they lack attention and awareness; they are alien to genuine human functioning. Exercising clear vision means distinguishing the human person (potentially powerful and intelligent) from the vices that obscure these potentialities—irresponsibility, cruelty, numbness.

How does one show hostility to murder but not the murderer? This distinction is made frequently and on solid moral and psychological grounds. Consider the following. A husband breaks a serious promise to his wife without any overriding moral reason, committing a clear ethical breach. The wife expresses her dismay, her condemnation of the action, her expectation that such behavior will never occur again. All the while, she also communicates that she loves him, respects him, and wants him in her life. It is unpleasant to be called to account for one's errors, but the wife is not inflicting painful suffering on him, although she is heaping plenty of condemnation on his behavior and demanding accountability. In contrast, a vengeful response—which justifies hostility toward the husband—might include such things as shaming him, locking him out of the house, refusing to talk or have sex with him, or leaving for the weekend without a note as to her whereabouts.

Every day presents opportunities to affirm others' humanity while deploring their habit-bound behavior. Revenge and retribution deny this possibility, holding that bad behavior requires the person be treated badly. These practices require an obscured vision in which a human is reduced to the worst thing he or she has ever done. Others are supposed to see only the offense, not the person with a story about how he or she came to do the evil deed. Such practices erase the human from view.

Some victims' family members believe that since the person responsible for killing their beloved did not bother to see her humanity, they are not obligated to see the murderer as a person. But such an approach comes from within the perspective of victimhood. The killer's failure of practical reason does not excuse theirs. The state unfairly expects murderers to exercise a discerning vision about others that it does not expect of survivors, bystanders, or state officials.

VICE #6: BELIEVING THAT SOME HUMANS DESERVE GRAVE HARM

The vice of attributing peoples' difficulties to their personhood results in another habit consisting of the belief that humans deserve harm. Why is this attitude a vice, not a rational perspective?

Once one trains one's practical reason to see every human as precious, dear, and unfairly saddled with all manner of encumbrances that no human in her right mind would ever freely choose, then one can see that every human on the planet deserves respect and compassion. The people who are weighed down by habits that prompt grievous wrongdoing need an extra dose of compassion because they have been so lost and disconnected from their own humanity that they have been blind and deaf to the humanity of others. This reality is cause for grief and outrage about a world that cares for humans so poorly that such vices are not prevented, or, absent prevention, people with them are not helped. The malefactor's identification with her vices needs to be exposed; her lack of integrity in acting on them needs to be condemned. She needs to be restrained until she is able to resist successfully the temptation to act on her vices. Many different things need to happen in response to the person who has demonstrated just how lost, confused, terrified, and damaged she is. Morally, practical reason demands this clarity of vision, rigor of condemnation, and firmness of restraint. Everyone's own humanity requires recognition of the human face of the other. Perpetrators' bad moral merit heightens the need for such recognition and responsiveness. Failing to respond to the humanity of persons is always a vice, and painful penalty constitutes such failure.

VICE #7: DO UNTO OTHERS AS WAS DONE UNTO YOU
"Do unto others as was done unto you" is a pervasive vice, an almost universal temptation. Both retribution and revenge feed desert cycles. The victim, feeling outraged, thinks, "I didn't deserve to be harmed," and rather than affirming that no human—innocent or guilty—ever deserves to be harmed seeks to pass her feelings of resentment and outrage along to another directly or through the courts. Of course, that is exactly why perpetrators hurt their victims—passing along their pain to another, hoping to cure their pain by harming others. People need to raise their heads out of this cycle of retaliation and declare that, as a matter of principle, they shall not pass along their pain to any other human being. Instead, they need to heal from it, find ways to help others to heal, work to prevent more wrongdoing, and establish institutions built on the principle that no human deserves harm. Otherwise, they remain locked into the vice of using their victimization as a reason to victimize others.

All the nonhuman habits without which revenge would collapse are incorporated into the practice of retribution, being informed by the same story. With the habits of revenge folded into retribution, they are given a patina of acceptability. Moreover, retribution feeds off an additional vice of nonpresence, which allows participants and bystanders to tolerate degrading and harsh punishments without a pang of guilt and, maybe, with a twinge of satisfaction.

Schooling in the three Rs, rather than inculcating virtues, actually reinforces vices and then exploits them. Thus the practice of punishment fails on all three counts. It fails to protect core goods, it pursues rules that unnecessarily harm, and it instills vices. These habits are imposed on innocent humans, often in the most brutal and coarse ways.

NOTES

1. Robert Solomon, *A Passion for Justice: Emotions and the Origins of the Social Contract* (Lanham, MD: Rowman & Littlefield, 1995); Susan Jacoby, *Wild Justice* (New York: Harper and Row, 1983); and Peter A. French, *Virtues of Vengeance* (Lawrence: University Press of Kansas, 2001).

2. Trudy Govier, *Forgiveness and Revenge* (London: Routledge, 2002), 13–15 and 177, n. 36.

3. The capacities to develop virtue are innate; virtues themselves are not. Humans acquire virtue easily, just as absent any impairment or deprivation, they learn to walk and talk readily. Virtues are never simply an individual acquisition, but are always acquired in communities informed by narratives.

4. See Martha C. Nussbaum, *The Therapy of Desire* (Princeton, NJ: Princeton University Press, 1994), 381. See also G. Simon Harak, *Virtuous Passions: The Formation of Christian Character* (Mahwah, NJ: Paulist, 1983), ch. 4.

5. Donald L. Nathanson, *Shame and Pride: Affect, Sex, and the Birth of the Self* (New York: Norton, 1992), 308.

6. Judith W. Kay, "Getting Egypt out of the People: Aquinas's Contributions to Liberation," in *Aquinas and Empowerment: Classical Ethics in Everyday Lives*, ed. G. Simon Harak (Washington, DC: Georgetown University Press, 1996), 15–23.

7. "Yet if we felt none of those emotions at all . . . there would really be something wrong with our life." Augustine, *City of God*, book XIV, ch. 9.

8. Nathanson, *Shame and Pride*, 366ff.

9. James Gilligan, *Violence: Our Deadly Epidemic and Its Causes* (New York: Putnam's Sons, 1996), 182.

10. French, *Vengeance*, 69.

11. Govier, *Forgiveness*, 18. Italics in original.

12. Dennis Sullivan and Larry Tifft, *Restorative Justice: Healing the Foundations of Our Everyday Lives* (Monsey, NY: Willow Tree, 2001), 8.

13. French, *Vengeance*, ch. 5.

14. Gilligan, *Violence*, 182, 85.

15. Pietro Marongiu and Graeme Newman, *Vengeance: The Fight against Injustice* (Totowa, NJ: Rowman & Littlefield, 1987), 115.

16. Gilligan, *Violence*, 42.

17. Reinhold Niebuhr, *Moral Man and Immoral Society* (New York: Scribner's Sons, 1932), ch. 2.

18. Quoted in Hannah Arendt, *Eichmann in Jerusalem*, revised and enlarged (originally published in 1963; New York: Penguin, 1994), 30.

19. Gil Bailie, *Violence Unveiled: Humanity at the Crossroads* (New York: Crossroad, 1996), 35.

20. George Kateb, *Hannah Arendt: Politics, Conscience, Evil* (Totowa, NJ: Rowman and Allanheld, 1983), 74. See also Ervin Staub, *The Roots of Evil* (New York: Cambridge University Press, 1989), 21–22, and Victoria J. Barnett, *Bystanders: Conscience and Complicity during the Holocaust* (Westport, CT.: Praeger, 2000), ch. 7.

21. Kant quoted by Kateb, *Arendt*, 74.

22. For a discussion of the virtues necessary to avoid nonhuman blankness in the death house, see Judith W. Kay, "In the Shadow of the Execution Chamber," in *Practice What You Preach*, ed. James F. Keenan and Joseph Kotva (Franklin, WI: Sheed and Ward, 1999), 115–27.

23. Sullivan and Tifft, *Restorative Justice*, 109.

24. French, *Vengeance*, 187.

6

Habits Begotten by Violence

The whole story of violence includes inescapably the lives of victimizers, and the moment we realize that, we are in the territory of tragedy.

James Gilligan, Violence: Our Deadly Epidemic and Its Causes

Every society has the criminals it deserves.

Albert Camus, Resistance, Rebellion, and Death

Is violence bad for people? Neither this question nor its answer is obvious.

The story proclaims that punitive violence restores equality, promotes social cohesion, and prevents chaos. The story preaches that painful penalty reorients the wayward to the right path. Killing people may even produce good. The story's silence about the effects of violence on human beings is deafening.

It is an achievement that citizens are finally able to ask whether this story is true. For centuries, people have not been able to pay sustained attention to the hurtful effects of violence. The unthinkable remained un–thought about, and cultures lay largely silent about the unspeakable. Even within psychology and psychiatry, attention to horrific violence has come in short bursts. Psychiatrist Judith Herman links three periods of psychiatric interest in violent trauma to political movements. In *Trauma and Recovery,* she surveys the social causes that made it possible to look where we were otherwise coached to "avert our gaze and shut our ears." Three movements pushed particular victims to the forefront, making it legitimate for psychiatrists to challenge the dominant story. First was the move toward the emancipation of women as part of the emergence of the modern state and its affirmation of political liberties for all, which enabled Sigmund Freud and others to study the effects of sexual abuse on women in pre-Holocaust Europe. The second social movement began with concern for the shell-shocked veterans of World War I and was reinvigorated during the 1960s antiwar movement and recognition of the disorientation of returning Vietnam War veterans. Third, the women's movement, opened the country's eyes to the realities of rape and domestic violence. In all three movements for social change, the dominant story failed to provide a meaningful narrative or adequate practices to help heal people with shattered selves.[1]

Political agitation and the pioneering efforts of mental health professionals brought widespread awareness of how violence affects people. The general public understood that several months after the events of 9/11, many New Yorkers suffered legitimately from disturbed sleep, irrational fears, intrusive flashbacks, or an inability to plan for the future. Similarly, recent revelations about sexual exploitation by priests shocks but does not surprise. Thirty years ago, no one talked about battered children; today their existence cannot be denied.

Lonnie Athens, a criminologist who carefully documented the life course of violent offenders, gained public attention through the book *Why They Kill* by Pulitzer prize-winning author Richard Rhodes. Athens, himself a survivor of childhood violence, studied violent offenders in prisons, gaining their confidence through private interviews over many months. He wanted to know how people are created who commit heinous violent crimes.[2] He concluded that the violent offender is a product of a "lengthy, odious, and cruel process" that "definitely ends, but which did not start, with a malevolent human being."[3] The benign human at the beginning of the process evokes our empathy, whereas the human with resulting violent habits typically elicits antipathy.

How is it that offenders come to acquire the habits that support and inform revenge, retribution, and a belief that violence rectifies? Although not all homicides can be explained by the following analysis—the kinds of mistreatment and resultant malformations are simply too varied to reduce to one prototype—they demonstrate how many violent offenders come to share the vices found in the three Rs.

The cases that follow are from Athens's second book, *The Creation of Dangerous Violent Criminals*. The interpretation of the habits they instill is mine. This excavation of the tortured lives of individuals with violent habits illustrates how murderers are schooled in the three Rs and share the same interpretive story that will ultimately justify their execution.

VIOLENT COERCION: ENGENDERING THE HABITS OF VICTIMHOOD AND DESERVING HARM

The following case represents a type of mistreatment Athens calls "violent coercion." Such experiences are characterized by the use of violence by a "bona fide or would-be authority figure" from one of the subject's primary groups (family, gang, group home, or military unit) to force the person to submit to authority. "Submission to authority" includes not only obedience, but also "showing the proper respect for them as superiors." The subject is a male in his midteens who was most recently convicted of armed robbery.

CASE 19

I was sitting outside in a lawn chair one Sunday morning. My father yelled from the door, "Go get ready for church." I ignored him and kept sitting in the chair. I hated church. I couldn't stand listening to those sermons about sinning and going to hell. That kind of preaching got under my skin. I hated all those church people. . . .

When I didn't get ready for church, my father came back and said, "I thought I told you to get ready for church." I said, "I'm not going to church." He said, "Oh yes you are going to church, now get ready." I said, "I'm not going to church any more", and then he said again, "oh yes you are", and went berserk on me. He started hitting me with his fists in the face and stomach. I yelled, "Leave me alone, stop hitting me, I am not going to church." But he kept on punching me saying, "You are going to church." When I fell

(continued)

CASE 19 (*continued*)

down on the ground, he grabbed me by the hair and started drag-
ging me into the house saying, "If I can't take you one way, then I'll
have to take you another." I was scared he would pull all my hair
out of my head, and my head and face were hurting bad, so I said,
"Okay, okay, I'll go to church. Stop, stop, stop. Please stop." Then
he finally let go of my hair and we went into the house. . . . When
I looked in the mirror, I saw that I had a black eye, swollen face and
fat lip. I was ashamed to go to church looking like that. I got so mad
and angry thinking about it that I hit the bathroom wall with my
fist. What he did to me was plain dirty. I wanted to get even with
him for doing it. I wanted to kill him and kept thinking over and
over again while we were sitting in church about shooting him.[4]

Violent coercion entails lessons in desert (who deserves a proper show of
respect) and the reality of inequality (some do not deserve respect). Violence
is used as a way to force the "subordinate" to be "respectful" to those deemed
worthy. Here, violence is used in order to align the adolescent with "correct"
values. In case 19, the "correct" value is adultism, in which adults assume that
young people are less worthy of respect than adults. Adultism entails the disregarding of young peoples' thoughts and feelings, and distribution of resources in favor of adults rather than children. (In the case of wife abuse, the
correct value might be the desert-based system of sexism, in which males are
set up to act as if a man's needs, desires, and feelings take precedence over a
woman's. In other settings, such as gangs or the military, the correct value
might be proper respect for those deemed "higher up," namely those with the
physical power to harm.)[5]

Violent coercion has the goal of forcing obedience to some command. In
case 19, once the son outwardly submits, the beating ends. The subject thus
retains some element of control—the appearance of submission brings the
battering to a halt. Athens's subjects report that they "emphatically deny the
right of authority figures to use brutal force upon them in response to their
misconduct."[6] Painful penalty, at this stage, has not produced compliance with

the belief that respect is based on social desert. The punishment, instead of achieving alignment with "correct" value, causes subjects to feel outrage—a sign that they believe they deserve to be treated according to their inherent human dignity and equal human worth.

What does such violent coercion do to a human? Athens describes in terse language the nightmare of those violently coerced. The "typical course" of beating may begin with the subject "acting defiantly," but "as the battery continues and becomes more severe, the subject's defiance erodes into fear." As the battering continues, fear escalates into "full-fledged terror, and panic sets in." The subject, on the "point of breaking," thinks "'How much more battering can I endure?' to which she sooner or later answers, 'no more.'" Submission and the cessation of the battering bring "a great sense of relief." However, "relief quickly turns into humiliation with the realization that she was brutally beaten into submission."[7]

If unable to secure the attention needed to heal from such battery, the subject becomes incensed by her powerlessness and humiliation. "Her burning rage becomes cooled only later when it is transformed into a desire for revenge. The subject's desire for vengeance expresses itself in passing fantasies in which she batters, maims, tortures, or murders her subjugator."[8] These "passing fantasies" offer only illusory relief, because although they place the person in the position of dominator rather than dominated, they do nothing to address the real source of the pain—the humiliation coupled with the violence. If the subject were enabled to grieve, rage, and heal from such terrifying experiences, the "fuel" of the revenge fantasy would also be drained away.[9]

An experience such as violent coercion becomes implanted upon a person's body and mind. The imprint literally records the entirety of the subject's feelings, sensations, and perceptions during the event. This inscription is like a tape recording that the subject replays when powerful triggers later remind the subject of it. Such repetitions form the core of an unthinking vice.[10]

What kind of internal formations might the subject acquire as a result of violent coercion? The person might chronically feel that all people in authority are potential batterers, that the only available role is victim, and that authority rests on the ability to wield a stick. Defiance is feared, as it may result in additional battery. Submission brings humiliation but also relief. In response to any future perceived coercion, the subject may activate the entire memory, including its fantasies of revenge and a "barely repressed sense of rage with vague notions about physically attacking other people."[11]

VIOLENT RETALIATION: GROUNDWORK FOR THE HABITS OF VICTIMHOOD AND "DO UNTO OTHERS AS THEY DO UNTO YOU"

Closely akin to violent coercion is violent retaliation. Athens suggests that both are forms of violent subjugation, because they both intend subjugation to a superior authority. Here, the subject is in his early teens, he was last convicted of armed robbery, and the subjugator was his mother:

CASE 29

I was sitting at the top of the stairs flipping through the pages of the Bible and scribbling in it with a pen. When my little sister came out of her room and saw me, she said, "I'm telling Mama on you" and yelled, "Mama, Johnny's writing in the Bible, Johnny's writing in the Bible." My mother told my sister to bring the Bible down to her. After my mother saw it, she said, "Come down here Johnny, you're going to get a whipping."

She took me in the bathroom and told me to take all my clothes off. I took everything off except my underwear. After she hit me with the belt three or four times, she said, "Take off your underwear too." I said, "Okay, okay." Then she started slashing me all over my raw body. I screamed and screamed, but she wouldn't stop. It hurt really bad. I thought she was going to beat me to death. When I started crying and begging her to stop, she said, "You must be made to be sorry for the terrible thing you did so that you will never do anything like that again." She kept beating me saying, "You must be made to repent, my son, you must be made to repent". . . . I could not believe how bad she was beating me. I knew there was no use in saying I was sorry to her any more. She had gone completely crazy, lost her head. After she got tired of hitting me, which seemed like two hours, she opened the bathroom door.

> I walked out in a daze, completely naked in front of my sister. I
> had big blue welts all over my body. I felt completely humiliated
> as I walked up to my room. I laid on my bed crying and getting
> madder and madder. I looked out the window and saw the
> clothesline. I wished I could get that line and strangle her with it.
> I wanted to wrap that line around her neck and pull and pull and
> pull until I choked her to death. I wanted to kill my mother.[12]

Athens concludes that the punisher justifies her violence by citing the subject's "past disobedience" or a "present display of disrespect." The subject deserves it. Notice that the punisher interprets the misconduct of the subject as a show of disrespect; that is, the parent interprets the situation through the lens of victimhood. A child who forgets to do his chores or fulfill his responsibilities may have many motivations and reasons, but disrespect of the parent need not be one. Because the authority figure feels like a victim, the beatings involved in retaliatory subjugation are "qualitatively different from those administered" during coercive subjugation. In situations of retaliation, the punisher refuses to accept the victim's "offers of submission." "During retaliatory subjugation, the battering is purposely continued to the point where the subject is beaten into an apoplectic condition or the subjugator becomes exhausted, whichever comes first." The subject is denied the "precious luxury" of controlling when the punishment will end.[13]

As in the practice of revenge, the violence doled out by the subjugator is not proportional to the offense. Designed to resolve the avenger's feelings of powerlessness, the suffering of the victim is obliterated from view. This type of violent subjugation affects the subject differently than does violent coercion. Athens summarizes succinctly. Experiences of violent retaliation may begin "with either dread or defiance, rather than only defiance." "If overcome by a strong enough sense of injustice at the anticipation of being battered, the subject may openly express outrage for her violent subjugation and sometimes even her disdain for the subjugator. Otherwise, the subject immediately becomes preoccupied with thoughts about the pain that will be suffered from the battering." The outrage or dread "gives way to fear" that, as the battering continues, gives way to terror and panic. "How much more battering can I possibly endure?" The answer, as with violent coercion, is "No more." Submission, however, does not end the battering, which is "cruelly and relentlessly" continued. The "terror changes into resignation"—nothing she does will change the outcome of the situation. In an apoplectic state, the victim becomes dissociated and numb, watching the beating as if from afar. By the end, "the subject has sunk into a stupor"; her intelligence shuts down. As the stupor wears off, humiliation "overcomes her," but this is "short-lived." Again, in the absence of an opportunity to achieve physical safety and heal from these painful wounds, humiliation is quickly "transformed into an intense desire for revenge against the subjugator," again replete with fantasies of gravely harming the subjugator.[14]

Here, the subject is imprinted differently than in violent coercion. The person may struggle with complete dissociation from any physical pain or emotions. Profound despair and resignation may alternate with burning anger and violent revenge fantasies—both of which replay polar opposite responses. Neither offers a way out of the story.

HORRIFICATION: INSTILLING THE BELIEF
THAT VIOLENCE RECTIFIES VICTIMIZATION

A third type of violent mistreatment reinforces the habits of the three Rs. A mistaken assumption is sometimes made that only those actually targeted with physical violence are harmed. However, ample evidence exists that witnessing violence aimed at a beloved member of one's primary group is also profoundly traumatizing. The clinical definition of post-traumatic stress syndrome recognizes that trauma may result solely by witnessing horrific acts, as happened to many New Yorkers who watched the attack of 9/11.

Athens also found that violent offenders he studied experienced this form of injury, called "horrification." Athens observes that this is not just any kind of violence being witnessed—such as the attack of 9/11—but either violent coercion or violent retaliation. In the next case, the subject is a male hearing his stepfather subjugate his mother:

CASE 9

One night I was woken up by loud voices coming from my parent's bedroom. I got a drink of water from the bathroom so I could find out what was going on. As I walked to the bathroom, I heard my mother say, "No, I told you not to do that, I don't like it." I thought to myself, "What could he be doing to her?" I started listening as hard as I could. My mother said, "please don't do that any more to me, it hurts," but he said, "I don't care whether it hurts or not." I heard noises which sounded like scuffling and my mother screamed, "Please stop, it hurts, it hurts bad, please stop now, no more, stop, stop." She would cry for a while, scream out in pain, and then start crying again.

As I walked back to my room, I knew that he must be hurting her awful bad to make her scream like that. It got me so mad and angry that I wanted to kill him. I thought about going in there, pulling him off her and kicking his ass good, but he was too big for me to handle. I knew there was nothing I could do. I wished he would stop, but he wouldn't. As I heard her crying from my bed, I felt bad because I couldn't do anything to help her. I wanted to get him off her and hurt him, but I was too afraid. I kept telling myself that I was just a little sissy. Then I tried to fall back to sleep and pretend it was all a bad dream.[15]

In this type of hurt, the subject is forced "to listen more keenly to the performance than he otherwise might have and fill out the unseen portion with mental imagery."[16] In cases of violent retaliation, the victim may close his eyes the entire time or become too dissociated to pay attention to the details of what is happening. In horrification, the images he conjures up are often more horrible than what is actually occurring.

Typically, the subject's "initial feelings of apprehension" that the intimate may be assaulted turn to anger toward the punisher. "The subject's attention now becomes riveted upon the assault itself, which is perceived almost as if it were happening in slow motion. Every blow of the subjugator and the victim's reaction to it is hammered into the subject's mind." The question arises, "How much more can I let the victim endure before I do something?" The answer, once again, is "No more." "The wrath rapidly building up in the subject climaxes in an urgent and powerfully felt desire physically to attack the intimate's subjugator." The decision, finally, to refrain from action is interpreted by the subject neither as a rational response of a terrified child nor as an appropriate assessment of his chances of success. The subject turns his anger inward and is filled with powerlessness and "intense shame."[17]

Horrification lays the groundwork for the fixation that powerlessness is resolved through violence. Failure to resort to violence is associated with shame and impotence, so he attacks himself as unworthy and inadequate. To avoid these painful feelings, the victim may entertain violent fantasies—fantasies aimed toward himself rather than others. Later, the mere threat of violence may be sufficient for the subject to replay the recording and submit, which "explains why people can sometimes undergo violent subjugation without themselves ever being physically harmed."[18]

VIOLENT COACHING IN THE THREE Rs

Violent coaching, Athens writes, involves a credible authority within the subject's primary group, who explains how the world works and how the subject must learn to act within it. The coach conveys the message that the "world is inhabited by many mean and nasty people, both inside and outside primary groups, and the novice must be properly prepared to deal with these people when he meets them." Implicit in such coaching is the belief that some people deserve grave harm. Coaching is a direct method of insuring that the subject acquires this habit central to the three Rs.[19]

Athens explains that subjects are *always* taught that violence "is a *personal responsibility* which they cannot evade," no matter if they are young, small, or female and despite what their own moral sensibilities might forbid. The subjects are seldom taught how to actually fight. The point of violent coaching is not "supplying the know-how" for prevailing, but "conveying the realization that grave harm should be done to certain people" and the subject's duty to embrace this concept.[20]

Enforcement techniques fall into four categories, according to Athens. The first is vainglorification, in which the coach "glorifies violence," with himself cast as the "hero" beating the bad guys. The coach here relies on the subject's "*vicarious enjoyment* of" imagining being the victimizer rather than the victim.[21] Here the subject longs to be the hero of a story, any story, rather than the victim.

Another coaching tactic is ridicule, in which "the coach belittles or threatens to belittle the novice for his reluctance or refusal physically to attack other people who provoke him."[22] The subject in this case is a man in his midtwenties who was last convicted of armed robbery.

CASE 21

My father told me that there were two things I better always remember: "If you ever get into it with somebody, don't ever run,
but stand there and fight. If something is worth fighting about
then it's worth killing somebody over. If you get into a fight with
anybody, try to kill them. I don't care who it is—a man or
woman—pick up a stick, board, rock, brick, or anything, and hit
them in the head with it. That way you won't have to worry about
having any trouble from them later."

One day my father brought home some boxing gloves. . . .
I thought we were only going to play. He started punching at
me and telling me to punch him back, but I could never reach
him. He said, "You ain't shit, you little punk, come on, hit me,
you ain't shit. Anybody could whip your ass. I'm going to get
your cousin over here to whip your ass. He's twice as bad as
you are." I felt frustrated and humiliated and started crying. My
dad kept grinning, laughing, and punching at me and calling
me a little punk. Finally my grandmother heard me crying and
came in and asked my father what he was doing. He said, "I'm
trying to make him become a man and not a punk. Since I'm his
father, I've got a right to make a man out of him any way I
want."[23]

Such ridicule embeds a recording with the feeling that status rests on being
able to harm others. Those without this ability deserve to be ridiculed. Communicated is the message that anything is better than being a victim.

Coercion is a third technique of coaching, in which the coach, much as in
violent subjugation, physically punishes the subject if she refuses to fight back.
The fourth form of coaching that Athens describes occurs in haranguing
through "incessant melodrama." If someone is told something with "enough
force and conviction," eventually it is "taken to heart," even if it is resisted initially. What is the narrative behind the melodrama heard by subjects? They

"should attack physically those who provoke them." The use of all four techniques Athens dubs "overkill."[24]

Violent coaching continues the snowballing of hurts. Such coaching could not be successful unless it built upon the deep wounds and painful recordings already set in place through violent subjugation and horrification. A person lacking such prior victimization might simply turn a deaf ear toward the violent coach. But in the traumatized subject, the coach's boasts, ridicule, and threats trigger painful recordings of humiliation and fear. Now the coach drives home how the subject has failed to follow the advice given to him, failed to be the kind of person his coach urges him to be. Four additional layers are added to the painful recordings already embedded in him.

First, the principle of action, "Do unto others as was done unto you," is enforced upon subjects through coaches who see themselves as victims and who encourage subjects to see themselves as victims. Violence, they maintain, is the way to escape victimization and assert status. Provocations are to be interpreted as genuine signs of disrespect. Interpreted as true communications, no provocation should go unpunished. (Coaches could teach their subjects the opposite, namely, that no provocation should be taken personally, because when people are disrespectful, they cannot be thinking intelligently about the subjects as humans. If provocateurs were to notice the subject as a person, they would have nothing disrespectful to say or do.) Prior brutalization has set the groundwork for interpreting many kinds of behavior as threatening—indeed, to regard all people as threatening. Violent coaching communicates that the only solution to victimhood is to be able to victimize others.

Second, coaches also force subjects to narrow their vision. Coaches make their subjects see their harassers as essentially victimizers, rather than as human beings with violent accretions. Coaches could teach their subjects to use discerning vision and see bullies as humans lost in habits of violence. Instead, coaches mistreat their subjects so that they cannot see the humanity of the bully. From within their recordings, subjects reduce the bully to his conditioning and respond only to it. (If coaches were to teach their subjects to see the humanity of the victimizer, then the violent coaches themselves would have to acknowledge the humanity of their victims—their sons, daughters, fellow gang members, and so forth. This clarity of vision then might force the realization that their subjects do not deserve to be violently coached, either.)

Why is harming others a duty? Because giving people what they deserve is the moral of the story. The other's bad behavior justifies one's own.

Third, coaching is harmful because it prompts subjects to lose discerning vision toward themselves. Coaching betrays subjects, who feel profoundly forsaken when someone they trust prescribes violence. Subjects want the humans they depend upon to act virtuously and to remind them of their worth. If violently coached, subjects will have a harder time maintaining a clear picture of who they truly are.

The fourth imprint is the conviction that people are rectified through suffering. Infliction of violent punishment is supposed to inculcate proper respect and "right" attitudes in the subject. But such experiences traumatize rather than edify, and any subsequent obedience is grounded in terror, not in free and voluntary choice. Hatred and vindictiveness, not respect, seem to be the "lesson" learned. Violence forces the subject's conformity to prevailing inequalities of power. Rather than being rectified, therefore, brutalized people, unless offered a helping hand, are likely to brutalize others.

All four types of maltreatment—coercion, retaliation, horrification, and violent coaching—in the absence of opportunities to heal, produce a chaotic interior life. Humans were simply not meant to handle such overwhelming experiences. Victims of these experiences do not have "selves" in the typical sense. Splintered and shattered, they often function with big chunks of themselves tucked away for safe keeping. They might hear in Sunday school about loving their enemies, but they are racked by guilt because they cannot. They are as yet unable to fight back, so the church's narrative of nonviolent resistance is interpreted as counsel to be passive and submit.

Believing they deserved it protects subjects from facing the hard truth of how helpless and subjugated they were. Such fantasy prevents total disintegration of the self. Jim Elledge, as we saw earlier, blamed himself for the accident with the scalding pot of lard. Jim became quite superstitious, believing that a mere thought could make things happen. He took coincidences as signs that he was in control of his environment, even though, as a youngster, he was totally at the whim of irresponsible adults.

For the vast majority of brutalized children, such mistreatment has gone unacknowledged, except by confidantes. No one has stood up and denounced it as wrong. No one has said that they did not deserve it. No one has praised them for being the valiant, brave little persons they were. With neither fanfare nor thanks, they have gotten on with their lives, forming friendships, finding work, raising children, and helping neighbors. They may, however, come to resent victims who are not able to pull their own weight, who seem to be unable to function as well as they do. They may point to their own hard-won ability to rise above brutalization and to pass along less of the hurt to their children than they received. Sick of the "abuse" excuse, they fail to see why murderers cannot exercise the same control, the same decision to rise above their circumstances.

Athens is careful to avoid the fuzzy category of "abuse." He refuses to divide the above brutalizing experiences into emotional, physical, or sexual abuse. A child might be sexually abused, but never experience the above three forms of subjugation. Or a child may be subjugated through horrification, but never suffer a blow. Athens urges observers to reject the imprecise term *abuse* in favor of obtaining information on specific social experiences and recordings that can be studied and verified. Gilligan concurs:

> Child abuse is neither a necessary nor a sufficient condition for adult violence, anymore than smoking is a necessary or sufficient cause for the development of lung cancer. There are, however, plenty of statistical studies showing that acts of actual and extremely physical violence, such as beatings and attempted murders, are regular experiences in the childhoods of those who grow up to become violent, just as we know that smoking is a major, and preventable, cause of lung cancer.[25]

Sometimes people, as a way to argue that killers should have been able to exert the same self-control that they do, claim that "they were abused but never felt violent urges." However, Athens's research suggests that people who endured other forms of mistreatment than he catalogues in his research do not end up with the same recordings that dangerous criminals do, because it typically takes a special combination of experiences to override a human's powerful practical reason and orientation to the good.

ARE SUCH HABITS INEVITABLE?

It is at this juncture that the paths of subjects begin to diverge. Some are able to achieve safety and begin a path of healing. Others move more deeply into the three Rs and eventually come to believe in the efficacy of violence. Humans who have been through the above experiences are not inevitably headed for a life of crime. They may escape the violent primary community. They may receive helpful attention from a caring teacher, neighbor, or peer. They may encounter a positive narrative that buttresses their belief that no one deserves such battery, a perspective they had almost lost.

Violent criminals are those who did not receive enough of such lifelines. Sometimes entire communities are virulent, and the individuals trapped within them lack access to the resources to help themselves. Some families or gangs are isolated in violent patterns, and the powerless have no ready avenues of escape. They are not given the opportunity to dismantle their recordings, heal from their hurts, and reclaim their ability to act as humans. Instead, they have merely begun their "schooling" in the three Rs.

Coercion, retaliation, horrification, and violent coaching leave the subject with imprinted feelings of bewilderment, fear, anger, shame, humiliation, and worthlessness. The subject is haunted with questions:" 'Why have I not done anything to stop my own and my intimate's violent subjugation?' 'What can I do to stop undergoing any further violent subjugation and personal horrification at the hands of other people?'"[26] Instead of a helping hand, they face an onslaught of distressing experiences that build on and solidify their embryonic vices.

NOTES

1. Judith L. Herman, *Trauma and Recovery* (New York: Basic, 1997), 7–32.

2. Athens conducted in-depth interviews with about one hundred violent offenders, closely comparing the oral narratives of the criminals with those found in their records. If the person lied, he promptly ended the interview. He did not ask them *why* they had committed their crimes. Rather, he wanted to know *what* they were thinking and feeling as they did their deeds. His goal was to obtain complete descriptions, and then to discern themes later. Rhodes compares Athens's "carefully framed narratives" to good maps, which "reduce the clutter while preserving the basic relationships." Athens's case studies "increased the visibility of the information" otherwise buried in a welter of data. "Athens still had to find the patterns, of course, but in order to do so he first had to make the necessary maps" (Richard Rhodes, *Why They Kill* [New York: Vintage, 1999], 63). The results of Athens's first research project can be found in his *Violent Criminal Acts and Actors Revisited* (originally published in 1980; Chicago: University of Illinois Press, 1997).

3. Lonnie Athens, *The Creation of Dangerous Violent Criminals* (Urbana: University of Illinois Press, 1992), 6.

4. Athens, *Creation*, 30–31.

5. Athens, *Creation*, 28.

6. Athens, *Creation*, 28, 29.

7. Athens, *Creation*, 29.

8, Athens, *Creation*, 29.

9. For a powerful account of a woman's eventual victory over compulsive fantasies of hurting others, see Katie Kauffman and Caroline New, *Co-Counselling: The Theory and Practice of Re-Evaluation Counselling* (New York: Brunner-Routledge, 2004), 103–111.

10. Harvey Jackins, *The Human Side of Human Beings*, 25th printing, revised (Seattle: Rational Island, 1994), and Donald Nathanson, *Shame and Pride: Affect, Sex, and the Birth of the Self* (New York: Norton, 1992), 95–96.

11. Athens, *Creation*, 58.

12. Athens, *Creation*, 34–35.

13. Athens, *Creation*, 31, 32.

14. Athens, *Creation*, 32, 33.

15. Athens, *Creation*, 41.

16. Athens, *Creation*, 38.

17. Athens, *Creation*, 39, 40, 41.

18. Athens, *Creation*, 41, 45.

19. Athens, *Creation*, 46, 47.

20. Athens, *Creation*, 47. Italics in original.

21. Athens, *Creation*, 48. Italics in original.

22. Athens, *Creation*, 49.

23. Athens, *Creation*, 51.

24. Athens, *Creation*, 54.

25. James Gilligan, *Violence: Our Deadly Epidemic and Its Causes* (New York: Putnam's Sons, 1996), 49.

26. Athens, *Creation*, 59.

7

Making the Three Rs Stick

It is not hypocritical to support victim family members and offenders. Real compassion does not betray anyone.

Jeanette Star Howard

Hence I have no mercy or compassion in me for a society that will crush people and then penalize them for not being able to stand up under the weight.

Malcolm X, The Autobiography of Malcolm X

Rarely are people exposed to the three Rs from a safe distance with the luxury of rational analysis; most have had them literally beaten into them. Violent criminals encounter the three Rs first through cruel conditioning. Their consequent adherence to the beliefs that support the three Rs is not simply a matter of false ideas or personal preferences. Rather, such adherence has emotional roots. Criminologist Lonnie Athens, among others, has identified the specific kinds of social experiences that mark the mileposts in the making of murderers. A clearer perception of the experiences and reactive choices that sabotage a person's reluctance to seriously harm others, such as offered by Athens, sharpens bystanders' perceptions of criminals' *affective* attachment, even "addiction" to the narrative of the lie.

Athens's analysis is limited to offenders he deems violent and dangerous, the kind whose heinous acts were initiated with little or no provocation and were out of proportion to the situations. "Those criminals who commit such acts are the most dangerous violent criminals, with perhaps the lone exception of certain white collar criminals whose actions jeopardize the health or safety of large numbers of people."[1] Athens defines "grievous violence" as that which results in a major physical violation, whether threatened or actual.[2] Typical offenses include armed robbery, rape, battering, and murder.

Albert Camus, in *Reflections on the Guillotine*, cautions against sniveling sentimentality or muddled relativity that places the murderer (being a poor victim, too) and the murdered on the same moral plane. "I am far from indulging," he writes, "in the flabby pity characteristic of humanitarians, in which values and responsibilities fuse, crimes are balanced against one another, and innocence finally loses its rights."[3] At the end, one breathes and the other lies dead—a moral world hangs in the difference. Romanticizing murderers is just as bad as demonizing them. Understanding is not excusing. Yet paying careful attention to the stories of violent offenders exposes the community's complicity in their formation.

Athens discovered that every violent offender he interviewed had been through the process of brutalization described in the previous chapter. The process, Athens found, does not end there, however, but has several more stages. The entire process from beginning to end Athens calls "violentization." Richard Rhodes writes that this process is not confined to the home at the hands of parental figures. Violentization occurs in gangs, foster homes, group homes, military schools, or the military itself. Not all are children when the process begins—adults can be violentized.[4] Yet each violent path is started by someone being brutalized, by someone literally having the wounds and story that support the three Rs beaten into them and being offered no help to recover.[5] These stages need not occur all at once, but may occur over time. There is a snowballing effect, in which later experiences build on earlier recordings, making later stages possible, but not inevitable. One can possess internal imbroglios from being brutalized without acting on them. The victim of violence makes choices at each fork in the road—although the decisions are often made from limited options constricted by circumstance—before progressing to the next stage.[6]

Thus far, the murderer-in-the-making, in the first stage of brutalization, has been mistreated into "believing" the three Rs, but only from the perspective of a victim. The decision to go from vanquished to victimizer occurs in the next stage—a momentous transition for any human. What happens to those who cannot escape a life of violence, but move from victim to perpetrator?

STAGE TWO. BELLIGERENCY: MAKING THE PAINFUL DECISION TO VICTIMIZE RATHER THAN FEEL VICTIMIZED

Athens characterizes the belligerency stage as a period of reflection that culminates in a decision to use violence, but only when seriously provoked. "After considerable thought, [the subject] concludes that there is a huge gap between the ideal and real way in which people interact."[7] Subjects "take stock"[8] and look for a narrative to make sense of their brutalizers, their own conflicted and tormented feelings, and the society that permitted their brutalization. What kind of story can victims form about themselves that will explain their pasts as nonviolent people and their current realities as targets of violence, and that will project themselves into a future? Is there a future beyond brutalization? Does the world consist only of victims and victimizers? Stage two is marked by a search for understanding.

Violent coaching was not a crash course in how to fight and win. Up to this point, these subjects have never been able to defend themselves physically. There is no guarantee that they will be able to defend themselves now. Risking physical defeat and physical injury again is not a welcome prospect.

However, most of the situations faced by the subjects will not be truly life-threatening. Nevertheless, they have been primed to feel that provocations really *are* matters of survival. Brutalized subjects have been heavily shamed. A provocation that may look to an outsider as utterly trivial may, within the distressful scripts of the subject, be perceived as life or death. Most people, psychologist Donald Nathanson observes, have nonviolent ways to reduce shame—they can point to their accomplishments, possessions, or social merit. But, too often, the brutalized lack such means of warding off shame. Nathanson says that once triggered and after a "transient inability to think," subjects rapidly "scan" their "shame library" to compare and contrast "the group of shame-related scripts." "It is the script (rather than the individual memories) that contains the real power."[9]

Nonviolent scripts are not readily available to most subjects. Walking away or ignoring the taunt would require not feeling like a victim by not taking the threat personally. But these subjects have habits of victimhood; they have been encouraged to believe they deserved their mistreatment.

Unable to locate a safe environment with caring attention and an alternate story while tormented by their scripts of helplessness and unworthiness, subjects resolve to fight back with physical force the next time someone comes at them.

This "emotionally-laden resolution," notes Athens, is not enough to *make* one violent. Intentionally injuring another human gravely for the very first time in one's life is not a casual matter. "It takes more courage than may be realized to cross the invisible line which separates those who will from those who will not deliberately jeopardize or take human life."[10] Athens observes:

> The dawning of this belated solution . . . takes on the guise of the sudden revelation of the real wisdom of the lessons earlier taught him during his violent coaching, but which only now does he fully understand and appreciate. It is *as if* the subject had earlier been partially deaf and has only now heard what his coach had been telling him all along: resorting to violence is sometimes necessary in this world.[11]

But this sudden realization is not the fresh thinking of an unconditioned human. It is akin to the alcoholic's sudden realization that what he needs is a drink. The thought appears fresh, and subjects are unable to see it as a product of their conditioning, rooted in enormously painful emotions and reinforced by the story.

With this decision, the subject gives internal agreement to the story and to the vices it spawns. This agreement "begins rapidly and steadily to influence his conduct toward other people, while at the same time, slowly but surely fades into his unconscious."[12]

There may be ample time for their decisions to roll around in their minds. Weeks or months could pass before they are challenged in a way that feels threatening. Until that time comes, the subjects are in a state of belligerency; they may be more verbally aggressive or more apt to talk back, exploring being an aggressor, not the victim.

For three reasons, this stage should *not* be interpreted as a period in which no new hurt is added. First, failure to find help leaves the subject resigned that he is on his own. It is up to him to find a way to stop people from brutalizing him—there are no fantasy rescuers, no protectors, no trustworthy adults.

Second, the brutalized suffer the additional wound of not receiving the attention they need. This inability to secure helpful attention adds another layer to their existing distressful recordings. For some, the additional imprint may be heavy isolation, an inability to notice that others are there. For others, the recording contains an inability to ask for help, even in dire situations. For yet others, the new layer may contain a compulsive seeking of help, a desperate effort to transform every interaction into attention for the subject.

Third, it is hurtful when there is a communal failure to tell a truer story. The brutalized individual's recovery task is to construct a story that includes the trauma in her life narrative, but in which she does not remain captive to her past.[13] In the belligerency stage, subjects look for a narrative with which to understand their terrifying experiences and unbidden feelings. "Without some narrative, we slide into a chaos," Catholic theologian Robert Schreiter says.[14] Subjects look to known sources of meaning making, such as their classrooms, religious institutions, and peers.

What interpretive frameworks will they find to explain their brutalization? Too often, they find not a community that condemns the harsh treatment they have undergone, but rather one that is oddly silent about it. Religious communities pray for the oppressed, who are usually portrayed as suffering from hunger in distant lands. Often, extended family members or neighbors do not intervene to interrupt the violence in the home, and they often advocate corporal punishment as a means of rectification.

The three Rs are built on a deadly delusion—that the perpetrator does not know what it is like to suffer and therefore must be made to understand "just how wrong what he did was."[15] On the contrary, the violentized know all too well the mortification of being brutalized, and in their desperate attempts for justice and respect are prepared to attack anyone who brings them too close to such powerful, painful emotions. Fighting back is one way to "ward off those catastrophic experiences."[16]

Their brutalization and consequent powerlessness and shame, the lack of help, and the story's murderous lies may make violent response look like the only path open to them.

This is only the appearance, however. Athens, Rhodes, Gilligan, and others argue that subjects at this stage can still be helped. Outreach to belligerent youth in particular can be highly effective. Efforts can be made to reduce family and school violence and to offer nonviolent coaching, such as training in negotiation, anger management, and conflict resolution.[17] Adolescents with a history of belligerency can be offered safe places with caring listeners where they can heal emotionally and physically from their wounds.[18]

But things do not go well for many people who have internalized the narrative of the lie. Such subjects, Athens argues, proceed to a third stage.

STAGE THREE. VIOLENT PERFORMANCES: ACTING ON HABITS
Having made the decision to fight back, Athens's research suggests, the belligerent subject awaits the right circumstance. The narrative is "tested for its accuracy." Is violence a good solution? The subject is still wondering, "When the time finally comes, will I be able to hurt somebody bad or not?"[19] The subject in this stage limits his use of violence to two types of situations—when he is maximally or moderately provoked and when he has a chance of prevailing. The subject may lose decisively; the fight may end in a draw; or he may win. Athens's report of another "male in his midteens" convicted of "aggravated assault" illustrates "moderate provocation and a major defeat."

CASE 21

I was playing pick up basketball in the school gym. The same guy on the other side kept guarding me when I had the ball. Every time I dribbled or took a shot, he was pushing or shoving me. I got mad and said, "Get the fuck off me, man." He said, "Tough, that's the way the game is played here." When he kept on doing it, I knew he was trying to fuck with me on purpose. He wasn't guarding me close, but playing dirty basketball. When he later knocked me down from behind, I got mad and said, "Man, you better stop fucking pushing me." He said, "Fuck you." I waited for him to do it again. As soon as he did, I turned around and hit him four or five times in the face, which made him fall down. When he got up, he ran and grabbed a folding chair and hit me across the arms and face with it. . . . I was laying on the gym floor almost knocked out with my face cut wide open and my eyes swelling up. I never really knew before how bad you could get hurt in a fight with somebody.[20]

A series of such defeats, Athens observes, may change the life course of such a person. Concluding that he does not have what it takes, the subject "sadly resigns himself to being a non-violent person in the future."[21] He basically undoes his earlier agreement with his habits. If he continues to lack assistance to deal with his brutal mistreatment, his functioning may remain handicapped, marred by deep internal divisions.[22]

In contrast, others may take one defeat or even a series of defeats as a lesson that they need to become better fighters. The subject concludes that "he should resort to more lethal violence and resort to it much more quickly than in the past. The subject learns the hard way that lesson expressed in the aphorism, 'If something is worth fighting about, then it is worth killing over', and is somewhat perturbed with himself for not having learned this important lesson sooner."[23]

A series of "draws" keeps the subject in this stage indefinitely, Athens continues. "If he loses," says Athens, "his oppression may become far harsher than before the rebellion was mounted."[24]

Often, the first violent performance is a "personal revolt" against the primary brutalizer. If he wins, the parent backs down. Here is how one nineteen-year-old in jail on assault and drug charges describes his experience:

> I was like, fifteen or something, and I came home and my stepdad, man, he was beating on my mother. I was in the front yard and I heard her crying all the way outside. I had had enough, you see. I couldn't stand to see her get beat up one more time. So I grabbed the baseball bat and launched into him. I couldn't stop. My sister was screaming at me to stop, but I ignored her, it felt so good. Man, I beat the shit out of the old man [said with real pleasure in his voice]. He needed to go to the hospital, but man, he never touched me after that. I finally did him good.[25]

One or more decisive victories move the subject into higher levels of dangerous violence.

For most people who have had the experiences described in these chapters, the emotional pull to regain a sense of power through becoming a victimizer is enormous. Lacking a chance to either escape brutalization or heal their wounds, subjects seek release through taking revenge. They are primed by an environment that has coached them to use violence, supported by a narrative that advises "do unto others as was done unto you," and encoded with the notion that some people deserve grave harm. Various distressful recordings are about to coalesce into a vice of seeking revenge. "Nothing expands a person's determination to be violent more than the repeated successful performance of violent action. The more successful the performance or the bigger the violent feat performed, then the more quickly the violent resolution of the person can be expected to deepen and widen."[26]

Athens observes that successful interventions are also possible for someone in stage three. Athens's own life demonstrates the point. He was "adopted" by a Jewish family who let him stay with them when the violence at his home got out of hand. Safety from immediate harm is the first need of victims. Of modest means, his substitute parents nevertheless dreamed of college for their own son and for Athens, too. They taught Athens to win battles with his wits rather than his fists. They gave him hope. Their encouragement of his academic gifts carved out a new territory where he could try out alternative ways of being.

But for those subjects who persist with violent performances, the fairly instant conversion from tormented soul to tough guy does not, of course, heal their underlying pain. It merely substitutes one form of pain, masked as pleasure, for another. They have found harming others "pleasurable" only because it offers relief from their own brutalization and shame. "Doing unto others as was done unto you" offers the perceived satisfaction that the story and the three Rs promise. Underneath this pleasure sits unhealed wounds and distorted thinking, which will continue to inform their behavior. This time, however, they have to become top dog.

The subject's first violent performance can be lethal. The stepdad could have died from his injuries. The legal system does a huge disservice by viewing such individuals as chronically dangerous, virulent offenders. One violent performance (despite its seriousness) is not yet a well-entrenched vice.

Athens finds that the response to the subject *by the people in the primary group* shapes the decision to persist. A critical factor is the narrative that *others* construct about the person newly become violent.

STAGE FOUR. VIRULENCY: THE LOSS OF DISCERNING VISION

After the subject's violent performance, his primary group suddenly sees him in a new light. His group now sees him as an "authentically violent individual instead of a person who was not violent or only possibly capable of violence only a few short days or even hours earlier."[27] Its interpretive story denies the humanity of the subject. His peers also suggest that the subject is mentally un-balanced. The story told—in terms teetering between admiration and fear—describes him as "a violent lunatic" or an "insane killer."[28] And even as the accolades tinged with fear start rolling in, his peer group and even his coach say, "He went way too far." With this narrative developed, "People treat him as if he literally were *dangerous*."[29] This script told by his peers makes the subject the victor, not the vanquished. When he walks down a hallway, people uncon-sciously move aside. The subject now experiences both notoriety and social trepidation. These surprising experiences pose a new choice for him.

Being seen as strong—as the victor, not the victim—gives the subject an "almost irresistible" taste of power after years of subjugation. Subjects, once seen as "wimps" or "babies," are now treated as persons to be reckoned with; they have made the successful move from played upon to player. "The ques-tion of whether to embrace or reject the violent notoriety is virtually a forgone conclusion."[30] Suffering in the first two stages from poor self-esteem, the sub-ject now "becomes overly impressed with his violent performance and ulti-mately with himself in general." The subject internalizes the image of himself as a violent person, capable of doing harm, and willing to do it.[31] He has swal-lowed the story and now sees himself as "invincible."[32]

For former victims, this is heady stuff, indeed. Subjects do not see them-selves as scared and shamed people who have acquired a habit of violence, but as essentially violent (this being desirable, because it is feared rather than dis-respected). They lose discerning vision about themselves.

Painful feelings recede from view but do not disappear. Violent offenders are highly motivated to avoid any return to the shameful feelings from their brutalized past. The sense of power they now experience does not erase their former pain. Seemingly trivial events (an insulting letter) have the potential to reactivate their wounded past. Violent offenders become trapped into shame-shame cycles, feeling humiliated over how easily they can be triggered. Ulti-mately, destroying shame becomes translated into destroying the other's ability to shame them.[33] Gilligan observes, "Truly, the more tiny and trivial the cause, the more powerful, deadly, and violent the result." The false sense of power that is sought through violence hides even from the perpetrator his emotional deadness. Gilligan continues, "When they say they feel dead, they mean they cannot feel anything—neither emotions nor even physical sensa-tions." "For only the living dead would want to kill the living. No one who loves life, who cherishes and feels his own aliveness, would want to kill another human being."[34] Subjects' deeply violent resolution is encouraged by the story and the habits of bystanders.

Absent a different story and fresh approach, the subject "now firmly resolves to attack people physically with the serious intention of gravely harming or even killing them for the slightest provocation or no provocation whatsoever."[35] He has gone from defensive violence to offensive attack. Athens observes that such people have progressed to the final stage of the violentization process, which he calls "virulency."[36]

Moving to "unmitigated violence" renders the person an "ultra-criminal." The proverbial violent outcast and loner of American folklore emerges here, because people close to the subject avoid him in order to avoid feeling threatened. Shunned, he may be welcomed by malevolent groups for whom violence is a requirement of membership. However, Gilligan observes, "once they have seen that killing others does not bring them back to life, many murderers find that the only way to feel alive . . . is to feel physical pain," for "the experience of physical pain is preferable to feeling nothing." "Many more murderers kill themselves than are ever killed by the state. . . . The suicide rate among men who have just committed a murder is several hundred times greater than it is among ordinary men of the same age, sex, and race, in this country and elsewhere."[37]

Once habits of violence are acted upon, they are reinforced by threats of retributive punishment and rectification through suffering. Punishment did not challenge Jim Elledge's most painful recordings, but supported his deepest hurts and his most wounded "conclusions" about the world. Jim was not a moral outsider, but a true believer. An unjust system has much invested in denying that a social problem such as murder is the bitter fruit of its own practices. Americans are led to believe that murder is an aberration, not a symptom, and that capital punishment is a cure, not a prop of an oppressive social order.

NOTES

1. Lonnie Athens, *The Creation of Dangerous Violent Criminals* (Chicago: University of Illinois Press, 1992), 5.

2. Athens, *Creation*, 4.

3. Albert Camus, "Reflections on the Guillotine," *Resistance, Rebellion, and Death*, trans. Justin O'Brien (originally published in 1957; New York: Vintage International,

1995), 178. Camus writes: we must [not] give way to that modern tendency to absolve everything, victim and murderer, in the same confusion. Sure purely sentimental confusion is made up of cowardice rather than of generosity and eventually justifies whatever is worse in this world. If you keep on excusing, you eventually give your blessing to the slave camp, to cowardly force, to organized executioners, to the cynicism of great political monsters; you finally hand over your brothers" (231).

4. Richard Rhodes, *Why They Kill* (New York: Vintage, 1999), chs. 12–18.

5. Athens's notion of brutalization needs to be broadened to include systematic mistreatment of target groups and non–target groups in oppressive societies. Growing up in a society twisted by racism, the oppression of disabled persons, and the pervasive disrespect for children account for more types of crime than those discussed by Athens.

6. Athens, *Creation*, 20–21.

7. Athens, *Creation*, 57.

8. Athens, *Creation*, 58.

9. Donald Nathanson, *Shame and Pride: Affect, Sex, and the Birth of the Self* (New York: Norton, 1992), 308.

10. Athens, *Creation*, 62, 63.

11. Athens, *Creation*, 59–60.

12. Athens, *Creation*, 62.

13. For the importance of narrative in recovery, see Theodore R. Sardin, ed., *Narrative Psychology: The Storied Nature of Human Conduct* (New York: Praeger, 1986).

14. Robert J. Schreiter, *Reconciliation: Mission and Ministry in a Changing Social Order* (Maryknoll, NY: Orbis, 1992), 34.

15. Robert Nozick, *Philosophical Explanations* (Cambridge, MA: Harvard University Press, 1981), 370.

16. James Gilligan, *Violence: Our National Epidemic and Its Causes* (New York: Putnam's Sons, 1996), 64.

17. For a good overview of possible steps, see the last chapter of Rhodes, *Why They Kill*.

18. "At the maximum-security lockup in St. Joseph [Missouri], two cats, Midnight and Tigger, curl up on laps as the state's toughest teenage offenders explore the roots of their anger, weep over the acts of abusive parents and swap strategies for breaking free of gangs." Jennifer Warren, "Spare the Rod, Spoil the Child," *Los Angeles Times*, 1 July 2004, A-1.

19. Athens, *Creation*, 63.

20. Athens, *Creation*, 65–66.

21. Athens, *Creation*, 68.

22. Athens, *Creation*, 68.

23. Athens, *Creation*, 69.

24. Athens, *Creation*, 66.

25. Author interview.

26. Athens, *Creation*, 71.

27. Athens, *Creation*, 73.

28. Athens, *Creation*, 73.

29. Athens, *Creation*, 74.

30. Athens, *Creation*, 75.

31. Rhodes, *Why They Kill*, 133.

32. Athens, *Creation*, 75.

33. Gilligan, *Violence*, 69.

34. Gilligan, *Violence*, 136, 33, 32. Gilligan believes that any human who "approaches the point of being . . . overwhelmed by shame" will conclude that the only way "one can preserve one's self (as a psychological entity) [is] by sacrificing one's body (or those of others)" (110).

35. Athens, *Creation*, 75.

36. Athens reminds us that, although dangerous violent criminals are created "through the passage of these few stages, the mere entrance into any stage does not guarantee completion of that stage, much less the completion of the process as a whole. The completion of each stage is contingent upon the person fully undergoing all the experiences that comprise that stage, and the completion of the process as a whole is contingent upon the person undergoing all the stages." *Creation*, 80–81.

37. Gilligan, *Violence*, 38, 39, 41.

Of Monsters and Men

When a modern mob experiences the nonhumanity of its victim, what it sees in the victim's stead is some deranged animal, a source of social pollution, a beast, a pervert. . . . [I]he human victim disappears, only to be transfigured into an icon in the sacred system that his victimization generated or regenerated.

Gil Bailie, Violence Unveiled

I found it very difficult to see him as a person—his crime kept getting in the way, concealing him, so to speak.

James Gilligan, Violence: Our Deadly Epidemic and Its Causes

Almost every person can think of at least one person or group she regards as a monster, be it Hitler, Osama bin Laden, Ted Bundy, or Jeffrey Dahmer. Middle schoolers, asked to name a person or group they were most tempted to regard as nonhuman, with some embarrassment responded: teachers. This was a group about which they fantasized revenge, singing rhymes of burning down the school. Others identify the severely mentally retarded or physically disabled. Some loudly proclaim on the internet the inhumanity of blacks or Jews or homosexuals.

The projects of revenge and retribution feed off the view that some people are monsters. This view goes beyond the fact that some people act abominably to the claim that they are abominable by nature. Two paths lead to this essentialist view—one biological, the other religious. Since the Enlightenment, scientists have searched for the cause of violence in an individual's biology, in the essence of the offender. Instinct, drives, biochemistry, brain lesions, and epilepsy have at one time or another been held up as "the" causes of violence. Others refer to bad seeds or, more ominously, bad blood. Genetic research has given these old biological determinisms legitimacy. Modern sciences have not fully displaced older religious views, which attributed violence to original sin. Criminal psychologist Craig Haney states:

> Citizens are treated to widespread media mystifications about "natural born killers" that even seep into academic commentary on the issue. Serious-looking but over-simplified treatments of the topic have instructed members of the public that much crime reduces to the problem of "evil people" caused in part by the defective biology of its perpetrators, and warn that our society is at risk of being overtaken by an epidemic of the "disease" of murder.[1]

Whatever the specific mechanism, nature defines the person.

Narrow and deterministic arguments from nature are very old and often very damaging, regardless of their scientific or religious dress. Ironically, instead of explaining violence, such arguments justify it. As James Gilligan puts it, "In the history of human violence, biological concepts have been among the most potent stimulants of violent behavior."[2] The same holds for religious concepts. Those people in cahoots with the devil could be killed, with the blessings of the community, because they deserved it.

BAD BY NATURE

Biological essentialism contains three premises: (1) humans are not equal, and social inequalities are the fault of the individual; (2) the causes of violence also lie within the individual; and (3) biological mechanisms are determinative and causative. These premises justify a public policy that absolves the collective of any responsibility for violence, denies the injustice of the current social order, and mystifies the damaging effects of social oppression. Threatened by unnamed oppressive forces, people blame them on monsters. By attacking the personifications of evil, bystanders delude themselves that their world is safer. Bystanders appeal to biological essentialism—boys will be bad—to support capital punishment.

The belief that some people are monsters abandons the deeply held American ideal that all people are created equal. Biologist Richard Lewontin notes that the bourgeois revolutions of the seventeenth and eighteenth centuries carried the banner of "*liberté, égalité,* and *fraternité*" for all, lending hope to the oppressed that these concepts applied to them as well. Faced with "immense inequalities of social status, power, and wealth among individuals, among races, and between the sexes," liberal reformers sought legal and educational remedies. Yet, Lewontin notes, persistent inequalities plagued the Enlightenment project of social reform. In the United States, for instance, the gap between rich and poor has widened significantly over time. Reformers found a way to adjust to such stubborn inequalities. Enlightenment philosophy "provided a tool for legitimizing inequality through its implied claims that the individual is supremely responsible for causing the unequal situation he or she occupies."[3] The reason certain individuals did not succeed must reside within them.

The philosophes drew on a rich tradition. The *ancien régime* thrived on blaming individuals—or God's will for individuals—for being at the bottom of the class hierarchy. The sixteenth-century Protestant Reformer John Calvin and his heirs, the English Calvinists, presumed that God had foreordained each individual's salvation. A poor woman's hard work here on earth could do nothing to sway the intentions of a sovereign God, who had consigned her to poverty and then hell. As Max Weber has shown, such a bleak view, rather than leading to resignation or caprice, led to a fervent desire to demonstrate, through one's worldly success, that one was among the saved. After all, the saved could be distinguished by their industry, sobriety, simple living, good deeds, and thrift. The saved, certainly, wouldn't look like the lower classes—slovenly, unemployed, drunk, vulgar, violent, and criminal. Even if the rich were not necessarily saved, it was evident the criminal class was damned.

Over time, Calvinist meritocracy lost its religious inspiration. The eighteenth-century philosophes put into secular language meritocratic classism.

Lewontin writes, "Individuals are said to acquire their position in society by their own efforts"—it is a matter of individual desert. "Individuals are ontologically prior to the collectivity in this worldview, and so the properties of society are simply the accumulated consequences of the properties of individuals."[4] The story says that since an even playing field exists and yet poor people of African heritage continue to occupy a lower station in life,

> then we must look into the properties of blacks as individuals for the causes of that inequality. . . . [If] the properties of society are the properties of individuals writ large, then the study of society must become the study of individuals, for social causes, are, ultimately, individual causes. To understand the origin and maintenance of social structures, we must, in this view, understand the ontogeny of individuals. Thus political economy becomes applied biology.[5]

The first premise leads to the second. If the cause of social inequalities lay within individuals, so must the cause of violence. Eugenicists hoped to eliminate moral defectives in order to prevent the pollution of the normal population. Eugenicists believed natural selection had ended due to medical advances, which allowed the lower class to reproduce rather than be weeded out. They made proposals for the "segregation of the feeble-minded" and the "sterilization of the unfit," arguing, "The drunkard, the criminal, the diseased, the morally weak, should never come into society."[6] William Rathbone Greg wrote in 1872,

> Among savages, the vigorous and sound alone survive; among us the diseased and enfeebled survive as well; . . . with us, thousands with tainted constitutions, frames weakened by malady or waste, brains bearing subtle and hereditary mischief in their recesses, are suffered to transmit their terrible inheritance of evil to other generations, and to spread it through a whole community.[7]

Modern science, having ended natural selection, now needed medical men to make the necessary selections. Always included in the list of those to be excluded or extinguished was the criminal class.

Criminal anthropology has its roots in the eugenics movement. "The first serious 'scientific' study of the internal biological causes of social position was Cesare Lombroso's late-nineteenth-century criminal anthropology, which claimed that criminals were born and not made."[8] Lombroso suggested that criminals were easily recognized by their long arms, sloping foreheads, and jutting jaws. These pseudoscientific efforts persuaded the middling classes that the real threats to their safety came from inferior lower classes, not from above. These efforts also justified the belief that all humans are not human, since some are criminally defective by nature.

Perhaps as a reaction against the eugenics movement of the 1930s and the horrors to which it led under the Third Reich, the 1950s saw a rise in the belief that humans have no nature. A narrative of cultural determinism replaced that of biological essentialism. Humans have no nature, biology plays no role, and people are totally products of environmental variables. Philosopher Mary Midgley observes, "Trouble only arises when these schemes are taken to compete with and annihilate the individual point of view—to prove it unnecessary by demonstrating that everybody is only the pawn or product of their society." She concludes that this was not a perspective but "a manifesto."[9] This manifesto gave rise to a liberal effort of social reform through social engineering.

Yet even for environmental determinists, the individual reigned supreme once again. The individual was seen as a product of his or her experiences, primarily within the family. Such adherents unflinchingly affirmed the prospect of individual fulfillment despite an oppressive social order. If any force beyond the family was acknowledged, it was poverty, reducing the individual to, that marvelously vacuous phrase, "the disadvantaged."

However, such a restricted notion of environment was inadequate to explain why middle-class white boys could become violent. How could this framework explain a serial murderer such as Ted Bundy, who had such nice parents? Within this limited notion of "environment," there appears to be no other possible cause except biology, wickedness, or the devil. The narrative of individual fault and difference denies the effects of pervasive social conditioning and relieves bystanders from their responsibility in violentization.

Nor did the liberal project of reform through social engineering prove successful. When liberal programs failed to deliver on their promises to rehabilitate prisoners or reduce crime, President Ronald Reagan announced the end of the environmental manifesto. Science analyst Dorothy Nelkin recalls:

> In 1981 President Reagan, speaking to a group of police chiefs, blamed crime on the utopian belief that social programs could prevent criminal behavior: Hindering the swift administration of justice was a "belief that there was nothing permanent or absolute about any man's nature." America was unable to control crime, said Reagan, because it was in the grip of the idea that man was a product of his material environment and that by changing that environment we could permanently change man and usher in a great new era.[10]

She notes that ten years later the editor of *Science* magazine promulgated the truth of biological determinism: "The brain can go wrong because of hereditary defects that are not related to environmental influences."[11] Now there is an entire industry devoted to finding the biological causes of deviant behavior.

The biological model of criminality has so permeated attitudes that locating the problem within the interior of the criminal is taken as dogma. The prospect of mapping the human genome emerged in the 1990s, launching the search for criminal chromosomes. By the 1990s, the public once again accepted the genetic basis of criminal behavior, almost in terms reminiscent of Lombroso. Renewed visions of social control through genetic manipulation filled the media. If those most likely to become violent were identified, the analysts predicted, experts could prevent their birth, abort them, control them through surgery or medication, or failing that, execute them.

Two opposing perspectives are grounded in fear of the other pole. One pole of radical individuality denies any mitigating circumstances and the effect of the social on the individual. The second pole, whether in the form of genetics or victimhood, eliminates individual freedom or choice. Rather than cobble these two views together, we should use them to correct each other.

In a 1987 book, social scientists argued that discovering a partial biological etiology for criminal behavior need not lead to a "'lock 'em up and throw away the key' attitude."[12] They noted that "evidence indicates that biological deficits can be compensated for by appropriate environmental intervention," for instance; studies indicate that adolescents engage in less criminal behavior if they have "high SES [socioeconomic status], low levels of family conflict, availability of counseling and remedial assistance."[13] But if giving children good lives is the solution, does it matter what the biological deficits are? All children deserve adequate resources, healthy adult interaction, and lots of loving attention.[14]

Biological essentialists hold that nature is determinative and causative. "Bad seeds," "bad blood," or defective genes are believed to cause very specific behaviors—such as the decision to pack a gun as one heads off to rob the bank. Moreover, such biology determines that such a person will actually use the gun. Despite the best environment, ultimately the violent individual cannot escape her determinative nature.

Much like what the gentleman claims in Shakespeare's *The Winter's Tale*, nature prevails over breeding. The natural disposition "of nobleness, which nature shows above her breeding and many other evidences—proclaim her, with all certainty, to be the King's daughter."[15] The interior is believed to be dominant over the exterior.[16] Where once "bad blood" was blamed for poverty, feebleness, or criminality, now innate personality or genes express one's fate. Everyone can tell a story about "good parents" whose child ran afoul of drugs and the law, and how someone who was "disadvantaged" prevailed against the odds.

Families are studied to identify heritable traits. Yet the classical method of the statistical geneticist—the estimation of heritability—cannot satisfactorily resolve the question of how much genetically transmitted characteristics are implicated in violent crime. Psychologist Gordon Trasler writes, "The reason is straightforward: Where heritable characteristics are invested with social meaning, so that physical attribute and social advantage or handicap are closely linked, it is not feasible to distinguish the biological from the social effect." Trasler gives the example of skin color: "In a society that places multiple handicaps on people who have a particular skin pigmentation, occupational features will have, on the face of it, a high degree of heritability."[17]

Another problem with the concept of heritability, Lewontin points out, is that a trait could be 100 percent inheritable, yet its effect could be easily changed. Lewontin suggests, "If that were not true, medical genetics would lose most of its interest." Lewontin provides the example of Wilson's disease, in which the inheritor of the trait (a deficiency in an enzyme) from both parents inevitably died in adolescence or early adulthood. "Now they survive by taking a simple pill that makes up for their chemical deficiency."[18] Thus, heritability is not determinative.

Children "inherit" the class standing of their parents, but this should not be attributed to the "rich" gene (nor to "smarter genes," nor to "bluer blood"). Yet, the effects of social inequalities are often blamed on genes: "Recidivist property offenses such as petty theft are particularly heritable."[19] As with Wilson's disease, would daily doses to counter the inherited deficiency—say $100 a day—"treat" and eliminate the heritable "disease of petty theft"? That petty theft is heritable under present circumstances makes it no predictor of its expression under conditions of plentitude.

Knowing the heritability of a trait reveals "nothing useful about the pathways of mediation," argues Lewontin. Wilson's disease is preventable because an enzyme can repair the metabolism; "nothing has been added by the knowledge that the disruption is a consequence of a genetic mutation."[20] Similarly, a determination that some violence may have a genetic basis should not alter preventive efforts.

The 2 August 2002 news reported "Gene links child abuse with later violence." The article proclaimed that "scientists have discovered a gene that appears to help explain why some boys who are abused or mistreated are more likely than others to grow up to be aggressive, antisocial or violent adults." The hope is that by showing how abuse leads to violence in some children rather than in others, services could be directed at those most prone to become violent. The researchers themselves were much more cautious than the reporter, indicating "in the interplay between this gene and the environment, researchers found the environment dominant. Absent abuse, the gene, which helps regulate brain chemicals, did not predict whether a boy would grow up to be violent or aggressive. And some boys without the genetic variation became aggressive if they grew up in an abusive setting."[21] The known mediation for preventing some violence is to prevent abuse or to assist the abused to heal from their trauma. Knowing that some—but not all—boys carry this form of the gene should not alter proven methods of prevention. And brutalized boys without that gene formation need intervention, too. There is no benefit to knowing about an alleged defect.

The authors of a book on the biological causes of crime conclude, "Because we can only inherit biological predispositions, the genetic evidence conclusively admits biological factors among the important agents influencing some forms of criminal behavior."[22] What does genetic predisposition or being influenced by genetic factors mean? All humans have genes that limit freedom. Humans lack the eyes of an eagle, the nose of a bear, the lungs of a whale, or the speed of a cheetah. But the moral and philosophical notion of free will contains the unstated premise that human freedom is appropriate to humans, not eagles or supermen. Humans are free, but with freedom appropriate to the nature of humans, not turtles or turtle doves. Human freedom accounts for genetic limitations and predispositions, but also for endowments. Humans are able to care for children over decades, communicate with enormous complexity, recover from trauma, and use intelligence to extend their limits. With technology, humans now see better than eagles or stay under water longer than whales, and so on. Referring to a genetic predisposition is a fancy way of not saying much. Genes, after all, are part of the environment to which *Homo sapiens* have always flexibly adapted.

Geneticists have identified about four thousand single gene defects that are responsible for specific ailments, but these are rare conditions. Cystic fibrosis, Huntington's disease, and Down's syndrome are some familiar ones. What has this knowledge brought? So far, genetic illnesses cannot be cured, and most cannot be treated; the only option is to prevent people with them from being conceived or born. Elimination of the adult with genetic defects is not a morally permissible option, although it was tried in Nazi Germany.[23] This hope for a single "cause" infects the genetic search for the root of violence. People naïvely hope that genetic findings will be both straightforward and deterministic.[24]

The scientific optimism that hopes to find the "cause" of violence sits alongside socially accepted habits of greed, racism, or complacency about poverty. Arguably, racism, grounded in biological concepts, has contributed to many more deaths throughout human history than have individual murderers not motivated by racism. The death tolls include forty to one hundred million indigenous peoples in the sixteenth century, several million Africans during the Middle Passage, and 5.8 million Jews during the Holocaust. And yet one never hears of testing white people for a gene called "racism."

Biological essentialism relieves the need to question prejudices. Men are presumed to be inherently more violent than women and allegedly do not feel pain as women do. Evidence for such prejudices is sought by looking either at men's behavior or their biological makeup. Missing is an analysis of how institutions such as the criminal justice system routinely violentize men. Critical social analyses of the institutionalized mistreatment of men cannot be found in these industries of determinism.

Biological determinists deny the effects of oppression on humans, and especially deny the victimization of men. They argue that criminals have violent genes; they were not violently mistreated. Complex social problems—injustice and violentization—are ignored. With this story, people dismiss as improbable that someone would become indifferent to human life by being disrespected, humiliated, shamed, expected to be wicked, or by losing family and friends to gun violence while growing up.[25] Blaming the biology of the individual leads to an acceptance of violence as inevitable and absolves the rest of us.

Biological essentialism also infects the mental health system. Not only do judges and prosecutors—and death-row inmates themselves—think of some people as inherently monsters, but so do many psychologists, psychiatrists, and social workers. Many professionals believe that some people deserve to be subjected to unwanted treatments. The story of the monster shapes how they should handle criminals (the morally defective) and the criminally insane (the mentally defective). They converge in the belief that some people are "bad by nature."

Some scientists have wanted to explain political economy by using applied biology, locating the causes of social inequality and violence within the individual. Eliminating the defective individual would solve the social problem. But before the advent of science, religion offered a similar explanation. The problem lay in the will.

EVIL BY FALLEN NATURE

Three Christian views parallel the claims of biological determinism. First is a common interpretation of original sin; second is a belief in the devil; and third is the belief that people "become" their habits. All three views locate the cause of violence within the individual offender, shut a blind eye to the oppressive society, and justify executing the evil among us.

First, most Christians accept uncritically that the Garden of Eden story reveals humans' original sin and consequent punishment. Eve ate the forbidden fruit and blamed the serpent. God punished Adam and Eve for their disobedience by banishing them from the Garden. From that point on, fallen nature will triumph over nurture.

Church historian Elaine Pagels' provocative and carefully researched work, *Adam, Eve and the Serpent*, however, calls into question this naïve view. First, she explains how Jews and early Christians did not interpret the story as an account of original sin tainting subsequent generations. Prior to the fourth century of the Common Era, "most Jews and Christians would . . . have agreed that Adam left each of his offspring free to make his or her own choice for good or evil. The whole point of the story of Adam, most Christians assumed, was to warn everyone who heard it not to misuse that divinely given capacity for free choice."[26] "Christians regarded *freedom* as the primary message of Genesis 1–3—freedom in its many forms, including free will, freedom from demonic powers, freedom from social and sexual obligations, freedom from tyrannical government and from fate; and self-mastery as the source of such freedom."[27]

Pagels argues that a full-blown doctrine of original sin as inherited corruption did not enter the church until the fourth century, when it was prompted by the dramatic change in the political status of the church. Once a persecuted religion under an indifferent-to-hostile Roman Empire, Christianity became the coin of the realm. The conversion of Emperor Constantine and the consequent conversion of masses under him brought new political and religious challenges to the church. Heretofore, under Roman oppression, proclaiming Jesus as one's savior meant possible martyrdom in the arena. Baptism under such conditions meant that converts were willing to lead the upright life called for by a tight-knit Christian community. The new "life in Christ" meant refusal to be soldiers or executioners. Baptism did indeed lead to a (relatively) sinless life.

But with the offices of the Empire needing to be filled by Christians, baptism no longer insured that converts could avoid getting blood on their hands. Finding his pews filled with baptized judges, soldiers, and executioners, the bishop from Alexandria, Augustine, forged a doctrine of original sin, about humans' primal sin and God's just retribution of perpetual disobedience.[28]

Original sin was a theological response to a new political reality. The locus of the problem was in the individual—not a violent and oppressive empire that Christians had failed to truly Christianize. Pagels argues, "By insisting that humanity, ravaged by sin, now lies helplessly in need of outside intervention, Augustine's theory could not only validate secular power but justify as well the imposition of church authority—by force, if necessary—as essential for human salvation."[29]

Executions took up at a quick pace in the new Christian empire. Brutal Roman law, under which Jesus and thousands of other Jews and Christians had been executed, was now joined with literal interpretations of ancient Hebrew codes. Catholic historian James Megivern concludes, "Ironically, the lethal combination of the Bible and Roman law provided surprisingly cruel penal codes, invariably viewed as directly willed by God. The entire repressive system of Roman law was brought to bear actively on the project of 'Christianizing' the Empire."[30]

The doctrine of original sin is tempered in the thirteenth century by the absorption of Aristotelian thought as found in Thomas Aquinas. God, as the unmoved mover and creator, produced a good creation. The goodness inherent to creation, this ontological goodness, could not be obliterated by any sin—original or otherwise. The good of nature persisted; even fallen angels such as Lucifer could not have the glow of original goodness erased in them. Humans' original bent toward the good might be dimmed, but it persisted, and explained why humans could become virtuous, achieving the potentialities of their nature. The conviction that God revealed himself in creation—in human nature—resulted in a type of natural law ethic that enabled people to determine what was "according to nature" and what was not. Humans acting contrary to nature meant that they lacked practical reason and acted against basic goods—life in community, justice, responsibility. Natural law conceived thusly allowed even a mainstream theologian such as Aquinas to argue that neither slavery nor private property was "natural."

But the subtleties in Aquinas's thought—and his occasional inconsistencies, when he regards the natural as the biological—meant that the Catholic Church had no trouble endorsing a darker view of original sin as an evil will within.

Later, Protestants abandoned human nature altogether as a major site of God's revelation. The deeds in the Garden of Eden snuffed out humans' original lights; human nature is now infected with original sin. Reason, will, and passion are thoroughly corrupted. This Protestant inheritance most informs the story told in the United States, given its Calvinist roots. Given fallen nature's corruption, humans deserve damnation in hell.

Original sin most damaged the will. Malefic action—despite knowledge of the good—is the result of willed wickedness. In this model, a healthy, rational person could freely choose evil without any other motivation. In contrast, most other models of depravity focus on the question of motive. That is, they assume most murderers know murder is wrong, but think it is the "best" and most "fitting" response given the situation. In such models, no rational human just goes out and kills for no reason. Jim Elledge, for instance, knew that murder was wrong and that he would be punished for it. But overriding his own considered judgment were his impulse for revenge and his emotional sense that eliminating the source of shame was the only way to save himself. But the Protestant concept of malice allows for sheer perversity.

That evil is chosen gleefully and knowingly for no good reason is a moral fiction, but a fiction made plausible by original sin. The focus on evil as residing in the will—and the belief that resisting evil takes will power—are deep-seated in the story. Haney observes:

> Armed with this conventional and pre-existing narrative about why people do bad things, jurors are predisposed to posit violent acts as the product of an odd combination of equally free and unencumbered evil choices, on the one hand, and monstrously deranged, defective traits, on the other. . . . [This combination makes all defendants] dehumanized monsters rather than real people.[31]

The second view of essentialism is a belief in the devil. In Gnostic forms of both Christianity and Judaism, there are two powerful forces in the world—good and evil, God and Satan. The devil wields a genuine, negative power by tempting people to act on their evil impulses. In its Protestant version, the devil is wholly evil—a fallen angel, an adversary of God and all good intentions. With such a split in the fundamental ontology of the world—good and bad, light and dark, armies of glory and armies of darkness—it is easy to think of humans as being similarly split. Thus, some contemporary Christians speak of evil people in language reminiscent of the medieval view that Jews and females (witches) were infected by the devil. It is not a question of a good person (ontologically) behaving badly (morally), but of some people becoming evil in their inherent nature. Good and evil here are not moral terms, but ontological ones.

The third view—one definitely not limited to Christian or even religious perspectives—is that vices do not obscure human potentiality, but consume it. A person can lose one's humanity to one's vices. A Hitler has so let vice overtake his personhood that there is no human potentiality remaining. Here, nurture replaces or overtakes nature.

Psychologist Robert Rieber writes that true psychopathy "indicates something more than a tendency to care about others only as means to one's own self-centered aims; it indicates a *lack of capacity* to do otherwise. The true psychopath is lost to humanity, utterly incapable of human concern and involvement with others except at the most superficial and exploitative level."[32] Later, Rieber returns to the notion of inherent capacity: "Since time immemorial, humankind has outlined in figures of the demonic an inherently human capacity to fuse despair and . . . [the innate drive toward aggression] in an antisocial posture."[33] Such a soul, he continues, being inherently asocial, "goes beyond the categories of evil and sin; theologically, the true psychopath is incapable of forming any relationship to God or to humans. These are the souls who reside in Dante's Inferno, these are the damned of Jonathan Edwards's theology."[34] Such a view, however, cannot explain why some psychopaths are able to abandon such behaviors in middle age.[35]

The muddled thinking about people with violent habits surfaced in the following front-page story from the *New York Times* of 12 July 2002. Patrick, a thirteen-year-old from Brooklyn, ran afoul of Delon Lucas, eighteen, and his girlfriend, Clarine Jones, twenty-one, whom a neighbor described as "natural born killers." Luring Patrick to their apartment, the couple tied him up and took turns beating him with a baseball bat, the authorities said. Then, they said, Lucas stabbed Patrick and stuffed his lifeless body into a closet. The article reports that Lucas once told Clarine's sister: "Well, my mother didn't care about me. My father didn't care about me. That's why I don't care about anybody else. I'll kill anybody. I don't care." The article also reports Clarine's sister saying that Clarine was a once-sweet girl who had descended into rage and mental illness years before, adding "There's something that's in her that's not in other people." When asked what, she paused and then replied softly, "Mister, the Devil. The Devil himself." Apparently, complete abandonment, hopelessness, being hurt so badly that one cannot feel loved or feel love for others are not sufficient explanations for violent behavior—we also need an inexplicable force.

Haney observes: "'the myth of demonic agency' . . . serves to deny the humanity of the person who commits capital murder by substituting the heinousness of their crimes for the reality of their personhood. This myth is essential to maintaining the system of death sentencing in the United States."[36] Without this substitution, bystanders would need to look upon the human countenance of the about-to-be-executed and see, not the devil incarnate, but a violentized human.

ARE THERE TWO KINDS OF PEOPLE?

The story told of monsters and men is predicated on the belief that there are two essentially different types of humans—good and evil.

Instead, the story should relate that there is one kind of human. Humans are more alike than they are different; fundamentally, all are one sort of being of equal human worth. Any other moral position leaves some human group potentially outside the moral community of care and concern. Over the centuries, the moral circle has grown wider and wider to now include Jews, people with African heritage, women, children, homosexuals, and people with physical or mental defects. It is time now to bring humans with murderous patterns and committers of dreadful deeds into the fold. Universalizing moral principles of respect to include people who behave monstrously does not mean asking Andrea Yates (who killed five of her children) to be one's nanny. It does mean that she should not be killed. With a different narrative, citizens can instead reach for the human under weighty rubble of distress while holding her accountable for the tremendous harm she has done.

Americans could reject the belief that there are two kinds of humans and that evil is a separate force in the universe. Aquinas had a robust respect for the devil, but he resolutely defended the commonality of human creation. The devil, in his view a created being, was good. This ontological goodness inherent in creation by a good God—could never be blotted out. Sin and evil behavior might obscure this goodness, but it could never snuff out the light.

The resulting perspective—that no human would want to harm another for no reason—should not be confused with romantic individualism. Nature endows humans with the potential for virtue; the acquisition of virtue requires social learning, full of mistakes along the way. Yet if humans are not overly hurt, this learning should be easy for them, and they should develop the virtues. Thus, for example, humans are not born with the virtue of cooperation, but they are born with the capacity to acquire such skills easily in a particular historical context. Cooperation in an American family might look quite different than in one in Tibet, and how to be cooperative in a particular context takes learning. But this view means that humans are not inherently mean or selfish. Greed and jealousy are the by-products of mistreatment and may become the causes of violence, but it is not necessary or accurate to ascribe any vice to inherent nature.

EXCUSE OR EXECUTE: THE ONLY TWO OPTIONS?

Many may remain committed to the view that some people are monsters by nature. If a biological or religious cause of individual violence could be determined, what does such a view imply legally? Does knowing the "cause" of violence affect the evaluation of a person's responsibility? A belief that some people are monsters renders people victims of their environment, victims of their biology, or expendable.

The First Temptation: Not Responsible

In a culture that skewers individuals with blame, an initially appealing defense alleges "I am that way by nature." If so, then it makes no sense to argue that there was criminal intent. There have been some successes in using "genetic defenses" to secure life sentences rather than the death penalty.[37]

In 1924, defense attorney Clarence Darrow argued before the jury that his defendants, Richard Loeb and Nathan Leopold Jr., charged with kidnapping and bludgeoning to death a young schoolmate, were inheritors of a deformed nature and therefore bore less responsibility for their actions. Darrow spoke thus to the jury:

> I know that they cannot feel what you feel and what I feel; that they cannot feel the moral shocks which come to men that are educated and who have not been deprived of an emotional system of emotional feelings. I know it and every person who has honestly studied this subject knows it as well. Is Dickie Loeb to blame because out of the infinite forces that conspired to form him, the infinite forces that were at work producing him ages before he was born, that because out of this infinite combination he was born without it? If he is, then there should be a new definition for justice.[38]

The trial judge subsequently spared the boys from hanging; instead, they received life imprisonment plus ninety-nine years.

Victimhood has become a high art in U.S. society. Defenders of biological determinism attack the "environmental determinists" as excusing the individual's behavior. Attacks are made on "sappy" liberals who see people as nothing but victims of their surroundings. Bystanders have become disgusted with efforts to use environmental factors to excuse malefactors. The "abuse excuse" is ridiculed by a public tired of individuals not being held accountable for the damage they cause. Yet biological determinism also fails to hold people accountable, saying, "It was the fault of their nature." Low blood sugar (the Twinkie defense), premenstrual tension, postpartum depression, the possession of an extra Y-chromosome—these biological defenses have also been used to excuse. When people are seen as captives of their heredity, blame may shift to parents, doctors, or juries for failing to identify and remove harmful biologies from our midst.

Defense lawyers play on the turf established by the criminal justice system. Since the story identifies individual biological fault as the cause of crime, they try to argue that a causative biological mechanism reduces responsibility. Although "bad by nature" arguments may save some individuals from the death chamber, such reasoning could just as easily lead to the conclusion that defective people are expendable.

The Second Temptation: Marginalization or Elimination

If a person can be excused because her behavior is "caused by nature," then she can just as easily be exterminated on the same grounds. Agents of an oppressive society can either accept so-called defective people because "that's just the way they are" or deny them a right to live. In the case cited above, what was to prevent the arguments from going the other way? The Loeb brothers—being genetically flawed—could have been recommended for death as incorrigible and incurable.[39]

Being "mad" by nature often results in exclusion. People found not guilty by reason of insanity serve longer terms than the maximum prison terms for those deemed mentally sound.[40] Being "mad by nature" may excuse from responsibility, but not from oppressive control, such as permanent institutionalization. That's why biological claims, like dangerous explosives, must be handled with extreme care.

Isolation and maltreatment are also proposed for the criminally poor. "A writer for *Science Digest* wondered whether children who are suspected of being genetically prone to criminal behavior should be isolated or operated on, just as defective cars are recalled to the factory."[41] Such fear of the criminally prone among us led to the formation of the Bush administration's Violence Prevention Initiative. Treating the poor as "natural carriers" of violent strains of behavior, the initiative sought to identify and inoculate them. The program intended to screen about 100,000 inner-city school children (the sons of the elite apparently lack any criminal predisposition) to identify potential criminals.[42] But they lacked a vaccine for violence. In the absence of a vaccine, public health managers decided to send the biologically doomed to camps for remedial, behavior-modification training. Such harmful policies have not advanced beyond Lombroso.

Biological essentialism has justified slavery and lynching of Africans, the mass murder of Native Americans, forced sterilization of the retarded, "mercy killing" of physically disabled persons, and the genocide of European Jews. Such rationales also justify execution of the incurably wicked. Criminal "tendencies" are seen as unchangeable, rendering the miscreant impervious to rehabilitation.[43]

Why has seeing malefactors as essentially evil justified their execution? Classifying people as nonhuman places them outside the moral community, so that moral obligations to "true" humans do not apply. Beasts such as gorillas once fell outside the community of care and were caged or killed without moral restraint. However, as our earlier portrayal of these animals as "wild beasts" has been replaced with insight into their complex behavior and natures, many moralists have begun to move higher primates into the moral circle of respect and protection. No longer do citizens think it humane to confine primates in concrete, windowless rooms for twenty-three hours at a stretch. As many commentators note, gorillas in zoos are treated better than humans on death row.

If offenders are essentially evil, then they are not human. If not human, then it is not clear what they are owed morally. The story says that subhumans or nonhumans are dispensable and may be caged in institutions or killed outright. Rieber notes how career criminals share this story: "when trouble arises, the psychopaths are the first to go."[44]

In summing up the direction of applying essentialism to crime, Mary Coombs concludes, "The objects of that control will be the usual suspects: disadvantaged groups, primarily African American men. The public's perception of a genetic explanation for crime will serve not to exculpate individuals but to justify the control of populations."[45] Biological essentialism as criminal justice policy also justifies reducing funds for prevention and healing. Economic cost saving looms large—why waste funds on the incorrigible? Already, the prison industry has backed away from rehabilitation in favor of retribution. Complex social questions of responsibility and free will, social influence and individual freedom, the nature of the human being, and the dynamics of oppression are solved with the flick of the switch.

If violence is a product of nature, little can be done. But if violence results from human activity and institutional arrangements, then it is not inevitable. Rather it is both preventable and surmountable. For persistent offenders, this means there is hope for them to desist from crime.

RENOUNCING THE STORY

Can offenders give up a life of crime and step out of the narrative of the lie? Criminals face the task of coming to terms with not only their own troubled pasts and vices, but also the fact that they have gravely, perhaps lethally, harmed others. Leading a life of respect for the law, responsiveness to their fellow humans, and responsibility for themselves entails renouncing the story and its practices and habits. Success with these tasks requires a better story. Not any story will suffice. Jim Elledge completely internalized the narrative of the lie, revealing a thorough identification with its rhetoric of essentialism ("the evil part of me"), a subscription to the three Rs ("I deserve to die"), and a desperate hope that his suffering would achieve rectification ("my voluntary execution will somehow make it right with God"). Unlike Jim, offenders who learn to abstain from crime tell a different story, one that aligns with reality more adequately. What is impressive about the accounts of offenders who have "gone straight" is how perpetrators manage to throw off almost all the stigmatizing and negative assumptions made about them within the criminal justice system and by the wider community. In his book *Making Good*, criminologist Shadd Maruna contrasts the system's "reality based" assumptions to these ex-convicts' quite different views of reality.[46]

Two key themes emerge from the stories that Maruna collected from his study, based in Liverpool, England, of offenders who were able to desist from criminal acts: their latent humanity and their sense of personal power. These former offenders display a sturdy belief that their "core self" is different from their bad habits, effectively discarding the tunnel vision that there is something inherently wrong with them.

Reclaiming Their Latent Humanness

Perhaps most key is the ex-convicts' discerning vision about themselves. That is, they reject biological or religious determinist views that they are essentially deviant, defective, dumb, or diabolical. Instead, they identify with their potential humanity, which remains available despite their evil habits. They talk about a "core self" that was always there but that became obscured for a long period by their hurts, painful recordings, and ruinous choices.[47] Ex-convicts often identify this basic capacity for goodness by noticing "recurring themes" or "significant episodes" in their past, such as the times they were able to resist wrongdoing, their ability to stand for principle against peer pressure, or even their innocence as a baby. Remembrance of these moments in which they manifested some goodness provides needed leverage against pressures to identify with their habits: "Even though I feel and used to act like X, I'm really capable of acting like Y now."

Desisting offenders who emerge from their vices to reclaim their humanity do not amputate, suppress, or cut off "bad parts" of themselves. Instead, they own their negative past and integrate it into their life story without aligning with it. They take responsibility for their vices without essentializing them. Thus, they reject the perspective that "the devil is in me" or that "the devil made me do it," which destroys personal responsibility, mystifies painful conditioning, and blocks condemnation of oppressive social arrangements.

Offenders who desist from crime require a new vision of the self. According to criminologists John Braithwaite and S. Mugford:

> The self of the perpetrator is sustained as sacred rather than profane. This is accomplished by comprehending: (a) how essentially good people have a pluralistic self that accounts for their occasional lapse into profane acts; and (b) that the profane act of a perpetrator may bear some shared responsibility.[48]

This new perspective directly contradicts the cover story, in which if people admit to doing a wrong deed, then that becomes their defining characteristic. Once a person prevails in her first violent act, the surrounding community's judgment that she is now an inherently violent person jams her further into a stunted perspective. The story makes the bad action an essential part of who she is, making it easy for her to become identified with her budding vices. She then becomes a different kind of human than everyone else, the story goes. Thus, the narrative of the lie rejects the very perspective that desisting offenders adopt in order to make good.

Reclaiming Their Personal Agency

Unhealed offenders say they want to make a change but feel "powerless to change their behavior because. . . ." They then provide a list of external factors they feel rob them of choice.[49] Maruna speculates that the passive rhetoric ("something made me do it") shields ex-convicts from overwhelming blame and shame. However, the convicts' approach—using a posture of victimhood to protect against painful feelings—is self-defeating.

In contrast, ex-offenders eschew the habit of victimhood sufficiently to enable them to cease acting on their habits—a tremendous victory. The first step in taking charge of their lives often comes through "empowerment from some outside course." Maruna underscores the importance of external help that broadens convicts' narrow worldview: a program, individual, or belief system that provides them a new perspective on themselves. Two key past choices—first, their agreement with the narrative of the lie and, second, their abandonment of practical reason and parts of their humanity—were sacrifices they made to keep themselves from disintegration or suicide. Helpful bystanders should condemn thoroughly the inhumanity of putting any human in a position in which capitulation and truncation of one's humanity are the only two choices. These are "choiceless" choices, created by injustice and mistreatment, and people are not blameworthy for choosing to survive at the expense of their integrity. Indeed, taking the perspective that they are flawed heroes rather than victims seems to help some offenders discard the powerless way of describing their behavior.

Offenders who decide not to act on their vices successfully do not blame themselves for having acquired painful recordings. Instead, they see themselves as responsible for having acted upon them in the past, for choosing not to act on them now, and ultimately for undoing their allegiance to them.[50]

Philosophically, this squares with the perspective that the past cannot be changed, but that the future dawns bright and each person is responsible for choosing to act inside or outside a virtue or vice. Each person's intelligence, caring, and desire to make things right is always available to be acted upon, even for the person heavily identified with her vices. Vices do not determine a person's character—her human capacities for moral choice, personal control, and right action remain.

Most importantly, emergence from an identification with one's vices is made easier with validation from outsiders. Often, the perspective of someone else is a convict's lifeline until she can begin to think more accurately about herself. Many cling to a letter from a teacher or girlfriend who insisted on the goodness of their abilities, brains, or hearts. Many "borrow" confidence from others that they can make it, until they can have this confidence for themselves. Again, the messages from the criminal justice system too often conform to the narrative of the lie—"you are a deviant," "you are a psychopath"—and set the person back, rather than offer a usable perspective that allows her to acknowledge the harm she has done and her possibilities for transformation.

The significance of hearing a new narrative cannot be overstated. Maruna says "At five times the proportion of persisting narratives, desisting narratives described scenes in which, 'The subject is enlarged, enhanced, empowered, ennobled, built up, or made better through his or her association with something larger and more powerful than the self.'"[51] Most often, the person needs to be told directly, over and over, of his potential for moral goodness, intelligence, and efficacy. For many, this may be the first time they encounter a narrative in which they are told they are of value.

A woman named Sylvia, age twenty-nine, had experienced since she was in fourth grade repetitive fantasies of "going crazy" and "killing people" because she thought it would be "fun and exciting." She could make no sense of why she felt this way and had even proceeded as far as buying weapons with the intent to kill. She eventually found her way to a peer counseling community whose members were able to affirm her inherent humanness. The perspective they were able to offer her from outside the narrative of the lie countered the false information encoded within her vices that "killing would be fun." Taking this new attitude toward herself served "as a guide," she later says, and exposed her habit of "loving and being intrigued by what I feared and what upset me. I 'loved' weapons and wanted to own and use them because, when I was small, I had been threatened with them and they frightened me." When the specific distorted perspective was contradicted sufficiently, she was able to release the painful emotions from her early exposure to violence that heretofore had been lost to her conscious memory. Over time, "the pattern lost its power to generate any prolonged emotion or desire."[52] A thorough healing of painful emotion combined with a helpful perspective provided by caring allies ultimately freed her from violent habits and corrected her moral vision.[53]

When serial murderer Gary Ridgway had to confront surviving family members of the forty-eight young women he had killed, almost all the families aimed their grief, rage, and disgust at Ridgway, telling him that they hoped he'd "rot in hell," that he was a worthless person. Ridgway sat numbly staring at them, expressionless. But when one father rose to tell Ridgway that he was a child of God, Ridgway burst into tears. For a brief second, one could see the humanness of Ridgway, and for a brief second, maybe his own capacity for human feeling was reawakened. Only from a platform outside his heinous habits could he even begin to take a peek at the enormity of the pain he had caused. As one member of the South African Truth and Reconciliation Commission says, "It's that element of humanity, isn't it? You want to see that they are not monsters after all. [You want them to] show, in a genuine way, that they truly look back, and regret, and are full of remorse. And then you feel at least there is hope for humanity."[54]

Bystanders could offer hope to perpetrators by renouncing the story of the lie and instead telling a story that rejects the ascription of acquired habits to inherent nature. But bystanders may resist a new story, because by blaming the individual they avoid their responsibility for their role in the story and the difficult challenge of changing themselves and existing practices. Ascribing the wide array of violent behaviors to biology permits them to close their eyes to the violence perpetuated by an oppressive society. But bystanders can take the first step in becoming accountable by listening to murder victims' families who tell a different story.

NOTES

1. Craig Haney, "Mitigation and the Study of Lives," in *America's Experiment with Capital Punishment*, ed. James Acker, Robert Bohm, and Charles Lanier (Durham, NC: Carolina Academic, 1998), 355.

2. James Gilligan, *Violence: Our Deadly Epidemic and Its Causes* (New York: Putnam's Sons, 1996), 209.

3. Richard Lewontin, *It Ain't Necessarily So: The Dream of the Human Genome and Other Illusions*, 2nd ed. (New York: New York Review of Books, 2001), 200, 201.

4. Lewontin, *It Ain't So*, 201.

5. Lewontin, *It Ain't So*, 201, 202.

6. Grant Allen and Hiram Stanley, quoted by Alfred Russel Wallace, *Social Environment and Moral Progress* (New York: Funk & Wagnalls, 1913), 142. Wallace opposed the eugenicists, who were mistaken to think that "criminals are essentially bad in nature." *Alfred Russel Wallace: An Anthology of His Shorter Writings*, ed. Charles H. Smith (New York: Oxford University Press, 1991), 181.

7. William Rathbone Greg, *Enigmas of Life* (originally published in 1872; Freeport, NY: Books for Libraries, 1972), 105.

8. Lewontin, *It Ain't So*, 202.

9. Mary Midgley, *Wickedness* (New York: Routledge, 1984), 53.

10. Dorothy Nelkin and M. Susan Lindee, *The DNA Mystique: The Gene as a Cultural Icon* (New York: Freeman and Company, 1995), 132.

11. Daniel Koshland, quoted in Nelkin and Lindee, *DNA Mystique*, 133.

12. Sarnoff A. Mednick, "Biological Factors in Crime Causation: The Reactions of Social Scientists," in *The Causes of Crime: New Biological Approaches*, ed. Sarnoff A. Mednick, et al. (Cambridge: Cambridge University Press, 1987), 4.

13. Mednick, "Biological Factors," 5.

14. Mednick, "Biological Factors," 5.

15. William Shakespeare, *The Winter's Tale*, V, ii.

16. Lewontin, *It Ain't So*, 203.

17. Gordon Trasler, "Cautions for a Biological Approach to Crime," in *Causes of Crime*, ed. Mednick, 14.

18. Lewontin, *It Ain't So*, 37, 38.

19. Steven O. Moldin, "Genetic Research on Mental Disorders," in *Genetics and Criminality: The Potential Misuse of Scientific Information in Court*, ed. Jeffrey R. Botkin, William M. McMachon, and Leslie Pickering Francis (Washington, DC: American Psychological Association, 1999), 130.

20. Lewontin, *It Ain't So*, 38, 39.

21. "Gene links child abuse with later violence," Tacoma *News Tribune*, 2 August 2002, A-16.

22. Mednick, "Biological Factors," 6.

23. Hitler's first act of mass murder was authorizing the killing of physical and mental "defectives" within Germany—over 170,000, eventually. See Henry Friedlander, *The Origins of Nazi Genocide: From Euthanasia to the Final Solution* (Chapel Hill: University of North Carolina Press, 1995).

24. A genotype refers to one's genetic makeup. A phenotype is the observable manifestation and may result from a variety of genetic defects or environmental causes. The same genetic mutation may have varying expression. Except for a handful of genetic illnesses, environmental factors affect whether the genotype will ever be overt. To complicate matters further, different genetic mutations may result in the same phenotype. Thus, assessing how much of violent behavior is genetic remains imprecise guesswork. Botkin, "Introduction to Part II," in *Genetics and Criminality*, 96–97.

25. "Between 1980 and 1990 the federal government withdrew $260 billion from direct support of inner-city communities." Nelkin and Lindee, *DNA Mystique*, 136.

26. Elaine Pagels, *Adam, Eve, and the Serpent* (New York: Random House, 1988), 108.

27. Pagels, *Adam, Eve*, xxv. Italics in original.

28. Augustine, *City of God*, Book XIV, ch. 13.

29. Pagels, *Adam, Eve*, 125.

30. James Megivern, *The Death Penalty: An Historical and Theological Survey* (New York: Paulist, 1997), 27.

31. Haney, "Mitigation," 352.

32. Robert W. Rieber, *Manufacturing Social Distress: Psychopathy in Everyday Life* (New York: Plenum, 1997), 40–41. Italics in original.

33. Rieber, *Social Distress*, 48.

34. Rieber, *Social Distress*, 48.

35. Harpur T. Hare, "Assessment of Psychopathy as a Function of Age," *Journal of Abnormal Psychology* 103, no. 4 (November 1994): 604.

36. Haney, "Mitigation," 353.

37. "Heritable traits" in the form of depression rather than "genes" successfully mitigated punishment in *South Carolina v. Susan Smith*. See Daniel A. Summer, "The Use of Human Genome Research in Criminal Defense and Mitigation of Punishment," in *Genetics and Criminality*, 185.

38. Kevin Tierney, *Darrow* (New York: Thomas Y. Crowell, 1979), 340.

39. Also see Mary Coombs, "A Brave New Crime-Free World?" in *Genetics and Criminality*, 230.

40. Michael L. Perlin, "Big Ideas, Images and Distorted Facts," in *Genetics and Criminality*, 53.

41. Nelkin and Lindee, *DNA Mystique*, 158.

42. Nelkin and Lindee, *DNA Mystique*, 159.

43. One Polish police officer responsible for rounding up the Jews in his town could not order them to be shot without first reading the death warrant. However, they were condemned to death, not for their actions but for who they were.

44. Rieber, *Social Distress*, 41.

45. Coombs, "Brave Crime-Free World?" 227.

46. Shadd Maruna, *Making Good: How Ex-Convicts Reform and Rebuild Their Lives* (Washington, DC: American Psychological Association, 2001), 9, 88. "All of the research participants who have offered their life stories for this project were nonrandomly identified because they fit the profile for what has been called the 'career criminal' or 'persistent offender.' That is, each has at some point in their life been engaged in a sustained period of very high-frequency offending. . . . They represent the infamous 5% or 6% of offenders who are responsible for over half of all recorded crimes. It should be noted, however, that these offenses tend to be relatively 'ordinary' crimes such as burglary, theft, and drug sales, and very rarely more serious offenses like rape or murder" (13). Thus these cases do not apply directly to the murderers primarily examined in this book; however, their stories indicate the kind of research that should be undertaken and the type of approach that might help violent offenders also desist.

47. Maruna, *Making Good*, 88.

48. John Braithwaite and S. Mugford, "Conditions of Successful Reintegration Ceremonies: Dealing with Juvenile Offenders," *British Journal of Criminology* 34, no. 2 (1994):146, quoted in Maruna, *Making Good*, 140.

49. Maruna, *Making Good*, 74.

50. For four models of blame and responsibility, see P. Brickman, et. al., "Models of Helping and Coping," *American Psychologist* 37 (1982): 368–84.

51. D. P. McAdams, *Coding Autobiographical Episodes for Themes of Agency and Communion*, 3rd ed., revised (Evanston, IL: Foley Center for the Study of Lives, Northwestern University, 1992), quoted in Maruna, *Making Good*, 96.

52. Katie Kauffman and Caroline New, *Co-Counselling: The Theory of Re-Evaluation Counseling* (New York: Brunner-Routledge, 2004), 103–07.

53. Thomas J. Scheff, *Catharsis in Healing, Ritual, and Drama* (originally published 1979; Lincoln, NE: iUniverse.com, 2001), 48–67.

54. Quote from a member of the Truth Commission in Frances Reid and Deborah Hoffman, directors, *Long Night's Journey into Day: South Africa's Search for Truth & Reconciliation*, video (San Francisco: California Newsreel, 2000).

9

The Story's Broken Promise

The traumatic event challenges an ordinary person to become a
theologian, a philosopher, and a jurist. The survivor is called upon to
articulate the values and beliefs that she once held and that the trauma
destroyed. She stands mute before the emptiness of evil, feeling the
insufficiency of any known system of explanation. Survivors of atrocity of
every age and every culture come to a point in their testimony where all
questions are reduced to one, spoken more in bewilderment than in
outrage: Why?

Judith L. Herman, Trauma and Recovery

Retribution, according to the formal rules of the game, is not fundamentally
about victims. Rather punishment is exacted on behalf of the injured state.
The rules of retribution disallow this chapter on murder victim families. Although their experiences are tragic, they have no bearing on the determination of just deserts, argue retributivists. The state should not be concerned
whether surviving family members drown in bitterness, experience vindication, or find forgiveness.

The state, however, has made room for homicide families by portraying itself
as a compassionate agent that executes for their therapeutic benefit. Survivor
families must follow the script that says they should feel rancor and demand retribution; they must want the satisfaction of seeing the perpetrator locked away
forever or executed. Today, families are expected to help the prosecution secure

the harshest sentence possible, by demonstrating to the judge and jury the depth of their suffering, through victim impact statements. Virtuous survivors, reads the script, should accept the court's final decision, quelling resentment. If they do not, cracks appear in the veneer of the notion that differentiates retribution from vengeance. Since retribution allegedly does not create new victims (as in vengeance), it ends the need for further retaliation. The "stop" is achieved as the family finds closure. This story is widely accepted by Americans even in the absence of evidence of what closure means or how it works. "Closure is a story we tell, not a function we pursue."[1]

Eugene Kennedy, professor of psychology, writes that closure is achieved because execution is a "real human exchange." It is not revenge, because "it issues into peace restored and life recovered." This "transaction" is "integral to the question of capital punishment" and is an "invisible reality." He disagrees with Pope John Paul II, who wrote in *The Gospel of Life* that the death penalty is no longer necessary as a means to defend society, except in extremely rare circumstances. Defense and public order must be secured, the Pope wrote, through "bloodless means" whenever possible, "because they better correspond to the concrete conditions of the common good and are more in conformity to the dignity of the human person."[2] Kennedy rejects the Pope's pleas to respect human dignity, preferring the abstraction of exchange. He admits that how this transaction works is a "spiritual mystery . . . that can be better understood only if we factor this wound of death and its healing by another death into this complex moral judgment."[3]

Phyllis Hotchkiss, whose son was murdered, pursued this illusive alchemy as if it were the Holy Grail. A mutual friend introduced me to Phyllis, whose initial responses to her loss showed deep habituation into the three Rs. In the absence of a narrative that promotes connection to their humanity, family members grasp first at the story in which they have been steeped since childhood—the story behind the death penalty. Phyllis recounts:

> Saturday, June 24, 1989 was a beautiful day. I had dropped off our 19-year-old son, Brian, at his job at Pier One Imports in Saugus, Massachusetts. He was a stock room supervisor. After we had returned home from supper at Friendly's, Brian went to see if his friends were around. They had already left, except for 21-year-old Paul Watterson, who didn't live in the neighborhood at the time. Brian, seeing Paul in his car, went over to talk to him. Brian came in the house, telling

me that they were going to pick up Paul's girlfriend and baby on their way to the carnival in town. I asked Brian not to go with Paul, as I had a very bad feeling. Brian was not friends with Paul, but was very good friends with Paul's girlfriend. They were like brother and sister. Brian told me that he would be home early as he was tired from working all day. He hugged me and said, 'Don't worry ma, I love you.' Those were the last words that Brian said to me. It got to be midnight, but no Brian. I had a sick feeling that not all was right, as Brian always called if he were going to be late. Needless to say, Brian never came home. At ten Sunday morning, two police officers showed up at our door, instructing us to get to the hospital. Brian's body had been found in an auto body junkyard early that morning. He had been bludgeoned to death; the young man who found him said, "Half his head was gone." I told the detectives to get Paul Watterson; I knew that he had murdered Brian. I can't even begin to tell you how much rage and hate were inside of me. If Paul had been there, I would have killed him with my bare hands.

Phyllis recalls with bitterness how "Paul walked the streets for 18 months, frequently in our neighborhood. He would sit across the street from our house and laugh at us when he saw members of my family. He was so cocky because he felt he was literally getting away with murder. But not for long." She continued:

We went public, hitting every newspaper and television station. I said that I knew who murdered my son and would go to my grave to get him behind bars. Finally, in December 1990 Paul was arrested. The day of the trial he decided to plea-bargain. He knew if it went to trial that he would have received life. Instead, he received 15–20 years, which in Massachusetts meant that he would serve 10.

Only someone who has lost someone to murder knows the anger and hate that you have. If Massachusetts had the death penalty, I would have pulled the switch myself. I started going to the Boston Chapter of Parents of Murdered Children [POMC], which is a national support group. I met other parents with whom it was safe to vent my anger. As time went by, I started my own chapter in the North Shore, which I ran for three years. A support group is supposed to help, which it did to some degree, but the need for revenge was still there. I had visions of what I wanted to do to Paul. I thought of him and all murderers as human garbage. I realized that my fixation was not a good thing: I had seen other parents who never let go of the anger, and what it did to them years down the road.

Phyllis has great faith and prayed to God to give her guidance, which she believes finally came. She decided to go into prisons to meet with murderers. "I wanted to let them know what they had done to the victim's family. Boy was I going to give it to them. I eventually met with groups of five to six men for a period of three months."

For survivors, *healing*, like *closure*, is a word abhorred, implying as it does "getting over it." As Amy Mokricky said after the murder of her sister in 1994, "It's like a shattered glass." Even to mention the possibility of healing appears either as a tease, an insult, or a judgment. There is neither promise nor guarantee that the traumatized will succeed in this task. Many flounder. Lost souls abound, disconnected, dissociated, unable to feel, and profoundly isolated. Yet some garner the resources to glue the pieces together. Mokricky says, "You can take superglue and glue the pieces back together but the cracks are always going to be there."[4] Professor of restorative justice Howard Zehr, in his book of interviews with victims of violent crime, recasts the term "healing" as the ability to renarrate life stories that "are no longer just about shame and humiliation, but are ultimately about dignity and triumph."[5]

Thus, the survivor's task involves more than holding together the splintered self and fractured life. It involves fashioning a story that integrates the past and projects the protagonist into the future. An authentic story helps survivors reknit the web of relationships ripped by violence. When such a story can be told, survivors can give up the perspective of themselves as victims. How are they able to do this? The narrative with which Phyllis interpreted her tragedy began to change when she told her story to the prisoners and listened to theirs. She described her process of transformation:

> I told my story, saying that I thought murderers should be put to death. I read my victim impact statement to those prisoners. I think I shocked them, because one of them, almost in tears, said, "Wow, I never realized that someone may hate me as much as you hate Paul." My main goal was to make them see what they had done to not only the victim's family but to their own. Then they told their stories.
>
> As time went by, I was the one being helped the most. I no longer thought of murderers as "human garbage," but as human beings, who had feelings. It's weird to say that we actually became friends. Friendship became a possibility because every single man said he regretted what he did and was truly sorry for the pain he had caused. Whether or not they were sincere (one can never really

tell with prisoners), they said it. An apology was one thing that we never got and probably never will get from Paul. But as time went by, I realized he would have to deal with his failure to be accountable.

Genuine human acknowledgment by the perpetrator of the wrong done and his responsibility for it offers dignity to survivors and validation of their experience. Taking responsibility is also how the offender begins to reclaim his own humanity. These prisoners' apologies and her newfound ability to see the humanity of murderers drained away some of Phyllis's animosity, freeing up her practical reason:

> I started changing my mind about the death penalty. I gave up my chapter of POMC since, as chapter leader, I could not speak either for or against capital punishment. When I began speaking against it, reporters started calling me for stories. I knew that some victims would turn against me, but I followed my heart, doing what God wanted me to do. I met a two-time murderer who had had his sentence commuted years ago. Ironically, he and I started speaking together throughout New England against the death penalty—me as a mother of a murdered child, he as a former prisoner.

Then Phyllis joined Murder Victims' Families for Reconciliation (MVFR), an organization founded in 1976 out of concern for how the death penalty affects all society—families opposed to the death penalty, families of the executed, and families of people under sentence of death. Members' opposition to the death penalty "is rooted in our direct experience of loss and our refusal to respond to that loss with a quest for more killing. Executions are not what will help us heal."[6]

Phyllis paused:

> I have come full circle. I went from being bitter to better. I don't have hate and anger in me anymore. I now know that if there had been the death penalty in Massachusetts and Paul had been executed, his death would not have brought Brian back. It certainly would not have made me miss him any less. The ache and pain will always be there, no matter what. But I would not want someone killed in Brian's name.

Phyllis came to understand that the only story available to her in a period of intense grief and shock was a trap. It ensnared rather than liberated, deceived rather than elucidated. Phyllis intuitively understood that she needed to draw a line around the past and separate it from the present. Although the effects of that murder would always be with her, she needed to be defined by more than a mother of a murdered son. She, too, was a human with a story and a full life ahead of her, which couldn't be stuffed into the narrow box of this horror. Regaining discerning vision about murderers came with greater clarity about herself—she was more than her hurts:

> Do I hate Paul? To be truthful, I don't even think about him. He is not worth my energy. I just know that I will try to do the best I can. I would rather think about the good things in life, living in a positive way. In this way I honor Brian more than if I were full of hate and anger.

In 1997, Phyllis testified against the reinstatement of capital punishment in Massachusetts.[7]

The shock of murder—which is both a death and a crime—overwhelms family members. Oftentimes, the police, as a matter of security, deny the family an opportunity to see the deceased. Or the police may not release the body for burial for weeks or months as the investigation unfolds. If the family proceeds with a memorial service without a casket, then months later, when the body has been released to them, the family may have a funeral at a gravesite, prompting new rounds of grief. Families must deal with the immediate crisis, endure the memorial service, determine who will raise bereft children, replace lost income, pay for counseling, and get a crash course about the legal system.

Trauma rivets the mind upon the deceased's victimization. Many family members cannot put the murder scene from their minds. Bill Pelke recounts how he could only picture his grandmother, Ruth Pelke, lying on the dining room floor, stabbed thirty-three times with such force that the floorboards splintered under the carpet where she lay—"the same room where our family celebrated Christmas, Easter, Thanksgiving, birthdays, and other joyous occasions."[8] Shock temporarily shuts downs practical reason, restricting vision.[9] The full humanness of the victim is temporarily lost to view. Survivors cannot see both; with tunnel vision, they see only the murdered body.

It should be expected that the trauma of murder throws some people more deeply into the narrative of the lie. Sometimes, former abolitionists of capital

punishment become nonabolitionists after experiencing a murder. "Sometimes their opinions fluctuate during the trial, and later, the appeals process,"
social work professor Cecile Guin observes. "The victim's family is foundering
[*sic*] around trying to find anything to take the pain away."[10] Rage is fueled by
the focus on the murderer by the criminal justice system, the media, and abolitionists. Everyone knows the names of Ted Bundy or Jeffrey Dahmer, but few
can name their victims. The victim's life, achievements, and talents are snuffed
out a second time, after the murder. Ann Pace became a nonabolitionist after
her daughter, Charlotte Murray Pace, was murdered shortly after receiving a
master's degree. Ann felt that her sense of safety could only be restored by removing forever the possibility of another murder by the perpetrator.[11]

But for some, over time, a different shift occurs. For Bill Pelke it came when
he was at the end of his rope. A crane operator at the Bethlehem Steel Company, one day Bill arrived before his fellow workers. Alone in his cab, sixty feet
above the plant floor, he recounts:

> My life had been unraveling, and now it was in complete tatters. . . . I felt so
> hopeless that I decided to pray, which is something I hadn't done in a long time.
>
>   As I prayed, I started to get this image of my grandmother and what she stood
> for. I began to think of Nana's love of Jesus, and then thought about all the
> things that Jesus had said about forgiveness. I felt like Nana's spirit was speak-
> ing to me through the prayer. . . . [B]ut the problem was that I did not have an
> ounce of compassion for Paula [the fifteen-year old girl responsible for the
> murder]. I sat in the crane, not knowing what to do, with tears streaming down
> my face, and I begged God to please, please, please give me love and compassion
> for Paula Cooper. . . . I decided . . . I could share Nana's faith with Paula. As soon
> as I made this decision, I no longer wanted Paula to die. . . . [N]ow I had an im-
> age of her [Nana] alive—vibrant and filled with love.[12]

Finally, he could remember Ruth other than as a victim; he could once again
entertain pictures of her teaching Bible classes and cuddling grandchildren.
He could have sought escape from victimhood through revenge, which would
have drawn him deeper into a vision of his grandmother's trauma. But healing some of his grief restored his practical reason, enlarging and correcting his
view of reality; a violent death, he realized, hadn't erased Nana's seventy-eight
years of compassion and generosity. Thus reoriented, Bill sought to connect
Nana's humanity to Paula's.

Once survivors emotionally heal from some of their grief and rage, vision broadens. Gradually, Bill began to see the murderer in a new light, too. No longer defining Paula, the killer, solely by her crime, Bill began to think about her as a person with a story, a past, and most importantly, a future. At this point, the thought of executing the person becomes unbearable.

For Sally Senior, seeing the court documents about the defendant's personal history was enough to snap her vision into focus. Sally told me her story in the sunny living room of her California bungalow.

Her only granddaughter, Jenny, age thirteen, had been walking to a friend's house, kicking leaves while she licked an ice cream cone in her quiet town north of San Francisco. As she walked by a church, the man raking leaves asked for her help. He then offered her some lemonade. She followed him into church, where he raped and murdered her.

Upon reading his file, Sally learned of the killer's "appalling upbringing," his decades-old obsession with pornography, and his fantasy of a young girl who liked to be tied up while having sex. She learned that he had been shocked when Jenny had started to cry and protest, rather than react like the females in his fantasies. Suddenly realizing that Jenny might tell someone—rather than thank him—he faced the prospect of public humiliation and the loss of the only community he had known for many years. Sally could not hate him when she saw his lack of an adult sexual experience, his "aberrant sexual fantasies," and his understandable, though highly disturbed, decision-making process. Sally saw that Jenny just happened to be in the wrong place at the wrong time. Sally's overriding response was that Jenny's murder should have been prevented. Rather than "focusing so much" on the death penalty, she believed, the state "should spend that money on prevention."

Sally could hold in view that the man who had raped and murdered her only granddaughter was a person with a story, a story that included a lack of intervention that might have prevented the crime. Seeing both the person and his vices, she had different objects for both her compassion and her disgust and fury.

Once survivors see the humanity of the person who murdered their beloved, seeing another human die cannot be satisfying. In this way, some survivors avoid the vice of "doing unto others as was done unto their beloved." More than one family member has said, "Knowing the pain our families have gone through, I could never bear to have this inflicted on anybody else."[13] Survivors understand, more clearly than most, that capital punishment does not end suffering, does not end violence, and does not end murder. Instead, it creates a whole new set of grieving family members. Within the story, the offender's family members are not supposed to be seen as new victims because the state's violence is legitimate and somehow the offender's death isn't supposed to hurt. The horror of the victims' family members' loss builds the resolve that no one should ever have to suffer like this. Rejecting the story means they take responsibility for their pain rather than pass it to others.

But prior to regaining their full moral vision—and reclaiming the humanity of themselves, the victim, and the perpetrator—many victim families spend months or years filled with rage and vindictiveness, humiliation, and terror. It may take a long time for aggrieved individuals to move from vengeful fantasies to seeing themselves as capable of having a good life, remembering with joy the deceased, or viewing the perpetrator as a person worthy of life.[14] This necessary journey of reclaiming themselves, their connection to their deceased, and a place in the community provides an important reason for not rushing to execute (as some advocate, in order to reduce the costs of lengthy trials and appeals).[15]

The concern for victims' rights began in the 1970s as a backlash against a system of justice that systematically excluded victims. Before then, police, detectives, and prosecutors did not have to inform the family if a suspect had been found, when the trial started, or if a plea bargain had been struck. The defense often barred victims' families from the courtroom, and the prison did not inform them if the offender escaped or was released. Survivors of violent crime concluded rightfully that the accused had more rights within the criminal justice system than survivors did. But survivors did not go quietly into that good night, as the retributivists might have preferred. Under pressure from victims and their allies, individual states now grant victims the right "to be notified, to be present, and to be heard," although these rights are often ignored in practice.[16] However, there is a trade-off for families who get their day in court. They must support the three Rs.

Some families do not go along with the script, and they challenge the story that the state acts in victims' interests. Two relatives who did not follow the script were told by a Nebraska court they were not "victims." This determination came near the end of Randy Reeves's trial for the murder of Vicki Zessin and Janet Mesner on 28 March 1980. Randy Reeves had known Janet her

whole life; he occasionally called her when he needed a place to stay. While the
women were sleeping, Randy broke into the house and without any known
motive picked up a knife in the kitchen and stabbed Janet. Vicki probably
woke up and was going to her friend's aid when Randy "stabbed Vicki in the
liver, severing major arteries and killing her instantly with one blow." "Janet
lived long enough to call 911. When help arrived, Janet told a rescue worker,
"It was Randy, he had a knife. I don't know why he did it. I don't understand."[17]

When investigators were combing through the house, they opened a bedroom door and "found a small towheaded girl who asked, 'Where's my
mom?'" Apparently, two-year-old Audrey, daughter of Vicki, never saw or
heard anything that happened that night.

Audrey returned home to Oregon with her father, Gus Lamm, after the funeral. They got on with their lives as best they could, the pain of their loss settling into a steady ache over time. Back in Nebraska, Reeves's case slowly made
its way through the system. Eighteen years after the murder, Gus received a
phone call from a friend that Randy had received an execution date.[18]

Gus opposed the execution—which seemed absurd to him after so many
years—but he knew other members of the family felt differently, and he was
reluctant to involve Audrey in a family conflict. But determined to "be a force
for good" and not wanting "to live with myself knowing that I had not tried,"
Gus called Audrey, now twenty-one, who agreed to go to Nebraska to fight for
Reeves's life. The Pardons Board held a clemency hearing but decided to not
hear from victims' families. However, they read one letter from the Zessin
family advocating the death penalty. Gus and Audrey brought suit, arguing
that the Pardons Board denied their constitutional rights as victims of crime
to be heard during criminal cases.

The Lancaster County District Court ruled that no constitutional rights
had been violated since Gus and Audrey were not victims of the crime because
they were acting on behalf of Reeves.[19] Victims' families who do not speak the
script are not recognized as victims, but instead are treated as "saints or
kooks."[20] Since the state assumes families want an execution, no services are
offered to those families that oppose the execution and will experience it as a
traumatic obstacle to their own justice seeking.[21]

Some families of murder victims eschew the habits of victimhood, seeking
satisfaction through the suffering of another and reducing a person to her

vices. They deny retribution's story that the punishment ends the cycle of violence, does not create new victims, and provides closure to families.[22] But what about just deserts? What alternative story do some families tell about what murderers deserve?

The moral line between victims and perpetrators is enormous, yet it is often small things that prevent one from becoming both. John O'Keefe lives in the hills about an hour outside a major city.[23] John's story is particularly interesting because he was so brutally conditioned into the three Rs, yet he eventually emerged from them, despite the murder of his son, Benjy.

John, as a young boy, lived with a brother, a submissive mother, and an alcoholic, abusive father. "My father terrified me," he recalled. "I was always scared of him. All the men I knew were violent—my uncles, everybody." He recalled experiences that fit the description of violent coercion and violent retaliation. The violence also directed at his brother horrified and generated intense shame. Violent coaching came in the form of ridicule and overt threat.

Over the years, John watched family and friends go to jail. One nephew went to prison for fifteen years for multiple rapes. "My nephew," he explained, "was traumatized as a child. At eighteen months he would wake up screaming in terror."

John engaged in some violent performances in high school, but abandoned this behavior after a series of losses. He attributes his ability to escape a life of violence to his stepdad, Sean, who moved in when he was eleven. Sean was the first nonviolent man he had ever met.

His stepdad offered more than a cessation of brutalization. Sean gave John a bigger picture, a different narrative. Sean was Irish and taught John about the poor in County Kerry and the Irish diaspora. John got the picture that he was just one poor boy among many who had suffered. Violence and humiliation were universal issues, not unique to his little corner of hell.

With a new story and effective help, John was able to begin his own slow climb out of a life of violence. He eventually married a teacher named Rachel Block and adopted her toddler, Benjamin, nicknamed Benjy. The family was living in the city when adolescent Benjy started a hip-hop band called Killing Time that included African American and Hispanic members. Benjy believed in them and learned to use his middle-class white privilege to their advantage. After Benjy got the band interested in abolishing the death penalty, they gave concerts to raise money for Mumia Abu-Jamal's defense.[24]

Benjy also worked with the mentally disabled and at-risk youth in the poorest section of the city.

John recalls that members of Killing Time were always saying, "'One of us will probably die.' It was the fate of black or poor kids to get taken down, but not youngsters like Benjy."

Several members of Killing Time were in the car with Benjy when he was shot in 1996. His last words, at the age of twenty-three, in hope of calming the deranged stranger, were "Peace, brother, One Love." His friends in the car immediately went to the police shouting, "We need help." The police asked, "Were drugs involved?" They cried out, "Fuck that, our friend is dying!" The police immediately "copped an attitude" toward this crime. By the time John arrived at the police station, the officers were treating Benjy's friends like suspects. Once they saw that Benjy's parents were white and middle class, they treated the boys well. But the police had separated the friends in different rooms; John kept insisting that these young men had just been traumatized and needed care.

The police offered John and his wife closure if the killer were captured. "What do you want to happen? Come to the trial? Speak to the jury?" John didn't want any part of it. Yet for a while John had the idea of tracking down and killing the perpetrator himself. The murderer was never apprehended.

The death left a huge hole that John and Rachel tried to fill with the young adults who loved Benjy. Out of concern, one young man called John daily for the next eighteen months. Despite this network of friends, for three years John tried to think of a way to end his life without harming those he loved. He still does not sleep through the night.

The turning point in his grief process occurred when a member of the band, Donnell, asked to be married at their home in the hills. John said, "It was like the shroud coming off the house." Finally, John realized that he was alive, and life was going to go on. "If life was going to have a point, it was that I was going to have to live. It was up to me to determine how I was going to live."

"What I needed," he said, "was to fit this [homicide] into my world. Into my reality. I wanted to live life in a real way, with community, with family."

John spoke with passion about fundamental justice and his concept of social, human, and moral desert. "The root of violence," he said, "is the division into social classes. Philosophers say that some deserve and some do not deserve. Hogwash. We are all humans, we all deserve. Justice," he continued, "is about asking the question 'What do humans have in common as a species'? Our common human needs unite us." What do all humans need? He rattled off his list: "food, drinkable water, housing, clothes, respect, love, justice, community, democracy in which people participate in decisions, where the leadership trusts the people, even if they make mistakes. We live in a culture," he expounded, "in which some are thought to have needs and some do not. This myth of rugged individualism is not what we are about as a species; the reality is that we need each other. We are social animals."

He continued:

> The death penalty is not a question of just deserts. It has to do with what we need to survive. Therefore, rejecting the death penalty is not about exonerating the felons, excusing them, relieving them of blame. Justice is not fundamentally about blame. Justice, when pictured as scales, implies commerce. But social and criminal justice aren't about economic exchange. Justice means people are not exploited and legal violence is not permitted.
>
> We are where violence comes from. All humans deserve a safe place to sleep and parents who will not beat them. . . . But instead, we focus on building gated communities and prisons, rather than ensuring that people's needs are met.
>
> We are all responsible. We tolerate this violent world we live in. Murderer and murdered. Both are victims. There is a moral line between them, but that line is less wide than we think. It is wrong to pin responsibility solely on one individual for his act of injustice when we don't indict ourselves for our acts of injustice toward that individual. We are responsible that some have so lost their humanity that they could kill another.
>
> The rich are free to steal in this country, but no one blathers about retribution for them. We have the choice with regard to the death penalty, because there is so much more we can do with murderers than simply waste their lives.

As with many survivors, John would like a genuine apology from Benjy's murderer. Perhaps partly because the man has never been caught, John embraces neither the concept of forgiveness nor reconciliation. John said, "Maybe I need to forgive him. But he doesn't need me to forgive him." "I'm only interested in him if he is interested in learning, in understanding, in asking, 'Why?' We need to help perpetrators understand the big picture, to know that they deserved to be in a family who loved and respected them." "They need help," he said, "to figure that out. That's what we owe them."

John explained:

> Rachel and I went to the MVFR conference in June 2002 with trepidation. We're not into reconciliation with the offender because murder is not just between individuals. Murder is a community problem. It's invalid to use the idea of reconciliation if it is a trick to help people with their anger. People are so desperate to get past their anger. I'm interested in real justice, and I was glad to find that MVFR is too.
>
> My wife and I are working on a documentary whose theme is "We are all responsible for working to make the world better." With whatever skills you have—poetry, carpentry, music. There is no reason not to engage in this work. There is no excuse. If you don't, you have no right to complain. In the documentary, we want to show what these young people have achieved after Benjy's death.
>
> When I turned fifty [before Benjy's death], I thanked everyone who had helped me reach this day. I told Benjy that he was the next generation; it was up to him to carry things forward. But look at what's happened. I'm still learning from him. In Cuba, they built a community center in the poorest section, naming it after Benjy, and a teenager from the U.S. painted a mural on it. A poem of Benjy's adorns a mural in a Palestinian refugee camp. [A group of Jewish women from the United States were invited by a group of Palestinians to paint a mural on a four-story building in a camp outside Bethlehem. The top story of the building was to represent hope for the future, and the women decided to include Benjy's poem in that portion of the mural.]
>
> My greatest hope is to join with him in making the world a better place. I want there to be understanding, learning, and action. Can we make it so that fewer are killed and fewer are treated with disrespect and with violence? That's the best we can do. The past is gone. My child is gone. But I can look at the children in this world now.

John went into his house and returned with a poem.

> When I die if you need to weep
> Cry for your brother or sister
> Walking in the street beside you

And when you need me
Put your arms around anyone
And give them
What you need to give me

I want to leave you something
Something better than words or sounds

Look for me in the
People I've known or loved

And if you cannot
Give me away—
At least let me
Live in your eyes
And not on your mind

You can love me most
By letting hands touch hands
By letting bodies touch bodies
And by letting go of that
Which needs to be free

Love doesn't die,
People do
So when what's left of me is love

. . . give me away.

Anonymous
10 March 2002

John grew quiet. "Continuing Benjy's story let me rejoin the human race."

NOTES

1. Statement by Franklin E. Zimring at the national conference "The Impact of the Death Penalty on Victim's Families," Skidmore College, Saratoga Springs, NY, 11–13 September 2003.

2. John Paul II, *The Gospel of Life: On the Value and Inviolability of Human Life (Evangelium Vitae)* (Washington, DC: United States Catholic Conference, 1995), 99, 100.

3. Eugene Kennedy, "Inner Peace Restored for Victims' Families When Murderer Is Executed," *National Catholic Reporter* 35, no. 33 (2 July 1999): 21.

4. Quoted in Howard Zehr, *Transcending: Reflections of Crime Victims* (Intercourse, PA: Good Books, 2001), 35.

5. Zehr, *Transcending*, 19.

6. "Murder Victims' Families for Reconciliation [MVFR] is a national organization of family members of both homicide and state killings who oppose the death penalty in all cases. Our mission is to abolish the death penalty. . . . We advocate for programs and policies that reduce the rate of homicide and promote crime prevention and alternatives to violence." *Murder Victims' Families for Reconciliation, Inc.*, available at www.mvfr.org/ (accessed 20 June 2003).

7. Personal communications, June–August 2003. Also see Barbara Hood and Rachel King, eds., *Not in Our Name: Murder Victims' Families Speak Out against the Death Penalty*, 3rd ed. (Cambridge, MA: Murder Victims' Families for Reconciliation, 1999), 33.

8. Rachel King, *Don't Kill in Our Names: Families of Murder Victims Speak Out against the Death Penalty* (New Brunswick, NJ: Rutgers University Press, 2003), 89, 94, 97.

9. Donald Nathanson calls this "cognitive shock," a "transient inability to think." *Shame and Pride: Affect, Sex, and the Birth of the Self* (New York: Norton, 1992), 308.

10. Quoted by Marlene Naanes, "Victim's Mom Changes Death Penalty Stance," *Baton Rouge Advocate*, 17 September 2003, 7B.

11. Naanes, "Victims' Mom," 7B.

12. King, *Don't Kill*, 97.

13. Said to me by Jeanette Star Howard, who lost her fiancé, a police officer, to second-degree murder.

14. Some view vindictiveness as a step in a therapeutic process, not a settled moral judgment. See Judith L. Herman, *Trauma and Recovery* (New York: Basic, 1997), 138, 189–90, and Trudy Govier, *Forgiveness and Revenge* (London: Routledge, 2002), 19–22.

15. Bobby and Barbara Curley's son, Jeffrey, age ten, was lured from his neighborhood in Massachusetts by the promise of a bicycle. After resisting sexual advances, he was molested and murdered by two men, Charles Jaynes and Salvatore Sicari, on 1 October 1997. They stuffed his body into a concrete-filled container and dumped it in a Maine river. When the boy's body was discovered and the two men were charged, Bobby joined an effort to reinstate the death penalty in Massachusetts. If anyone needed a spokesperson for the death penalty, Bobby was it; he would stand on median strips of busy highways with a sign pleading, "Reinstate the Death Penalty." Bobby was invited to be present in the Massachusetts capitol building during a vote to reinstate

the death penalty. The measure had already passed the state house by a single vote, but then Representative John Slattery changed his mind and the bill died on an 80–80 tie.

It was quite a surprise when, on 7 June 2001, Bobby told New England Cable News that he was now against the death penalty. He told them, "I am now troubled by how the death penalty is applied differently to the rich and the poor." He went on to say that he admired Slattery's stand against the death penalty. "I guess he did the right thing," Curley said. "People knew more than I did at the time. But not many people experience anger like me and my family have." *Boston Globe*, 7 June 2001.

Having shed some of his anger and grief, having spoken with two brothers of murderers on death row, he now saw that the deaths of Jaynes and Sicari would not change his reality for the better but might actually make matters worse. Nothing would bring his beloved Jeffrey back; killing would not right the balance or pay off the murderer's debt to society.

16. Typically, victims are guaranteed "the right to be notified in advance of any court hearing in a case, the right to be consulted before a plea bargain, the right prior to sentencing to give a statement about the crime's impact, and the right to be notified of a criminal's parole hearing, release date, or escape from prison. Crime victims and their families also sought the right to remain in the courtroom through a trial." Eric Schlosser, "A Grief Like No Other," *Atlantic Monthly* 280, no. 3 (September 1997): 47. Also see Hannah Arendt, *Eichmann in Jerusalem*, 2nd ed., revised and enlarged (New York: Penguin, 1994 (1963), 260–72.

17. King, *Don't Kill*, 190.

18. King, *Don't Kill*, 197.

19. The Nebraska Supreme Court overturned the lower court's ruling that the Lamms were not victims, because "the legislature had failed to pass enacting legislation to protect" crime victims. King, *Don't Kill*, 217.

20. This phrase is Rachel King's from *Don't Kill*.

21. Robert R. Cushing and Susannah Sheffer, *Dignity Denied: The Experience of Murder Victims' Family Members Who Oppose the Death Penalty* (Cambridge, MA: Murder Victims' Families for Reconciliation, 2002), 27.

22. See Antoinette Bosco, *Choosing Mercy: A Mother of Murder Victims Pleads to End the Death Penalty* (Maryknoll, NY: Orbis, 2001).

23. The names and places from the "O'Keefe" interview are fictional. Any use of names of real persons is coincidental.

24. Abu-Jamal is a journalist who exposed police brutality. He was sentenced to die for killing a police officer, Daniel Faulkner, in 1981. An international movement has emerged defending his innocence and demanding a fair trial.

Living a New Story

Do not abandon the living for the dead.

Richard Zimler, The Last Kabbalist of Lisbon

I had found a third way: Transformation. Revenge does not have to be about destroying your enemy, it can mean transforming him, or yourself.

Laura Blumenthal, Revenge: A Story of Hope

Human beings are not our enemy.

Thich Nhat Hanh, Anger

Murder victims' families who oppose the death penalty tell new stories with liberating perspectives. Their new ways of seeing counter the narrative of death. What virtues, projects, and interpretations of core goods are suggested by the stories from such survivors? How might bystanders—those community members who do not experience a particular crime, participate in the criminal justice system, or bear witness to executions—take and use such a story?

THE VIRTUE OF RESPONSIBILITY: TAKING STOCK
Responsibility requires, ethicist Mary Elizabeth Hobgood argues, "a moral assessment of social relations" and "discerning unjust power arrangements."[1] The task involves analyzing bystanders' own role in the story: their relation to

the institutions, practices, and habits that sustain crime and punishment. As with all virtues, responsibility requires practical reason exercised in this case in the form of taking stock.

We saw in earlier chapters how societies' prevailing classism has derailed the criminal justice system from its intended purposes of protecting society and serving the goods of justice and responsibility. For instance, the ruling elites' definition of what constitutes a crime and who is a criminal draws deeply from pervasive class inequalities—the misdeeds of the poor are deemed particularly heinous, warranting the severest punishments. Although all societies deplore murder, classism distorts the definition of murder so that the intentional killing of certain people—for example, slaves in the United States or Jews in the Third Reich—is not classified and prosecuted as murder. The decision by company leaders to cut back on safety measures in order to save money, knowing that death of workers is likely, is regarded not as murder, but as a regulatory violation. Classism is both institutional (encoded in laws and social practices) and attitudinal (embedded within individual consciousness). It involves both power and prejudice. Classism, educator Lee Anne Bell writes, is also hierarchical, "in which dominant or privileged groups benefit, often in unconscious ways, from the disempowerment of subordinated or targeted groups."[2] Ruling elites have "access to social power and privilege not equally available" to all, meaning that they enjoy such things as more money, better health care, and less targeting by the criminal justice system.

Classism is pervasive, Bell writes, because it is structured not only in the criminal justice system, but "also within the human psyche." As we have seen, the story is internalized both by criminals and by those who make the criminal laws. "The idea that the poor somehow deserve and are responsible for poverty, rather than the economic system that structures and requires it, is learned by poor and affluent alike."[3] The ruling class "can project its particular way of seeing social reality so successfully that its view is accepted as common sense, as part of the natural order, even by those who are in fact disempowered by it." The narrative of the lie is one of the major mechanisms for creating acquiescence with such an unjust social order. The ruling elites do not have to rule with an iron fist, but rather, Bell continues, through "an ongoing system that is mediated by well-intentioned people acting as agents of oppression, usually unconsciously, by simply going about their daily lives."[4] Bystanders to the criminal justice system are such agents. The internalization of the narrative of the lie is a key mechanism in how the lower and middling classes end up supporting criminal justice policies and practices that are not good for them or society as a whole.

One of the most valuable insights from struggles against racism and other forms of oppression, Bell emphasizes, has been the understanding that not only do the dominated suffer from stigmatization and violence, but that oppression "does psychic and ethical violence to the dominator group as well."[5] In essence, both dominants and subordinates have to be mistreated into playing their respective roles within an oppressive society. The mistreatment suffered by the poor, middling, and upper classes are substantially different, yet people have to be groomed for their respective roles. Although such grooming may be accomplished by offering carrots of apparent privilege to members of dominant groups, it is often initially accomplished by wielding a stick.

The systemic mistreatment of children, called adultism, is the universal training ground for conscription into the narrative of the lie. The virtue of taking stock involves seeing that bystanders do not voluntarily subscribe to the story so many kill for: it is stamped on them through mistreatment. The systematic disrespect of their intelligence, caring, and needs while young— called adultism—sets them up to capitulate to a system of shame and blame.

Taking stock involves exposing how people acquire the habits that reinforce the three Rs. Children grow up in families and institutions built upon the three Rs. Infused from a tender age with the idea that their worth depends on their personal merit, children struggle to be obediently good, rather than having their inherent worth affirmed. In ways both obvious and subtle, well-meaning adults often override children's perceptions and choices, from which young people pick up habits of powerlessness. Children who harm others are not thought to deserve or need attention, just punishment. With the attention on fault and blame rather than redress and help, young people often conclude that they are bad. When adults coerce expressions of remorse from a guilty young person, they communicate the belief that the young person does not really care about the harm just caused. When a young person's actions upset her guardians, they often strike out at her for "making" them feel bad. Thus, children often see adults "do unto others as was done unto them" rather than handle their painful feelings responsibly. Young people whose own needs are denied often become alienated from their bodies and their feelings, which sets the stage for disconnecting from others' pain.

Taking stock involves investigating how bystanders internalize the story experientially.[6] For example, the story was not told at bedtime, but was a part of bedtime, during which rituals of confession and punishment were performed. Too often, children go to sleep stroking in the dark the still-smarting red mark on their face from the backhand slap for talking back. Taking stock involves understanding that the story is not so much told as enacted.

Taking stock recognizes how the story shapes all institutions, such as schools, which are run much like prisons. Seen as potential criminals rather than honor-roll candidates, students may be prohibited from speaking freely except when "in the yard," detained if caught outside their assigned room, put under surveillance, searched, marched through metal detectors, given "three strikes before they're out," or shamed. They are treated like objects whose worth is assessed by test scores or touchdowns scored rather than as intelligent beings whose voices and views matter.[7] Experiences in such environments condition young people to accept disrespect, thus preparing them to tolerate the disrespect of others. Adultism is thus the breeding ground for the habits that support the story behind the death penalty.

Because of the personal sacrifices young adults make—hiding their passion for a just world, abandoning friends in order to get ahead—they finally defend the idea that nobody's needs should be met without them "earning" it the hard way. They come to feel as though their worth depends on their ability to fit into the status quo. By adulthood, they are "snowed under"—buried in a veritable avalanche of inaccurate information and habits. The new story lays bare how all bystanders participate in social structures that are deeply punitive and how daily relationships partake of an economy of reward and punishment. Through a process of learning and conditioning (sometimes painful, sometimes numbing), by the time of adulthood, most silently condone a system that targets some for serious harm.

This blunting of moral sensitivities results in habits unresponsive to injustices. Alienated from their own wellsprings of desire for connection, separated from others by class and race, isolated from neighbors, bystanders may see no connection to what happens in their own lives and the lives of those snared by the criminal justice system.[8] Most bystanders feel unaffected by the prison-industrial complex. The lack of a robust debate about capital punishment—much less about punishment itself—signals that they feel untouched by the current state of affairs. Bystanders feel that dangerous criminals occupy a parallel world.

Most bystanders have been squeezed into tight quarters by the story of the lie and its accompanying practices. Frightened from one side by media portrayals of violent criminals on the prowl, they are angered from a second side by a criminal justice system that releases dangerous people into their community. They are overwhelmed from a third side by the sheer magnitude of the intertwined sources of crime and the challenges of providing for themselves and their loved ones in a competitive world. Finally, on the fourth side, they are paralyzed by self-perceptions as too small or powerless to make a difference. The dominant story allows bystanders to remain ignorant about the criminal justice system without appearing uninformed, blind to how this system privileges those with class and race status, and deceived about its moral pathology. The narrative of the lie results in what philosopher Jeffrey Reiman calls "historical inertia"—a muting of "effective demand for change." Predictably, bystanders steeped in the story and its habits clamor for more of the same—more draconian dungeons or an expansion of the death penalty.[9]

Bystanders need to take stock of their situation and own what is done in their name. The cover story obscures from view the painful processes by which people are conditioned into assuming their roles as agent of an oppressive society. Encouraged particularly to see themselves as victims, bystanders have a hard time identifying the short-term benefits that accrue to them by tolerating the violentization of others and by punishing others blameworthy for their vices. By blaming offenders, bystanders ignore their own role in the conditions that fail to prevent crime: the mistreatment of young people, the violentization of men and women, the installation of bad habits, the internalization of the narrative of the lie, economic injustice, racism, an incoherent practice of punishment, prisons that degrade, the death penalty.[10] "One out of every 142 Americans is in prison—and this does not include military prisons or INS jails."[11] How many neighbors must be incarcerated or executed before bystanders recognize their place in this system of injustice?

As agents of the oppressive society, bystanders lose. Projects such as capital punishment, argues Austin Sarat, "diminish us" by

> damaging our democracy, legitimating vengeance, intensifying racial divisions, and distracting us from the challenges that the new century poses for America. It promises simple solutions to complex problems and offers up moral simplicity in a morally ambiguous world. We need a new abolitionism that leaves

[humanist liberalism, political radicalism, or religious doctrine] behind, and assesses the injuries that state killing does to those who love America and its political and legal institutions, that allows and encourages more nuanced views of moral responsibility and of political action, and offers new narrative possibilities in the conversation about state killing.[12]

Bystanders can take the lead by cultivating the virtue of taking stock.

Taking stock means that bystanders need to tell their stories about how hurtful experiences set them up to acquire particular habits without their conscious assent. No bystander is born wanting to benefit from the punishment of the poor or the stigmatization of criminals. This conditioning to accept alienated forms of life is itself a form of mistreatment. At some point, people give in and settle for less than human and just relationships, falling into one of the available roles—bystander or victimizer.[13] Exposing the dynamics of systematic mistreatment demystifies the process by which people's capacities for responsibility and responsiveness are obscured. By taking stock, individuals are enabled to see how an oppressive society acts so that its members feel fearful, futile, or furious. Taking stock involves understanding how these systems hurt others, undermine respect for the law,[14] and constrict their own hearts and minds; it leads to taking responsibility for what is done with their passive consent.

THE VIRTUE OF JUSTICE: DISCERNING VISION

Telling a new story means rejecting the tunnel vision of the old. Humans deserve to be seen with discerning vision, which affirms their humanity while recognizing their vices. This entails understanding the fundamental difference between the potentially smart, capable, loving human and her nonintelligent and ineffectual habits.[15] With discerning vision, people can respond to another's human presence while thinking incisively about how to help her undo her enmeshment with her habits.[16]

Sustaining this clarity of vision requires a threefold commitment.

First, the full humanity of all victims needs to be affirmed, highlighting how they did not deserve what happened to them. Perpetrators bear a special responsibility to affirm the humanity of their victims, which will require affirming that perpetrators never deserved harm themselves. Many prisoners cannot feel compassion about their own brutal treatment at the hands of others. Casting off the lie that they deserved it, offenders can then challenge the deadly delusion that their victims deserved it, too.

Second, discerning vision includes seeing perpetrators as responsible for evil actions, not as essentially evil. By rejecting the cover story that says some people are inherently deviant, diseased, or demonic, bystanders can expose the process by which vices are acquired. By telling a new story that killers are worthy of respect and ontologically good, even though their actions are reprehensible, bystanders refuse to reenact one of their roles in the violentization process. If bystanders regarded newly violent people with discerning vision rather than as stereotypes, and offered assistance rather than avoidance, then perpetrators might be able to resist identifying with their own vices and retain clear vision about themselves. The media could refuse to portray malefactors as essentially bad while condemning their offenses. Survivors can exercise discerning vision by seeing the humanity of perpetrators, while remembering that such affirmation does not condone crime, undercut offenders' responsibility, or deny the depth of the loss.[17] Criminal justice practitioners can exercise discerning vision by ceasing to treat offenders as objects to be dominated in a misguided effort to vindicate the worth of the victim. Rather, practitioners should respect the humanity of the perpetrators and see that they get the assistance they need to own up to their deeds. With discerning vision, no wrongdoers can be said to deserve harm, even while being held responsible and restrained so that they do not harm self or others. Such discernment is a form of justice because, without excusing perpetrators, it exposes the community's responsibility for the violentization process.

And third, bystanders deserve to extend discerning vision to themselves. For everyone, this vision entails casting off the cloak of victimhood and seeing themselves as powerful rather than powerless, protagonists rather than pawns. With one eye firmly on their vices, they can commit to reanimating their capacities to act powerfully, responsibly, and responsively.

Exercising clear and compassionate vision serves justice. Failure to respond distinctly to the human *and* to the vice is at the heart of the injustice of the three Rs.

THE VIRTUE OF RESPONSIBILITY: RESPONSIVENESS TO THE OTHER

Crime bursts the myth of parallel worlds. When an individual kills someone across the great divides of race or class, the oneness of our world is revealed.

Crime shatters the fiction that a person can be morally decent while being indifferent to her fellows humans who are being maltreated.[18] Crime exposes a relationality denied by structures of injustice and their cover story.

Bystanders, in order to see themselves as part of the solution rather than as on the sidelines, must tell a new story about responsibility. The old story remains fixated on individual fault understood narrowly as liability—intentional misdeeds done from bad motives. This individualistic interpretation of responsibility is inadequate to deal with the kind of responsibility bystanders have when they act as agents of oppression but unintentionally and without bad motives. A new understanding of responsibility also requires responsiveness to people to whom bystanders are bound by neither past promises nor past wrongs. Moving beyond a sense of duty or what is "owed" someone, this type of responsibility calls bystanders to an expanded domain of responsiveness, a felt sense of connection to others because people have needs they cannot meet by themselves. For many, the point of connection is a sense of shared humanness. Being responsible means not just refraining from harm but also undertaking active deeds—preventing harm and correcting injustices.

Seeing themselves bound in a web of mutuality, bystanders can pursue the well-being of others to whom they are not narrowly obligated and address social problems that are not their individual fault.

A NEW PROJECT OF JUSTICE: DISMANTLING VICES

Oppression persists, Iris Marion Young argues, "through interactive habits, unconscious assumptions and stereotypes, and group-related feelings of nervousness or aversion." She observes that "many moral philosophers would find it odd to include gestures, informal remarks, judgments of ugliness, and feelings of discomfort under the rubric of issues of justice." Why is dismantling habits a matter of "social justice, not just individual moral action?" she asks.[19] For three important reasons, the new story invites people to make the commitment to eliminate their habits as a new project of justice.

First, the projects of revenge, retribution, and rectification have emotional underpinnings. People's allegiance to the three Rs is not a matter of rational choice or even false consciousness. Installed through mistreatment, habits involve an affective attachment, even "addiction" to the cover story and its projects.[20] Habits are like a second nature to which people have become accustomed. Living out a new story requires undoing one's emotional adhesion to the old.

Second, the projects of revenge and retribution specifically counsel taking out painful feelings on others. Indeed, many people think that hostile feelings justify punishment. In order for the new story to break with this legacy, it must provide an alternative project for handling aggressive emotions such as vindictiveness or rage.

Third, the dominant culture triggers bystanders' habits, unless people are aware enough to resist its cues. If bystanders do act unawarely within their vices, they reproduce the three Rs. Since, Young writes, "unconscious reactions, habits, and stereotypes reproduce the oppression of some groups, then they should be judged unjust, and therefore should be changed."[21] A sustained effort is required to undo one's allegiance to the habits that both result from and recycle the three Rs. The pursuit of justice must not reproduce injustice.

Thus, an important project of justice is the intentional dismantling of patterns of thought and feeling that fuel the three Rs. Even if bystanders withdraw their intellectual support from the death penalty, they still need to make a commitment to act on a new story *and* rid themselves of the habits that reinforce the three Rs.

Justice requires the dismantling of vices. It does not involve blaming bystanders for having capitulated to the story of the lie. Justice does, however, mean asking bystanders to take responsibility from this moment forward to "submit such unconscious behavior to reflection, to work to change habits and attitudes," Young writes. Change in such cultural habits can occur "only if individuals become aware of them and change their individual habits. This is cultural revolution."[22]

In order to set the process in motion, the habit of isolation needs to be tackled. Bystanders cannot change these habits by themselves. But if they were to participate in a mutual practice aimed at dismantling vices such as victimhood, they could help each other examine where they are tempted to hurt others rather than face their own painful feelings. This project could be called emergence from nonhuman habits. One vital activity of such a project involves asking for and listening to each others' stories about how they appropriated the three Rs. This activity of taking turns telling one's story can be informal, such as with friends over coffee or coworkers over lunch.

This practice could include joining a group of citizens involved in prisoner reform or death penalty abolition and initiating opportunities to explore feelings and stereotypes about criminals. In whatever setting, the project includes asking for and listening to each other's stories about their exposure to the three Rs.

The goals of such storytelling are not only to obtain a picture of how the narrative of the lie and the three Rs insinuate themselves into people's consciousness and operate in their daily lives. The goals also include healing and action, for only these together will actually dissolve habits.

Telling one's story to an attentive listener about how one acquired concepts of desert or recounting times when one felt vengeful permits the spontaneous release and healing of emotions. Telling friends with whom one feels safe about one's exposure to violence can easily lead to tears, a physical release of emotional pain. Such release actually heals the hurt, as a sort of "degriefing"[23] When people tell their stories and the tears flow, then they can access their own thinking and revive their clarity of vision rather than act unawarely upon their feelings.[24] The goals of an affective labor of healing are the enlargement of one's moral vision and capacity to care and act. Whereas the old story coached "do unto others as was done unto you," the new story counsels taking responsibility for healing the painful feelings that undergird one's allegiance to the three Rs.[25]

When bystanders heal from some of their isolation and indifference, they extend an attentive ear to others who need to tell their stories and heal. If they choose, bystanders might want to offer their attention to survivors of violent crime. Survivors who engage in this practice of emergence can begin to heal their anger by attending to its underlying sorrow and fear, eventually realizing that the past cannot be changed. Survivors say it is not helpful to be encouraged to stay angry for twenty years; such a peer-to-peer practice would help assuage their anger and enable them to find other ways to affirm the deceased's value, rather than by demanding the death penalty.[26]

American society systematically discourages and even suppresses the responsible release of painful emotions. Even for murder, popular media suggest that six to twelve months of mourning is all that is needed, when in fact, the process of grieving may take decades; a murder victim is never forgotten and never stops being missed. Such communal denial of the need to heal keeps people locked within their habits and trigger-ready to take out their pain on others.[27] Families of homicide victims may have vengeful feelings, which can also be healed. Allies can listen to survivors' angry demands for retaliation while encouraging survivors, as a matter of principle, to refrain from the vice of "doing unto others as was done unto you."

Telling their stories and healing from paralysis will enable bystanders to take action for change. They may find it easier to determine what may be best to do, if they take the time to heal and free up their moral vision from the story's confusions. Healing painful emotions does not diminish the need to take moral action. Nor does emotional catharsis dictate the course of future action. But its absence almost guarantees ineffective or even harmful responses. The cleansing of emotional wounds activates presence of mind and enables people to think of many creative ways to make a positive difference in their communities.

Any emotion, by itself, provides insufficient guidance for determining what is best to do. Decisions should involve comparing what one's feelings prompt one to do against what may be assumed to be true of humans. For example, if it is assumed that humans are oriented to the good and intelligent, then when a person treats someone, for example, as if he were inherently bad and stupid, she knows her emotions are impairing her moral vision and should not be acted upon. Virtuous action requires alignment with all that is excellent about humans, not with distorted perspectives and inappropriate emotions. Outrage at injustice is virtuous because practical reason sees that no human deserves harm. Similarly, vengeful feelings, because they fail to see the humanness in someone, cannot be the basis of virtuous action. In engaging in a project of mutual storytelling and healing, bystanders hope to liberate their minds and hearts so that they can act constructively and creatively, rather than reactively.

Bystanders are not the only group that needs to engage in an intentional project of dismantling habits. A new story also should support efforts to help offenders, as a project of justice, dismantle *their* vices. The need to protect society justifies selective incapacitation of dangerous, violent offenders. They need to be restrained until they can again be trusted. Defensive measures taken by communities to protect themselves from violentized people should use the minimum force possible.[28] However, the good of protection requires more than warehousing prisoners. Protection requires that offenders be offered a new story and set on the path of healing, so that they can eventually contribute to the community.

The focus of activities during incarceration should be the emergence of the human from his most dangerous vices, not punishment for punishment's sake. Such projects should help offenders make the commitment to undo their vices, free their intelligence, direct their existing skills to constructive ends, acquire new life skills, and release their generative desires to be productive citizens inside or outside prison. Offenders need to be helped to see that they are more than their habits and to confront the harm they have wrought by acting upon them.

Convicts' efforts to undo their habits must not be confused with either rehabilitation or therapy in the usual sense. Rehabilitation programs have the goal of producing predetermined behaviors (which convicts easily learn to fake) by coercing prisoners to meet the behavioral objectives of the prison system. Such programs are inevitably manipulative and driven by the old story's view of status and power. Deception and psychological manipulation are clearly immoral. Reconditioning ignores the qualitative and moral distinction between practical reasoning versus the determined, reactive promptings embedded in distressful recordings. The goal of dismantling vices is to release or free up the person's own thinking about how humans should treat one another, not provide him with a set of predetermined responses that he reactively calls forth. So-called counterconditioning may achieve short-term compliance, but it is not truly useful to a human in the long term. More conditioning just adds additional layers to their painful scripts from their previous violentization, especially their violent coaching. Significantly, in order to make good, offenders who give up a life of crime embrace a new story, which "is not seen as a matter of being resocialized or cured, but rather as a process of activating one's 'real me' and 'finding the diamond in the rough.' "[29]

The mental health model of therapy is also inappropriate to describe this new project. Too often, that model has focused on disorders or psychopathologies, which treat problems individualistically and without critical awareness of structural relations of power. Therapies encourage people to adapt or cope rather than counter the socially enforced forgetting of the traumatic nature of their conditioning and its socioeconomic roots.[30] The mental health model does not expect people to be able to act consistently outside their habits. Nor does it provide the necessary support for convicts to safely express the emotions that will inevitably arise as they begin to act outside their vices. By positing that there is something wrong with criminals, the medical model renders them passive organisms upon which pathogens wreak havoc. Most prisons view inmates as diseased, with inner pathologies.[31] In contrast, desisting offenders assume that their humanness enables them to be initiating, powerful, and responsible for changing the course of their lives. There is nothing wrong with them as humans, although there is much that is awry in how they have realized (or have not realized) their potentialities, how they have perceived themselves and others, and how they have acted.

If such services and attention are necessary to assist the offender's recovery, then doing evil seems to be rewarded, observes philosopher Lenn Goodman. But, he adds, restraint involves a significant loss of liberty that few voluntarily bequeath in exchange for help dismantling their habits.[32]

Programs aimed at dismantling habits require parameters to prevent their devolving into degraded retaliation. The moral limits on this project are not derived from the three Rs, but rather from the dignity of the criminal and those hurt by his actions. The dignities due each individual require that we morally condemn "the horrors of the familiar prison pecking order, sexual abuse, filth, brutality, or diminished health care."[33] Providing attention, creating safety, listening to stories, and facilitating emotional healing are not oppressive activities; offenders should be regarded as wanting to operate on a wider appreciation of their humanness, even if they cannot simply be trusted to do so at first and even if it takes great persistence to break through to the human inside them. Offenders, at minimum, need to give assent to receiving attention. Convicts need to be invited into such possibilities, not coerced. Assisting offenders to emerge from their conditioning can be done in ways that respect their autonomy. The justice-seeking intent of a new project, however, cannot guarantee that its own activities will be free from domination. Larger dimensions of injustice must also be addressed so that old habits do not corrupt this new project of justice.[34]

Significantly, this narrative about the human person who is identifiably distinct from the "not me" contradicts a main premise of the narrative of death. The old story assumes that offenders need to be shamed into owning up to their dreadful deeds, which leads to demeaning protocols such as placing prisoners in chains or in stocks.[35] "Shame-based 'technologies of the self' seek to 'subjectify' or 'responsibilize' offenders through the ritual of confession. In this framework, the only acceptable confession is one in which the person accepts complete and unmediated blame for an event."[36] Ironically, the very efforts of offenders to reclaim their humanness are condemned by the narrative of the lie. A correctional officer reports: "The inmate . . . believed he was a good person [and] he did not perceive this to be an error. . . . Clinging to this belief that he was essentially a decent person was deemed erroneous and further evidence of how deeply ingrained his criminal thinking was."[37] Maruna observes, "Importantly, interviewees rarely attributed negative behaviors to underlying personality defects or character weaknesses. . . . [T]he concessions used by interviewees regarded bad behaviors, not bad selves."[38]

U.S. culture is so thick with blame and shame that it is difficult for offenders to find a place outside that script. Taking the perspective of the lie means ascribing their difficulties to their nature, which "in Western culture would be tantamount to admitting they are irredeemable."[39] In order to render themselves forgivable, criminals must tell a "sad tale" or offer excuses.[40] Making excuses becomes an (ineffective) bid to be seen as a normal person, not a monster. The three Rs render excuses the "acceptable way" to deal with wrongdoing. As Maruna concludes, "Western societies may prefer pleasant lies ('it wasn't my fault') to the painful truth that good people [ontologically] often do bad things [morally]."[41] A truer narrative about the essential humanity of all people and the vulnerability of that goodness to corruption by damaging effects of unhealed mistreatment encourage truth telling, admission of guilt, and assumption of responsibility.

Convicts may perceive undoing their allegiance to their habits to be more onerous than serving time. Dismantling vices to the point that convicts can reliably be trusted not to act on them may take longer than a typical prison sentence. Responsibility requires something real from the offender. It means taking an honest look at what is inside them that has resulted in them causing such harm. Serving ten years may seem easy compared to facing, feeling, and dissolving mountains of pain and learning to live with who they were and what they did. Some will be unable to make the decision to abandon their habits.

Neither rehabilitation nor therapy demands anything comparable to what is required of offenders who, for example, participate in mediation programs, which assists offenders to step outside their habits and accept complete responsibility for their crimes.

Victim-offender mediations were initiated by Canadians in the 1970s in order to foster responsibility of juvenile offenders toward their victims. Mediations were intended for handling nonviolent crimes, but quickly expanded. The process must be initiated by the victim, and the offender has to take responsibility for the crime. The survivors, the perpetrator, and the mediator each go through about one hundred hours of preparation.[42]

Over a decade after fifteen-year-olds Gary Brown and Marion Berry raped and murdered Cathy O'Daniel, her now nineteen-year-old daughter, Ami, and Ami's grandmother, Linda White, participated in a Victim Offender Mediation/ Dialogue Program sponsored by the Texas Department of Criminal Justice. Linda recounts that it took her "13 years, two degrees, teaching in prison and a little coaxing to get to the point where she felt like she could meet the men who had raped and murdered Cathy."[43] Linda's granddaughter, Ami, "had always been ready." "I was always curious," Ami says. "They were 15 years old, and that really hit me, especially when I got to that age." Texas criminal justice officials forbade the participation of Marion Berry, deeming him psychiatrically "unsuited for the emotionally intensive process." "Despite nine months of preparation for this meeting, Brown was hyperventilating, trembling, and crying when the mediator brought him into the room with Ami and Linda. They, in turn, were shocked by how young he was, and "they never expected he would already be crying as he came in."

"The main thing I want you to get out of this Gary," Linda told him, "is I want you to know a lot about us and what the last 14 and half years have been like for us—not just the bad, the good things too . . . and I want to know the same things about you." She and Ami particularly wanted to know exactly what had happened the night of the murder. They met for six hours, with a break for lunch.

Mediations involve a process of symbolic reparation, which "depends on the emotional dynamics of the meeting and on the state of bonds between the participants," argues sociologist Thomas Scheff. He observes that "two separate movements of shame" occur in successful mediations. "First, *all shame must be removed from the victim*. . . . [I]t is the shame component—the victim's feeling that if only he or she had acted differently, the crime wouldn't have occurred—that leads to the most intense and protracted suffering." The offender removes shame from the victim by accepting "complete responsibility for the crime." However, "humiliating the offender in the conference makes it almost impossible for him both to accept responsibility and to help remove shame from the victim." The goal of the facilitator is to encourage the expression of painful emotions, such as grief and shame, and to "rechannel" the "aggressive ones, such as rage and anger." The latter can be "reframed" as being fueled by "hidden shame." The mutual reduction of shame accompanied by taking of responsibility is the "core sequence" of "emotional exchange," which "may be brief," yet "allows a preliminary bond to be formed between offender and victim." This bond is possible because the "offender's visible expression of emotion allows the victim to see the offender as a human being."[44]

Linda says in response to critics of such programs, "the process forces convicts to confront the personal tragedy they caused. If you commit an offense . . . you should *not be allowed* to go off and serve a passive prison sentence. You should have to face the victims." For those unable to fathom such meetings, she says, "They'll never get enough vengeance, because there isn't any." Gary, for his part, says "he's humbled by the kindness" shown him by the Whites. "I'm doing this because I done something wrong," he says. "I wanted to do everything I could to make things easier for them . . . any kind of relief that they could have, that's what I hoped would happen. I done something bad, but there's something good in me."[45]

Participating in mediation requires the willingness to feel, the courage to face reality, the cultivation of hope, and the determination to make change. Gary had to lay himself open in order to participate in a mediation program, confront his crime, show respect for the deceased as a person with a story and a community, find whatever ways he could to repair and mend by setting the survivors upright, and repent, even while acknowledging that his gesture of "setting things right" remained incomplete and partial.

Convicts' ability to function within society can be measured by their commitment to undo their vices, their ability to consistently drain away the tangled swamp at the root of their difficulties, their ability to act outside their vices for long periods, their commitment to secure help when they feel tempted to reactivate them, and their ability to regard themselves and others as humans worthy of respect.

JUSTICE AS MEETING NEEDS

The new story exposes an additional injustice: the community's failure to help people heal their wounds and emerge from their habits. People need sustained caring attention from interested others in order to shed the pain associated with heinous hurts. Being denied such help complicates peoples' justice seeking. The old story denies that humans need to or can heal, and therefore denies the injustice of failing to meet this need.

The vices that sustain the three Rs result partially from this injustice. Absent thorough emotional healing, mistreated people may persist in victimhood, vindictiveness, or vengeance. The desire to get even is not, therefore, a consequence solely of having been harmed, but also requires this extra wound of not receiving attention necessary to heal painful emotions systematically and thoroughly. Thus, vindictiveness is not a necessary moral or psychological response to harm, but one that results from additional deprivation. This injustice fuels the futile pursuit of the three Rs, thereby ensuring violence's repetition. It is only because so many are denied the opportunity to heal that they feel driven to seek relief through retaliatory violence.

The new story redefines the satisfaction of seeing "justice served." The satisfaction these survivors seek is not a vindictive desire to see their enemy suffer. Nor is it the satisfaction of the retributive desire to punish out of a sense of duty.

Rather, satisfaction comes, the new story suggests, from the confidence that civic trust will be restored by addressing the wrong, upholding the law, and helping people abandon their vices. Civic trust is restored partially by legal proceedings, public trials, and public condemnation of the crime. But restoring civic trust also requires meeting the needs of everyone affected by the crime. It means that the offender needs to be assisted in (not shamed or coerced into) acknowledging the harm done, making amends, offering redress, expressing remorse, offering an apology, and committing to undoing his vices. Justice involves helping offenders meet these needs without the imposition of sentences involving hard treatment, humiliation, or execution.

Using this new understanding of justice, restorative justice theorist Wesley Cragg proposes a new concept of sentencing that does not channel anger into retributive punishments, but seeks to dissipate it by constructive actions aimed at addressing genuine needs resulting from the crime.[46]

For offenses where the harm can be redressed through the making of amends, appropriate sentences might be restitution or reparation. By making gestures that acknowledge responsibility and express regret, such sentences "overcome the alienation" resulting from serious offenses. Reparations correct wrongs—not through some mysterious alchemy of rectification through suffering, but by meeting actual needs.[47]

Where the harms are intangible but real—terror or loss of trust—there is no redress that will "set things right." But survivors can heal from such wounds, if provided with enough attention over time.

There is no restitution for murder, strictly speaking.[48] But during the trial, steps can be taken to meet the needs of family members of the deceased. One key need is to have the offender become accountable for his crime. For example, an innovative program trains defense attorneys to help defendants acknowledge the harm they have wrought. Defense attorneys are coached so that they can help capital defendants become accountable, apart from what may or may not happen in the courtroom. Defense attorneys learn about how the criminal justice process affects victims and how homicide survivors are still hurt and angry, even though they may oppose capital punishment. Because murder victims' families who oppose the death penalty do not want to feel as though they are joining the defense, the emphasis of this effort is to teach the defense team to address the needs, concerns, and questions of the victim's family and to move the defendant to genuine statements that can mean so much to survivors.[49]

Homicide victims' families want to be included within justice practices, but not in ways that invite them to be vindictive, compete for victimhood with the killer, or become exploited by the state. Capital punishment cannot meet families' full needs for justice and healing.

JUSTICE AS RECLAMATION

Many homicide victims' family members who oppose the death penalty, however, continue to report dissatisfaction with almost every term in the lexicon of justice. Many reject revenge and retribution. But the idea of reparations or restitution strikes many as offensive and distasteful, as if there were some way to financially compensate for the loss of their family member. Many find the language of restorative justice distressing, because nothing will ever restore the deceased to life. These families reject the conclusion reached by many that the finality of death and the impossibility of adequate redress mean that execution is the only answer.

The concept of justice changes in this new story. Ultimately, the only response that will "fix" the situation is if people regain their humanity by emerging from their grief and rage, regaining their ability to connect with themselves and with others. In the long term, justice means the reclamation of human bonds. Able eventually to turn their attention from the crime scene to memories of the beloved's face, laughter, and humanness, for example, survivors' capacity for connection is slowly rekindled. Fellow feeling, a sense of belonging on the planet, a willingness to engage with others slowly returns to a life that had been reduced to the bare essentials of trying, sometimes unsuccessfully, to sleep, eat, or work. Establishing genuine connections with others enlarges one's capacity to take responsibility for how feelings are expressed and be responsive to the other. Justice enables *survivors* to reclaim themselves and to connect with others.

If survivors, perpetrators, and bystanders can reclaim their humanness, their discerning vision, and their birthright of connection, then there is hope that the retaliatory cycle will stop.

The new story cautions that reclaiming one's humanness can never be fully secured within an unjust society. People cannot be fully human themselves while remaining in institutions that fail to meet needs, withhold respect based on race, class, or gender, and pressure people to abandon important aspects of themselves, such as their caring, connection, and creativity. Complete integrity is not attainable while fellow humans are enslaved by external structures of domination or their internalization of lies. Healing from personal tragedy or injustice involves healing in relation to a society that fails to meet people's most basic needs for education, food, shelter, and caring attention, and that fail to prevent the violentization of its citizens in their homes and institutions. People cannot be fully restored to their humanness or their connection to others without jointly working to make the society truly just for all.

THE VIRTUE OF RESPONSIBILITY: GETTING INVOLVED
Responsibility entails involvement in efforts to correct and transform unjust social structures.

Bystanders cannot rely on politicians, bureaucrats, or experts in mental health or criminal justice "to fix it." Responsibility requires each bystander to clear up enough of her own hurts to be able to listen to others and help them enlarge their capacities for moral goodness and personal agency. Getting involved means acquiring the skills to lend a hand to others.[50] This mobilization is not about "doing good," but about fundamental human liberation through assisting people to regain their powers of responsiveness and responsible human agency.

The first question of the new story is not "What are my rights?" but "To whom am I bound in a web of mutuality?" The second question is not "Who is to blame for this mess?" or "Whose fault is this?" but "What can I do to move things forward; where can I make a difference?" And finally, the question is not "How can I help?" but "What is needed to reclaim myself and others and correct injustice?"

Bystanders can undertake initiatives in which they offer attention to fellow citizens. For example, an innovative program called United to End Racism sponsors "listening projects."[51] Participants are trained in the art of listening nondefensively. A small group then sets up a table in a public place with a sign with a single question on it such as "What do you think should be done to end racism?" The project could easily be adapted to ask "What are possible alternatives to the death penalty?" The trained listeners take turns listening to busy passersby, who stop to share their feelings and flashes of insight. Treated respectfully, people push through the anger, fear, or confusion to reach for their ideas. Such small measures encourage bystanders to notice their feelings about a problem and apply their intelligence to it.

Stigma still clings to victims of crime—associations with being lower class, dirty, or deserving of maltreatment persist. Bystanders can interrupt habits of silence and shunning by practicing hospitality. Bystanders can welcome survivors into their lives, listen to their stories, and welcome emotional healing. Bystanders can affirm victims' dignity by recalling their names and marking the anniversary of the crime. Bystanders can tell survivors a truthful story that they or their beloved did not deserve to be harmed, that explains both the malefactors' humanity and inhuman patterns, and that unflinchingly condemns the foul deed and the notion of the offender's lack of integrity. They can lend their ears and hearts to the children who have been brutalized, to the belligerent youth who see no option but to become violent, or to offenders locked within their habits. Rather than stigmatize offenders and isolate them, the community can usher them into an environment that *counteracts* the notion that some people deserve grave harm. The community can make demonstrable efforts to prevent crime. Such constructive actions build civic trust, foster accountability, and correct injustice.

   Liberation from the three Rs will require a two-pronged effort—to secure permanent attitude change and to change institutions. To create practices that protect life in community, secure justice, and foster responsibility, Americans must undo their profound habituation in the three Rs, liberating their voices and vision. If not, proposed alternatives are likely to remain stuck in old mindsets. Several U.S. states once prohibited the death penalty, only to reinstate it. Although the death penalty may be abolished eventually through legislative fiat, it will take a long-term commitment to transform attitudes and institutions. Cutting the cords that bind and blind—one by one and person by person—is necessary to successfully create a society that protects its citizens while correcting injustice.

   Liberating people's hearts and minds will be neither easy nor swift. But Americans can work now to build a legacy of hope and resistance by meeting genuine needs of survivors, perpetrators, and their communities; condemning hard treatment as self-defeating, incoherent, and immoral; and listening for an ever-truer story about humans, why they harm, and what restores people to their birthright of goodness. As Americans free themselves from habits and the cover story, they can honor and protect life, justice, and responsibility by means other than painful penalties. Justice envisioned as restoring humans to themselves and others is the only true "stop."

NOTES

   1. Mary Elizabeth Hobgood, *Dismantling Privilege: An Ethics of Accountability* (Cleveland, OH, Pilgrim, 2000), 9.
   2. Lee Anne Bell, "Theoretical Foundations for Social Justice Education," in *Teaching for Diversity and Social Justice: A Sourcebook*, ed. Maurianne Adams, Lee Anne Bell, and Pat Griffin (New York: Routledge, 1997), 5.
   3. Bell, "Theoretical Foundations," 5.
   4. Bell, "Theoretical Foundations," 11.
   5. Bell, "Theoretical Foundations," 7.
   6. See Philip Greven, *Spare the Child: The Religious Roots of Punishment and the Psychological Impact of Physical Abuse* (New York: Vintage, 1990).
   7. Dennis Sullivan and Larry Tifft, *Restorative Justice: Healing the Foundations of Our Everyday Lives* (Monsey, NY: Willow Tree, 2001), 104–105, 150–55.
   8. Laurence M. Thomas, *Vessels of Evil: American Slavery and the Holocaust* (Philadelphia: Temple University Press, 1993), chs. 2 and 3.
   9. Jeffrey Reiman, *The Rich Get Richer and the Poor Get Prison*, 6th ed. (Boston: Allyn and Bacon, 2001), 68, 159.

10. For an analysis of how no one takes responsibility for executions, see Robert Jay Lifton and Greg Mitchell, *Who Owns Death? Capital Punishment, the American Conscience, and the End of Executions* (New York: HarperCollins, 2000).

11. Paul Craig Roberts, "A Prison State, If Not a Police State," *LewRockwell.com*, 4 May 2004, available at www.lewrockwell.com/roberts/roberts43.html (accessed 6 May 2004).

12. Austin Sarat, *When the State Kills: Capital Punishment and the American Condition* (Princeton, NJ: Princeton University Press, 2001), 250.

13. Thandeka, *Learning to Be White: Money, Race, and God in America* (New York: Continuum, 1999), ch. 1.

14. Wesley Cragg argues that the death penalty undermines public confidence in the law, observing: "For a society to have to use this ultimate weapon, there must be real doubt that a significant number of people can be trusted to obey even the most fundamental of laws in the absence of this form of response." *The Practice of Punishment: Towards a Theory of Restorative Justice* (New York: Routledge, 1992), 189.

15. For a more thorough examination of the difference between virtues and vices, see Judith W. Kay, "Getting Egypt Out of the People: Aquinas's Contributions to Liberation," in *Aquinas and Empowerment: Classical Ethics for Ordinary Lives*, ed. G. Simon Harak (Washington, DC: Georgetown University Press, 1996), 29–33.

16. For an explication of the relation of vices to the human host, see Judith W. Kay, "Politics without Human Nature? Reconstructing a Common Humanity," *Hypatia: A Journal of Feminist Philosophy* 9, no. 1 (Winter 1994): 21–52.

17. For discussion of these elements within the context of forgiveness, see Robert D. Enright and Joanna North, eds., *Exploring Forgiveness* (Madison: University of Wisconsin Press, 1998).

18. For an analysis of "common-sense morality," see Thomas, *Vessels of Evil*, 45ff.

19. Iris Marion Young, *Justice and the Politics of Difference* (Princeton, NJ: Princeton University Press, 1990), 148, 149, 152.

20. Erica Sherover-Marcuse, *Emancipation and Consciousness* (Oxford: Basil Blackwell, 1986): 137–42.

21. Young, *Justice*, 150.

22. Young, *Justice*, 151, 152.

23. Thomas J. Scheff, *Catharsis in Healing, Ritual, and Drama*, reprint edition (originally published 1979; Lincoln, NE: iUniverse.com, 2001), 54–63.

24. Katie Kauffman and Caroline New, *Co-Counselling: The Theory and Practice of Re-Evaluation Counselling* (New York: Brunner-Routledge, 2004), ch. 4, and Harvey Jackins, *Reclaiming Power* (Seattle: Rational Island, 1983), 48–49.

25. Sherover-Marcuse, *Emancipation*, 137–42.

26. Many in the United States believe that anger justifies punishment, since as Diedre Golash says, punishment has been the old story's way of expressing the outrage of survivors and communities. She observes that U.S. culture "tends to glorify anger and to regard it as an inevitable feature of social interaction. The claim to be angry is often made with some pride; the person who strikes, or even kills, another out of uncontrollable anger is one kind of folk hero." "Anger," Golash notes, "fits in well with our rather egalitarian, yet competitive and atomistic view of social life; one has the right to be angry with almost anyone, and there is no particular reason to think they have considered your interests, or that you should consider theirs." Deirdre Golash, "Punishment and Anger," 21, available at gurukul.ucc.american.edu/golah/emotions.htm (accessed 1 April 2004).

27. Hatred comes from a profound disconnection of the person from herself and from others. There is nothing moral about hatred of humans, although condemning their vicious behaviors is morally appropriate.

28. Cragg argues, "The law creates a protective framework whose justification rests on its capacity to reduce the use of force in settling disputes and thus enhance the capacity of those falling under its authority to pursue goals in ways that would not otherwise be possible." *Practice of Punishment*, 176.

29. Shadd Maruna, *Making Good* (Washington, DC: American Psychological Association, 2001) 95.

30. Sherover-Marcuse, *Emancipation*, 140.

31. Maruna, *Making Good*, 139.

32. Lenn E. Goodman, *On Justice: An Essay in Jewish Philosophy* (New Haven, CT: Yale University Press, 1991), 60.

33. Goodman, *Justice*, 72.

34. For example, restorative justice focuses on financial restitution to victims by offenders, ignoring that the original motivation for the theft or drug use may have been poverty, lack of job training, or other barriers to economic parity.

35. Warren Richy, "In Alabama, Prisoners Fight Being Shackled," *Christian Science Monitor*, 17 April 2002, available at www.csmonitor.com/2002/0417/p02s02-usju.html (accessed 8 May 2004).

36. Maruna, *Making Good*, 132.

37. Maruna, *Making Good*, 132.

38. Maruna, *Making Good*, 136.

39. Maruna, *Making Good*, 145.

40. Maruna, *Making Good*, 145.

41. Maruna, *Making Good*, 145.

42. "Victim Offender Mediation/Dialogue," *Texas Department of Criminal Justice*, available at www.tdcj.state.tx.us/victim/victim-vomd.htm (accessed 2 May 2004).

43. All the quotes in this account are taken from Scott Nowell, "Face to Face," *Houston Press*, 27 September 2001, available at www.houstonpress.com/issues/2001-09-27/feature.html (accessed 3 May 2004).

44. Thomas J. Scheff, "Community Conferences: Shame and Anger in Therapeutic Jurisprudence," *La Revista Jurídica de la Universidad de Puerto Rico* 67, no. 2 (1998): 102, 105, 106, 117, 107.

45. Nowell, "Face to Face."

46. Cragg, *Practice of Punishment*, final chapter.

47. Vermont Department of Corrections director John Perry said at a national conference that the results of a state survey found that residents wanted offenders to give something back to the community, such as labor, service, or amending the wrong (where possible) rather than punishment. Remarks made at the Third Annual Justice Studies Association Conference on Restorative Justice, Norton, Massachusetts, May 2001.

48. Judith W. Kay, "Is Restitution Possible for Murder? Surviving Family Members Speak," in *Wounds That Do Not Bind: Victim-Based Perspectives on the Death Penalty*, ed. James Acker and David Karp (Durham, NC: Carolina Academic, forthcoming).

49. See "Working with Defense Attorneys," *The Voice: Murder Victims' Families for Reconciliation* (Spring/Summer 2004): 7.

50. Pamela A. Roby argues for extending mediations to schools and other arenas. "Community Conferencing in Therapeutic Jurisprudence: Perspectives on the Victim-Offender Emotional Exchange," *La Revista Jurídica de la Universidad de Puerto Rico* 67, no. 3 (1998): 645–51.

51. United to End Racism's pamphlet suggests various meeting formats. *Working Together to End Racism: Healing from the Damage Caused by Racism* (Seattle: Rational Island, 2002), 25, 40.

Bibliography

Amnesty International USA. "Killing with Prejudice: Race and the Death Penalty." Amnesty International's Campaign on the United States, May 1999. Available at web.amnesty.org/library/index/engamr510521999 (accessed 11 June 2003).

Aquinas, Thomas. *Summa Theologiae*. New York: Blackfriars, 1972.

Arendt, Hannah. *Eichmann in Jerusalem: A Report on the Banality of Evil*. Revised and enlarged. New York: Penguin, 1994.

Athens, Lonnie H. *The Creation of Dangerous Violent Criminals*. Chicago: University of Illinois Press, 1992.

———. *Violent Criminal Acts and Actors Revisited*. Chicago: University of Illinois Press, 1997.

Augustine. *City of God*. Edited by David Knowles. New York. Penguin, 1981.

Aynesworth, Hugh. "Banks' Execution Expected to Proceed." *Washington Times*, 12 March 2003, A05.

Bailie, Gil. *Violence Unveiled: Humanity at the Crossroads*. New York: Crossroad, 1996.

Baird, Robert M., and Stuart E. Rosenbaum, eds. *Punishment and the Death Penalty: The Current Debate*. Amherst, NY: Prometheus, 1995.

Banner, Stuart. *The Death Penalty: An American History*. Cambridge, MA: Harvard University Press, 2002.

Barcalow, Emmett. *Moral Philosophy: Theory and Issues*. Belmont, CA: Wadsworth, 1994.

Barnes, Harry Elmer. *The Story of Punishment: A Record of Man's Inhumanity to Man*. 2nd ed. Originally published in 1930. Montclair, NJ: Patterson Smith, 1972.

Barnett, Victoria J. *Bystanders: Conscience and Complicity during the Holocaust*. Westport, CT: Praeger, 2000.

Bedau, Hugo A., ed. *The Death Penalty in America: Current Controversies.* New York: Oxford University Press, 1997.

Bell, Lee Anne. "Theoretical Foundations for Social Justice Education." In *Teaching for Diversity and Social Justice: A Sourcebook,* ed. Maurianne Adams, Lee Anne Bell, and Pat Griffin, 3–15. New York: Routledge, 1997.

Bellah, Robert N., Richard Madsen, William M. Sullivan, Ann Swidler, and Steven M. Tipton. *Habits of the Heart: Individualism and Commitment in American Life.* Berkeley: University of California Press, 1985.

Billah, Yusuf, and Robert Scanlan. "Resonance, Tacoma Narrows Bridge Failure, and Undergraduate Physics Textbooks." *American Journal of Physics* 59, no. 2 (1991): 118–24.

Blumenthal, Laura. *Revenge: A Story of Hope.* New York: Washington Square, 2002.

Bosco, Antoinette. *Choosing Mercy: A Mother of Murder Victims Pleads to End the Death Penalty.* Maryknoll, NY: Orbis, 2001.

Botkin, Jeffrey R., William M. McMahon, and Leslie P. Francis, eds. *Genetics and Criminality: The Potential Misuse of Scientific Information in Court.* Washington, DC: American Psychological Association, 1999.

Braithwaite, John. *Crime, Shame and Reintegration.* New York: Cambridge University Press, 1989.

Braithwaite, John, and S. Mugford. "Conditions of Successful Reintegration Ceremonies: Dealing with Juvenile Offenders." *British Journal of Criminology* 34, no. 2 (1994): 139–71.

Brendtro, Larry, Martin Brokenleg, and Steve Van Bockern. *Reclaiming Youth at Risk: Our Hope for the Future.* Bloomington, IN: National Educational Service, 1998.

Brickman. P., et. al. "Models of Helping and Coping." *American Psychologist* 37, no. 2 (1982): 368–84.

Bright, Stephen B. "Discrimination, Death and Denial: The Tolerance of Racial Discrimination in Infliction of the Death Penalty." *Santa Clara Law Review* (1995): 437. Available at www.schr.org/racial/index.html, 14 (accessed 10 July 2002).

Brison, Susan J. *Aftermath: Violence and the Remaking of a Self.* Princeton, NJ: Princeton University Press, 2002.

Brock, Rita Nakashima, and Rebecca Parker. *Proverbs of Ashes: Violence, Redemptive Suffering, and the Search for What Saves Us.* Boston: Beacon, 2001.

Brugger, E. Christian. *Capital Punishment and the Roman Catholic Moral Tradition.* Notre Dame, IN: University of Notre Dame Press, 2003.

Brunk, Conrad G. "Restorative Justice and the Philosophical Theories of Criminal Punishment." In *The Spiritual Roots of Restorative Justice,* edited by Michael L. Hadley, 31–56. Albany: State University of New York Press, 2001.

Burggraeve, Roger. "Violence and the Vulnerable Face of the Other: The Vision of Emmanuel Levinas on Moral Evil and Our Responsibility." *Journal of Social Philosophy* 30, no. 1 (Spring 1999): 17–46.

Burnside, Jonathan, and Nicola Baker, eds. *Relational Justice: Repairing the Breach.* Winchester, England: Waterside, 1994.

Cabana, Donald. *Death at Midnight: The Confession of an Executioner.* Boston: Northeastern University Press, 1996.

Camus, Albert. "Reflections on the Guillotine." In *Resistance, Rebellion, and Death,* translated by Justin O'Brien. Originally published in 1957. New York: Vintage International, 1995.

Christoph, James B. *Capital Punishment and British Politics: The British Movement to Abolish the Death Penalty 1945–57.* Chicago: University of Chicago Press, 1962.

Coombs, Mary. "A Brave New Crime-Free World?" In *Genetics and Criminality: The Potential Misuse of Scientific Information in Court,* ed. Jeffrey R. Botkin, William M. McMahon, and Leslie Pickering Francis, 227–42. Washington, DC: American Psychological Association, 1999.

Cragg, Wesley. *The Practice of Punishment: Towards a Theory of Restorative Justice.* New York: Routledge, 1992.

———, ed. *Retributivism and Its Critics.* Stuttgart: Steiner, 1992.

"The Cruel and Ever More Unusual Punishment." *Economist,* 13 May 1999. Available at psy.ucsd.edu/~eebbesen/psych16298/162DeathPenaltyArticle.html (accessed 13 August 2003).

Cushing, Robert R., and Susannah Sheffer. *Dignity Denied: The Experience of Murder Victims' Family Members Who Oppose the Death Penalty.* Cambridge, MA: Murder Victims' Families for Reconciliation, 2002.

Dallas Morning News, 8 March 1992. Available at www.deathpenaltyinfo.org/article.php?did=108&scid=7 (accessed 13 August 2003).

Daly, Kathleen. "Revisiting the Relationship between Retributive and Restorative Justice." In *Restorative Justice: Philosophy to Practice,* edited by Heather Strang and John Braithwaite, 33–54. Burlington, VT: Ashgate, 2000.

Death Penalty Information Center. "Innocence: Freed from Death Row." Available at www.deathpenaltyinfo.org/Innocentlist.html (accessed 3 June 2003).

Death Penalty Information Center. "Juveniles and the Death Penalty." Available at www.deathpenaltyinfo.org/article.php?did=205&scid=27 (accessed 14 July 2003).

Denn, Rebekah. "Dispute Embroils Killer's Request to Die." *Seattle Post-Intelligencer,* 7 July 2001. Available at seattlepi.nwsource.com'local/30451_elledgex07.shtml (accessed 18 July 2001).

Dieter, Richard. "The Death Penalty in Black and White." Death Penalty Information Center. June 1998. Available at www.deathpenaltyinfo.org/article.php?scid=45&did=539 (accessed 11 June 2003).

Enright, Robert D., and Joanna North, eds. *Exploring Forgiveness.* Madison: University of Wisconsin Press, 1998.

Feinberg, Joel. *Doing and Deserving: Essays in the Theory of Responsibility.* Princeton, NJ: Princeton University Press, 1970.

Fingarette, Herbert. *On Responsibility.* New York: Basic, 1967.

Finnis, John. *Natural Law and Natural Rights.* Oxford: Clarendon, 1982.

Foucault, Michel. *Discipline and Punish: The Birth of the Prison.* Translated by Alan Sheridan. New York: Vintage, 1977.

French, Peter A. *The Virtues of Vengeance.* Lawrence: University Press of Kansas, 2001.

Friedlander, Henry. *The Origins of Nazi Genocide: From Euthanasia to the Final Solution.* Chapel Hill: University of North Carolina Press, 1995.

Garvey, Stephen P., ed. *Beyond Repair? America's Death Penalty.* Durham, NC: Duke University Press, 2003.

"Gene Links Child Abuse with Later Violence." Tacoma *News Tribune,* 2 August 2002, A-16.

Gilligan, James. *Violence: Our Deadly Epidemic and Its Causes.* New York: Putnam's Sons, 1996.

———. *Preventing Violence.* New York: Thames & Hudson, 2001.

Golash, Deirdre. "Punishment and Anger." Available at gurukul.ucc.american.edu/dgolash/emotions (accessed 1 April 2004).

Goodman, Lenn E. *On Justice: An Essay in Jewish Philosophy.* New Haven, CT: Yale University Press, 1991.

Gorringe, Timothy. *God's Just Vengeance: Crime, Violence and the Rhetoric of Salvation.* Cambridge: Cambridge University Press, 1996.

Govier, Trudy. *Forgiveness and Revenge.* London: Routledge, 2002.

Greg, William Rathbone. *Enigmas of Life.* Originally published in 1872. Freeport, NY: Books for Libraries, 1972.

"*Gregg v. Georgia,* 1976: The Death Penalty Is Not Per Se Unconstitutional." In *The Death Penalty in America: Current Controversies,* ed. by Hugo A. Bedau. New York: Oxford University Press, 1997.

Greven, Philip. *Spare the Child: The Religious Roots of Punishment and the Psychological Impact of Physical Abuse.* New York: Vintage, 1990.

Gross, Samuel R., and Phoebe C. Ellsworth. "Second Thoughts: Americans' Views on the Death Penalty at the Turn of the Century." In *Beyond Repair? America's Death Penalty,* edited by Stephen P. Garvey, 7–57. Durham, NC: Duke University Press, 2003.

Gross, Samuel R., and Daniel J. Matheson. "What They Say at the End: Capital Victims' Families and the Press." *Cornell Law Review* 88, no. 2 (January 2003): 486–516.

Haney, Craig. "Mitigation and the Study of Lives: On the Roots of Violent Criminality and the Nature of Capital Justice." In *America's Experiment with Capital Punishment*, edited by James Acker, Robert Bohm, and Charles Lanier, 351–84. Durham, NC: Carolina Academic, 1998.

Harak, G. Simon. *Virtuous Passions: The Formation of Christian Character.* Mahwah, NJ: Paulist, 1993.

Hare, Harpur T. "Assessment of Psychopathy as a Function of Age." *Journal of Abnormal Psychology* 103, no. 4 (November 1994): 604–609.

Harrison, Paige, and Allen Beck. "Prisoners in 2003 (NCJ-205335)." *Bureau of Justice Statistics.* Available at www.ojp.usdoj.gov/bjs/abstract/p03.htm (accessed 5 January 2005).

Hart, H. L. A. *Punishment and Responsibility: Essays in the Philosophy of Law.* New York: Oxford University Press, 1968.

Herman, Judith L. *Trauma and Recovery.* New York: Basic, 1997.

Hobgood, Mary Elizabeth. *Dismantling Privilege: An Ethics of Accountability.* Cleveland, OH: Pilgrim, 2000.

Hood, Barbara, and Rachel King, eds. *Not in Our Name: Murder Victims' Families Speak Out against the Death Penalty.* 3rd. ed. Cambridge, MA: Murder Victims' Families for Reconciliation, 1999.

Howard, Jeanette Star. "Compassion and Capital Punishment." *Washington Coalition to Abolish the Death Penalty Newsletter* 15, no. 4 (Autumn 2000): 6.

Jackins, Harvey. *Reclaiming Power.* Seattle: Rational Island, 1983.

———. *The Human Side of Human Beings.* 25th printing, revised. Seattle: Rational Island, 1994.

Jackson, Derrick Z. "Bush's Death Factory." *Boston Globe,* 25 October 2000, A17.

Jacoby, Susan. *Wild Justice: The Evolution of Revenge.* New York: Harper & Row, 1983.

John Paul II, Pope. *The Gospel of Life: On the Value and Inviolability of Human Life (Evangelium Vitae).* Washington, DC: United States Catholic Conference, 1995.

"Juveniles and the Death Penalty." Death Penalty Information Center. Available at www.deathpenaltyinfo.org/article.php?sdid=205&scid=27 (accessed 14 July 2003).

Kaminer, Wendy. *It's All the Rage: Crime and Culture.* New York: Addison-Wesley, 1995.

Kant, Immanuel. *Metaphysical Elements of Justice.* Translated by John Ladd. Indianapolis: Bobbs-Merrill, 1965.

Kateb, George. *Hannah Arendt: Politics, Conscience, Evil.* Totowa, NJ: Rowman and Allanheld, 1983.

Kauffman, Katie, and Caroline New. *Co-Counselling: The Theory and Practice of Re-Evaluation Counselling.* New York: Brunner-Routledge, 2004.

Kay, Alan F. "A New Framework for Our Prisons." *America* 141, no. 3 (August 1979): 46–48.

Kay, Judith W. "Politics without Human Nature? Reconstructing a Common Humanity." *Hypatia: A Journal of Feminist Philosophy* 9, no. 1 (Winter 1994): 21–52.

———. "Getting Egypt Out of the People: Aquinas's Contributions to Liberation." In *Aquinas and Empowerment: Classical Ethics for Ordinary Lives*, edited by G. Simon Harak, 1–46. Washington, DC: Georgetown University Press, 1996.

———. "In the Shadow of the Execution Chamber." In *Practice What You Preach*, edited by James F. Keenan and Joseph Kotva, 115–27. Franklin, WI: Sheed and Ward, 1999.

———. "Is Restitution Possible for Murder? Surviving Family Members Speak." In *Wounds That Do Not Bind: Victim-Based Perspectives on the Death Penalty*, edited by James Acker and David Karp. Durham, NC: Carolina Academic, forthcoming.

———. "Murder Victims' Families for Reconciliation: Story-telling for Healing, as Witness, and in Public Policy." In *Handbook of Restorative Justice: A Global Perspective*, edited by Dennis Sullivan and Larry Tifft. New York: Routledge, forthcoming.

Kennedy, Eugene. "Inner Peace Restored for Victims' Families When Murderer Is Executed." *National Catholic Reporter* 35, no. 33 (2 July 1999): 21

Kershnar, Stephen. *Desert, Retribution, and Torture*. Lanham, MD: University Press of America, 2001.

King, Rachel. *Don't Kill in Our Names: Families of Murder Victims Speak Out against the Death Penalty*. New Brunswick, NJ: Rutgers University Press, 2003.

Koestler, Arthur. *Reflections on Hanging*. New York: Macmillan, 1957.

Lewontin, Richard. *It Ain't Necessarily So: The Dream of the Human Genome and Other Illusions*. 2nd ed. New York: New York Review of Books, 2001.

Lifton, Robert Jay, and Mitchell, Greg. *Who Owns Death? Capital Punishment, the American Conscience, and the End of Executions*. New York: HarperCollins, 2000.

Liptak, Adam. "Sentences Are Too Long or Too Short. Rarely, Just Right." *New York Times*, 24 August 2003: WK3.

Lorde, Audre. "The Master's Tools Will Never Dismantle the Master's House." In Audre Lorde, *Sister Outsider: Essays and Speeches*. Trumansburg, NY: Crossing, 1984.

MacIntyre, Alasdair. *After Virtue*. 2nd ed. Notre Dame, IN: University of Notre Dame Press, 1984.

———. *Whose Justice? Which Rationality?* Notre Dame, IN: University of Notre Dame Press, 1988.

Malcolm X. *The Autobiography of Malcolm X*. New York: Ballantine, 1964.

Marongiu, Pietro, and Graeme Newman. *Vengeance: The Fight against Injustice*. Totowa, NJ: Rowman & Littlefield, 1987.

Marshall, Christopher D. *Beyond Retribution: A New Testament Vision for Justice, Crime, and Punishment.* Grand Rapids, MI: Eerdmans, 2001.

Maruna, Shadd. *Making Good: How Ex-Convicts Reform and Rebuild Their Lives.* Washington, DC: American Psychological Association, 2001.

Mednick, Sarnoff A., Terrie E. Moffitt, and Susan A. Stack, eds. *The Causes of Crime: New Biological Approaches.* Cambridge: Cambridge University Press, 1987.

Megivern, James J. *The Death Penalty: An Historical and Theological Survey.* New York: Paulist, 1997.

Menninger, Karl. *The Crime of Punishment.* New York: Viking, 1969.

Midgley, Mary. *Wickedness: A Philosophical Essay.* New York: Routledge, 1984.

Miller, William Ian. *Humiliation and Other Essays on Honor, Social Discomfort, and Violence.* Ithaca, NY: Cornell University Press, 1993.

Moffitt, T. E., and S. A. Mednick, eds. *Biological Contributions to Crime Causation.* Boston: Martinus Nijhoff, 1988.

Moldin, Steven O. "Genetic Research on Mental Disorders." In *Genetics and Criminality: The Potential Misuse of Scientific Information in Court,* ed. Jeffrey R. Botkin, William M. McMahon, and Leslie Pickering Francis, 115–49. Washington, DC: American Psychological Association, 1999).

Morris, Herbert. "Persons and Punishment." *Monist* 52 (October 1968): 475–501.

Murder Victims Families for Reconciliation. "Not In Our Names." Available at www .mvfr.org/ (accessed 20 June 2003).

Murphy, Jeffrie G. *Retribution, Justice, and Therapy: Essays in the Philosophy of Law.* Dordrecht, Netherlands: Reidel, 1979.

——. *Getting Even: Forgiveness and Its Limits.* New York: Oxford University Press, 2003.

Murphy, Jeffrie G., and Jean Hampton. *Forgiveness and Mercy.* Cambridge: Cambridge University Press, 1988.

Murray, Les. "The Averted." *New Yorker,* 17 March 2003, 68.

Naanes, Marlene. "Victim's Mom Changes Death Penalty Stance." In *Baton Rouge Advocate,* 17 September 2003, 7B.

Nathanson, Donald L. *Shame and Pride: Affect, Sex, and the Birth of the Self.* New York: Norton, 1992.

Nathanson, Stephen. *An Eye for an Eye? The Morality of Punishing by Death.* Totowa, NJ: Rowman & Littlefield, 1987.

——. *Economic Justice.* Upper Saddle River, NJ: Prentice Hall, 1998.

——. "Is the Death Penalty What Murderers Deserve?" In *Criminal Justice Ethics,* edited by Paul Leighton and Jeffrey Reiman, 416–23. Upper Saddle River, NJ: Prentice Hall, 2001.

———. "Why We Should Put the Death Penalty to Rest." Unpublished manuscript.

Nelkin, Dorothy, and M. Susan Lindee. *The DNA Mystique: The Gene as a Cultural Icon.* New York: Freeman, 1995.

Nhat Hanh, Thich. *Anger: Wisdom for Cooling the Flames.* New York: Riverhead, 2001.

Nichols, Michael P., and Melvin Zax. *Catharsis in Psychotherapy.* New York: Gardner, 1977.

Niebuhr, Reinhold. *Moral Man and Immoral Society.* New York: Scribner's Sons, 1932.

Nietzsche, Friedrich. *The Birth of Tragedy and The Genealogy of Morals.* Translated by Francis Golffing. New York: Doubleday Anchor, 1956.

Nowell, Scott. "Face to Face." *Houston Press,* 27 September 2001. Available at www .houstonpress.com/issues/2001-09-27/feature.html (accessed 8 May 2004).

Nozick, Robert. *Philosophical Explanations.* Cambridge, MA: Harvard University Press, 1981.

Nussbaum, Martha C. *The Fragility of Goodness: Luck and Ethics in Greek Tragedy and Philosophy.* New York: Cambridge University Press, 1986.

———. *The Therapy of Desire: Theory and Practice in Hellenistic Ethics.* Princeton, NJ: Princeton University Press, 1994.

———. *Sex and Social Justice.* New York: Oxford University Press, 1999.

Ostapiak, Mark. "Death Penalty Is Racist and Targets the Poor." *Socialist Action,* May 2001. Available at www.socialistaction.org/news/200105/death.html (accessed 13 August 2003).

Pagels, Elaine. *Adam, Eve, and the Serpent.* New York: Random House, 1988.

Parker, Rebecca. "The Cross, the Death of Jesus, and a Violent Culture." Lecture delivered at the University of Puget Sound, Tacoma, Washington, March 2000.

Pearson, Patricia. *When She Was Bad: How and Why Women Get Away with Murder.* New York: Penguin, 1998.

"The Percentage of Homicides Cleared by Arrest Has Been Declining." Bureau of Justice Statistics. Available at www.ojp.usdoj.gov/bjs/homicide/cleared.htm (accessed 2 June 2003).

Perlin, Michael L. "Big Ideas, Images, and Distorted Facts." In *Genetics and Criminality: The Potential Misuse of Scientific Information in Court,* ed. Jeffrey R. Botkin, William M. McMahon, and Leslie Pickering Francis, 37–66. Washington, DC: American Psychological Association, 1999.

Plato. *The Laws of Plato.* Translated by Thomas L. Pangle. New York: Basic, 1980.

Pojman, Louis P., and Jeffrey Reiman. *The Death Penalty: For and Against.* Lanham, MD: Rowman & Littlefield, 1998.

Prejean, Helen. *Dead Man Walking.* New York: Random House, 1993.

Primoratz, Igor. *Justifying Legal Punishment.* Atlantic Highlands, NJ: Humanities Press International, 1989.

Prothrow-Stith, Deborah, with Michaele Weissman. *Deadly Consequences: How Violence Is Destroying Our Teenage Population and a Plan to Begin Solving the Problem.* New York: HarperCollins, 1991.

Rawls, John. "Two Concepts of Rules." In *John Rawls: Collected Papers,* edited by Samuel Freeman, 20–46. Cambridge, MA: Harvard University Press, 1999.

Reid, Frances, and Deborah Hoffman, directors. Video. *Long Night's Journey into Day: South Africa's Search for Truth and Reconciliation.* San Francisco: California Newsreel, 2000.

Reiman, Jeffrey. *The Rich Get Richer and the Poor Get Prison.* 6th ed. Boston: Allyn and Bacon, 2001.

Rhodes, Richard. *Why They Kill: The Discoveries of a Maverick Criminologist.* New York: Vintage, 1999.

Richy, Warren. "In Alabama, Prisoners Fight Being Shackled." *Christian Science Monitor,* 17 April 2002. Available at www.csmonitor.com/2002/0417/p02s02-usju.html (accessed 8 May 2004).

Rieber, Robert W. *Manufacturing Social Distress: Psychopathy in Everyday Life.* New York: Plenum, 1997.

Roberts, Paul Craig. "A Prison State, If Not a Police State." 4 May 2004. Available at www.lewrockwell.com/roberts/roberts43.html (accessed 6 May 2004).

Roby, Pamela A. "Community Conferencing in Therapeutic Jurisprudence: Perspectives on the Victim-Offender Emotional Exchange." *La Revista Jurídica de la Universidad de Puerto Rico* 67, no. 3 (1998): 645–51.

Sarat, Austin. *When the State Kills: Capital Punishment and the American Condition.* Princeton, NJ: Princeton University Press, 2001.

Sardin, Theodore R., ed. *Narrative Psychology: The Storied Nature of Human Conduct.* New York: Praeger, 1986.

Scheff, Thomas J. "Community Conferences: Shame and Anger in Therapeutic Jurisprudence." *La Revista Jurídica de la Universidad de Puerto Rico* 67, no. 2 (1998): 97–119.

———. *Catharsis in Healing, Ritual, and Drama.* Originally published in 1979. Lincoln, NE: iUniverse.com, 2001.

Schlosser, Eric. "A Grief Like No Other." *Atlantic Monthly* 280, no. 3 (September 1997): 37–76.

Schreiter, Robert J. *Reconciliation: Mission and Ministry in a Changing Social Order.* Maryknoll, NY: Orbis, 1992.

———. *The Ministry of Reconciliation: Spirituality and Strategies.* Maryknoll, NY: Orbis, 1998.

Shaw, George Bernard. *The Crime of Punishment.* New York: Philosophical Library, 1946.

Sher, George. *Desert.* Princeton, NJ: Princeton University Press, 1987.

Sherover-Marcuse, Erica. *Emancipation and Consciousness: Dogmatic and Dialectical Perspectives in the Early Marx.* Oxford: Basil Blackwell, 1986.

Smith, Charles H., ed. *Alfred Russel Wallace: An Anthology of His Shorter Writings.* New York: Oxford University Press, 1991.

Snell, Tracy, and Laura Maruschak. "Capital Punishment 2001." *Bureau of Justice Statistics Bulletin.* NCJ 197020, December 2002. Available at www.ojp.usdoj.gov/bjs/pub/ (accessed 2 June 2003).

Socialist Action. May 2001. Available at www.socialistaction.org/news/200105/death.html (13 August 2003).

Soelle, Dorothee. *Suffering.* Translated by Everett R. Kalin. Philadelphia: Fortress, 1975.

Solomon, Robert C. *A Passion for Justice: Emotions and the Origins of the Social Contract.* Lanham, MD: Rowman & Littlefield, 1995.

Staub, Ervin. *The Roots of Evil: The Origins of Genocide and Other Group Violence.* New York: Cambridge University Press, 1989.

Steffen. Lloyd. *Executing Justice: The Moral Meaning of the Death Penalty.* Cleveland, OH: Pilgrim, 1998.

Steinbeck. John. *East of Eden.* New York: Penguin, 1952.

Strang, Heather. *Repair or Revenge: Victims and Restorative Justice.* Oxford: Clarendon, 2002.

Strang, Heather, and John Braithwaite. *Restorative Justice: Philosophy to Practice.* Burlington, VT: Ashgate, 2000.

Sullivan, Dennis, and Larry Tifft. *Restorative Justice: Healing the Foundations of Our Everyday Lives.* Monsey, NY: Willow Tree, 2001.

Texas Department of Corrections. "Victim Offender Mediation/Dialogue." *Texas Department of Criminal Justice.* Available at www.tdcj.state.tx.us/victim/victim-vomd.htm (accessed 2 May 2004).

Thandeka. *Learning to Be White: Money, Race, and God in America.* New York: Continuum, 1999.

Thomas, Laurence M. *Vessels of Evil: American Slavery and the Holocaust.* Philadelphia: Temple University Press, 1993.

Tierney, Kevin. *Darrow: A Biography.* New York: Thomas Y. Crowell, 1979.

Turow, Scott. *Ultimate Punishment.* New York: Farrar, Straus and Giroux, 2003.

Tutu, Desmond. *No Future without Forgiveness.* New York: Doubleday, 1999.

United to End Racism. *Working Together to End Racism: Healing from the Damage Caused by Racism.* Seattle, WA: Rational Island, 2002.

U.S. Bureau of Justice Statistics. "Homicide Trends in the U.S." Available at www.ojp.usdoj.gov/bjs/homicide/cleared.htm (accessed 2 June 2003).

Von Hirsch, Andrew. *Censure and Sanctions.* Oxford: Clarendon, 1993.

Wallace, Alfred Russel. *Social Environment and Moral Progress.* New York: Funk & Wagnalls, 1913.

Warren, Jennifer. "Spare the Rod, Spoil the Child." *Los Angeles Times,* 1 July 2004, A-1.

Waxman, Ben. "Currently Employed Prison Guard Supervised Iraqi Torture." *Political State Report.* Available at http://www.polstate.com/archives/005439.htm 005439 (accessed 7 May 2004).

Weaver, J. Denny. *The Nonviolent Atonement.* Grand Rapids, MI: Eerdmans, 2001.

Whitman, James Q. *Harsh Justice: Criminal Justice and the Widening Divide between America and Europe.* New York: Oxford University Press, 2003.

Wills, Gary. "The Dramaturgy of Death." *New York Review of Books* 21 (June 2001): 6–10.

"Working with Defense Attorneys." *The Voice: Murder Victims' Families for Reconciliation,* 7. Spring/Summer 2004.

Young, Iris Marion. *Justice and the Politics of Difference.* Princeton, NJ: Princeton University Press, 1990.

Zehr, Howard. *Changing Lenses.* Scottsdale, PA: Herald, 1995.

———. *Transcending: Reflections on Crime Victims.* Intercourse, PA: Good Books, 2001.

Zimler, Richard. *The Last Kabbalist of Lisbon.* New York: Overlook, 1998.

Zimring, Franklin E. *The Contradictions of American Capital Punishment.* New York. Oxford University Press, 2003.

Index

About the Author

Judith W. Kay has served as president of the Washington Coalition to Abolish the Death Penalty and works with death row prisoner and murder victims' family members. A professor of social and religious ethics, she has taught at the University of Puget Sound, Wake Forest University, San Francisco Theological Seminary, and Starr King School of Ministry. At Puget Sound, Kay also served as Vice President of Student Affairs and Dean of Students. Kay has been selected twice for participation in seminars at the Center for Advanced Holocaust Studies at the United States Holocaust Memorial Museum. Kay has volunteered in local jails, the Re-Evaluation Co-Counselling Communities, the Tacoma Urban League, and the National Coalition Building Institute.

Publications include "Is Restitution Possible for Murder? Family Members Speak," in *Wounds That Do Not Bind: Victim-Based Perspectives on the Death Penalty*, ed. J. Acker and D. Karp; and "Murder Victims' Families for Reconciliation: Story Telling for Healing, as Witness, and in Public Policy," in *Handbook of Restorative Justice: A Global Perspective*, ed. D. Sullivan and L. Tifft.

Kay holds a doctorate in social ethics from the Graduate Theological Union and a master's degree from the Pacific School of Religion, both in Berkeley, California, and a bachelor's degree from Oberlin College. She is an avid swimmer and lives in Washington with her husband, an engineer. Their son, a blues musician, resides in New York City.